*none of them un
vail jed tune*

# The Future of Modern Music

*A Philosophical Exploration of Modernist Music in
the 20th Century and Beyond*

*P 335
Harrison Birdwhistle
Benjamin Britten
Julio Estrada P284
Fartein Valen*

# James L. McHard

*Valen
Vermuelen*

*Gielen B.O*

ICONIC PRESS

Published by:
Iconic Press,  Divison of  J & A Music Enterprises, Inc.
Livonia, Michigan

ISBN 978-0-0778195-1-5

Printed in the United States of America

First published in the United States of America in 2001 by
American Publishing Group

Cover Design By: Anthony J. Fisher

Attention colleges and universities, corporations, and writing and publishing organizations: For information on discounts contact: Iconic Press at P.O. Box 510355, Livonia, Michigan 48151

# Dedication

For my wife, Alice McHard, in eternal gratitude for the many hours of hard work she cheerfully gave, by helping me proofread the original. My gratitude for her love and for her dedication cannot be expressed in mere words. Thus, I cannot express sufficiently my gratitude and love for her. Without her, this book would not be possible.

# Acknowledgements

I gratefully thank the following people for their assistance in the preparation of this book: Professor Karl Boelter, Music and Theater, Oakland University, Rochester, Michigan; William Brown, retired school principal, horn player, Detroit Symphony Orchestra; Bert Cooper, pianist, composer and electrical engineer; Dr. Julio Estrada, Professor of Composition, Universidad National Autónoma de México (UNAM), and member of the Institute of Aesthetics; Alice McHard, horn player (my wife); Gerard Pape, Lacanian psychologist, (Ph.D.) and Glen Price, principal horn player, Kansas City Civic Orchestra. Special thanks to Alice, Dr. Estrada, Mr. Pape, Dr. Boelter, and, most gratefully, to a terrific publishing editor, Lorna Lynch, for helping me edit this book.

Also, I am indebted to Dr. Estrada for his allowing me to include a score segment from his *Ishini'ioni* on the cover of this book.

# Contents

## PART III

(Karl Hartmann, Luigi Dallapiccola, Goffredo Petrassi, Giorgio Ghedini, Sergei Prokofiev, Albert Roussel, Alfredo Casella, Bohuslav Martinü, Arthur Honegger, Julián Orbón, Jón Leifs, Manuel de Falla, Ernst Toch, Fartein Valen, Harald Saeverud, Allan Pettersson, Aare Merikanto, Vagn Holmboe, Hanns Eisler, Egon Wellesz, Robert Gerhard, Carlos Chávez, Igor Markevitch, Artur Schnabel, Nikos Skalkottas, Silvestre Revueltas, Douglas Lilburn, Ahmed Saygun, Kamran Ince, Alois Hába, Josef Hauer, Henry Cowell, Conlon Nancarrow, Harry Partch, George Antheil, Luigi Russolo, Alexander Mosolov, Gavriil Popov, György Ligeti, György Kurtág, Luciano Berio, Bruno Maderna, Henri Pousseur, Karel Goeyvaerts, Krzysztof Penderecki, Henryk Górecki, George Crumb, Toru Takemitsu, Toshiro Mayuzumi, Toschi Ichyanagi, Yuji Takahashi, Yoritsune Matsudaira, Henri Dutilleux, Jean Barraqué, Pierre Barbaud, Sylvano Bussotti, Dieter Schnebel, Marticio Kagel, Franco Evangelisti, Aldo Clementi, Franco Donatoni, Hans Henze, Bernd Zimmermann, Friedrich Cerha, Gottfried Koenig, Avert Terterian, Galina Ustvolskaya, Wolgang Rihm, Gérard Grisey, Tristan Murail, Hugues Dufourt, Kaija Saariaho, Olga Neuwirth, Helmut Lachenmann, Salvatore Sciarrino, Stefano Scodanibbio, Heinz Hoffman-Richter, Chou Wen-Chung, Isang Yun, Morton

Feldman, Earle Brown, Christian Wolff, David Tudor, La
Monte Young, Pauline Oliveros, Donald Scavarda, George
Cacioppo, Bruce Wise, Robert Sheff, Roger Reynolds, Robert
Ashley, Gordon Mumma, Alvin Lucier, David Behrman, Yasunao
Tone, Toshiya Tsunoda, Otomo Yoshihide)

# Foreword

*The Future of Modern Music* is more than just a history or a who's who of early to mid-20th century art music--that which is most commonly called by musicologists and other art historians "the modernist era". McHard shows us that the "modern" in "modern music" refers not to just one specific historical era in the 20th century that is now over; it is, as he develops it, a compositional attitude that transcends any given era in music. For example, one might argue that, in the most general sense, the best music of any given historical era is always "modern" in that it is always experimental and groundbreaking; that is, of its time, as were the masterworks of Bach, Mozart, Berlioz, etc. in their time. It is only in retrospect, after a radically new work has become accepted by the critics and by the public, that one can say that it has become a "classic". It frequently can take, in our time, up to fifty years or more after a work has been composed for that to occur.

For McHard, any type of "post" music is decadent; a "post" music being one that looks back to previous eras, attempting to recover the lost listening satisfactions embodied in those beloved older musics by imitating, parodying, or collaging them. This may be due to nostalgia on the part of the composer, or possibly, in some cases, a cynical attempt to pander to the public's nostalgia. Another possible cause might be due to a failure of imagination on the part of the composer to get beyond his personal musical impasse. In any case, it would seem that McHard's point is that the only "authentic" attitude possible (in the existential sense) for the composer of any era to adopt is "modernist". We may define this "modernist" attitude, in the most general sense, to be that intransigent, uncompromisingly tough stance of the composer who says to himself and to his public: "On, ever on . . ." In other words, no turning back. No "post-music". If a musical impasse is reached, one must find the courage and imagination to compose one's way out of it; no return is possible to the halcyon days of past musics.

*The Future of Modern Music* is also a unique overview of music in the 20th century in that it focuses on composers who are either unjustly neglected (i.e., Malipiero, Ruggles, Varèse, etc.), or who have simply not yet been recognized for their great radical genius (i.e. Scelsi, Xenakis, Estrada, etc.). Mr. McHard's book gives us a very different picture of the 20th century's contribution to art music. This book does not emphasize sterile historical debates such as Schoenberg vs. Stravinsky, or, more recently, the blind alleys of neo-ro-manticism, post-modernism, or other pastiche-ridden musics that all seem to scream out that sincerity and originality are dead, no longer possible, or even relevant. Instead, the book focuses on those composers who are the very antith-esis of all that musical decadence.

What links all these figures, despite the heteroge-neously sounding qualities of their musics, is that they all adopted that tough, uncompromising attitude of "On, ever on...", often to their immediate personal and economic det-riment. Each composer studied in this book took the hard route, making music that was uniquely his own. Thus, not only is this book a lesson in musical history; it is also a study of artistic integrity and ethical courage.

The heart of this book, that which shows that "mod-ern music" is not dead today, is that part which describes the work of those composers who have contributed to the new paradigm of working with sound itself as the primary material to be developed in a musical composition. From Cage's admonition of "Let the sounds be themselves" to the Scelsian voyage into the "heart of sound", we find in these "sound-oriented" composers very unique contributions to a new kind of "modern music". It is a music which is the true music of our time, where a personal sound world is forged out of the very stuff of the inner musical imagination of the individual composer, as Julio Estrada so rightly emphasizes, both in his work as composer and composition professor.

McHard, himself, is also a composer of the very type of "modern music" of which he writes. He, quite modestly, never mentions his own music in his book. Having heard his music, however, I know that he knows, from his own direct personal compositional experience, what it means to attempt to translate personal sound fantasy into rigorous musical form. Such works as his *Tremors* for ensemble and tape and *Virtuals* for tape, attest to McHard's own experiences of composing, with the sound, itself, as the privileged vehicle for the transcription of inner personal experience.

McHard's book not only tells the story of some of the most interesting musical compositions of the early to mid-20th century; it also describes what is happening in the present, and what might happen in the future with "modern music".

Beyond describing the rich and interesting past of the historical "modern music" era, James McHard shows us the great potential benefit for the future of art music, which continuing to maintain a "modernist" attitude would give to the musical compositions of the future.

Gerard Pape
Lacanian Psychologist (Ph.D)
Director of Studio "Les Ateliers UPIC
Paris, France

# Preface –
# The Future of Modern Music

This book is intended to help today's listening audience come to grips with what most people consider the ogre of modern music. It's the word *modern* that causes consternation. Especially when one is faced with the purchase of a CD or listening to a concert, the appearance of the names Schönberg or Varèse, for example, seems to strike fear into the hearts of innocent concertgoers. This need not be so. While the music of many of the composers of the 20th century seems formidable upon first hearing, there are many ways a listener can prepare him or herself for the onslaught of sound so as to turn it into a productive and satisfying listening experience. This book is presented as a source for unlocking the secrets to a fully enriched and enriching listening experience. Enclosed herein are suggestions for approaching works that deserve *fair* hearing, as well as ideas that reveal a wholly new way of looking at modernism in music.

What do we mean by the overworked term modern (and, by association, its companion term *modernist*)? First, what don't we mean? The simplest idea of modern refers to anything in music history that is contemporary within a given time period. Certainly Bach's music was modern when it was composed in the 1700s, just as Schönberg's was in 1910.

A more recent definition of modernism refers primarily to art music written in the 1950s, 60s and early 70s. This is a functional, rather than temporal definition. This is the way that 20th century music has been characterized. It is a fixed-in-time reference to a style of a bygone era. It is a style no longer in use in the works of most composers today. So, here the word seems to refer to the *past*. When we take our mutual journey through the music discussed herein, how is it that we can talk of the *future* of an abandoned era? Can composers return to the past?

The answer lies in the reassessment of the idea of modernism. This book is intended to reconstruct the idea of modernism as a continuing term: a style that reflects an *attitude* of the composer; a living construct that can evolve with the times. For that reconsideration, we need to examine some attributes with which much important and overlooked works by advanced composers are richly imbued. This blueprint becomes a mind model that fosters all that is good in experimentation, innovation, and discovery clothed in a garb of shining fabric that, at the same time, can be approached by the listening audience, if given a fair chance.

To provide that fair chance, I have set out to share with you, the reader and listener, some of the many new ideas and concepts that are being brought to the act of composing in today's world. Many of these ideas are very new. Some of them have yet to find their way into print. Most haven't been compiled, together, within a single cover. All are intended to freshen the listening experience, and reawaken listeners to the notion of a new music that can be heard and understood, and that will become a powerful, memorable and rewarding event for you and me, the listeners. This will require something of a historical survey with a decidedly philosophical bent. New definitions will be traced as they were born, from the beginning of the century in works of Claude Debussy, through those of Arnold Schönberg, and in today's works by Julio Estrada, the Mexican revolutionary theorist.

What is the glue that can hold together such disparities? Is there a secret organizing impulse that makes these alchemies glimmer in ways that can move an audience? Yes! The best of what modernism exemplified, in the olden sense as well as what can be reascribed to advanced work of today, lies in a complete reconsideration of what constitutes a sound. A sound has many attributes, the most famous of which (and which garnered almost exclusive attention in the avant-garde music of the 1950s and 60s) are pitch and duration. Another dimension, far too long ignored, is just now receiving long overdue attention: it is depth (Giacinto Scelsi's *third dimension*). This has been the missing ingredient in the stew. The most common musical element of depth is timbre (tone-color resulting from a confluence of overtones). More broadly, it's the concept of color that provides the spice to enhance the flavor--in ways that provide *accessibility for the listener*, even in music of decidedly rugged terrain. These concepts slowly took on flesh with the work of composers in successive generations, until a formalized concept was born: that of sound-based music. Coupled with composers' understanding of psychoacoustics (how we perceive sound), this approach has led to startling new results that are striking at their very least, and deeply rewarding at their best.

So what is modernism? I link the chains of the groundwork sown in the seminal work of Iannis Xenakis, Luigi Nono, Giacinto Scelsi, Julio Estrada, and John Cage to provide a template for the rebirth of a higher, more vibrant, and evolving new *modernism.* How does this modernism differ from the olden, now shorn modernism (serialism etc.)? It (the new) is freed, flexible, and couched in an attitude of discovery, and yet it also joins hands with the listening audience to form a partnership in a new --and fun --way to listen (Luigi Nono - free the body, the ear, the mind). So this is a modernism that is living in real time. How, then, does this modernism differ from the consolidations in today's so-called 'post-modernism'?

To answer that we need to diverge momentarily to consider what has happened as reaction to the 'olden' modernism. So much public outrage was generated by the near-incestuous ideal of the (then) radical composers of total serialism. Some of the works of its practitioners seem so dense and dry that they are almost unreachable, except by a select few university professors. It seemed as though the goal was to generate a pseudo-mathematical/visual art form. The correlative listening experience, though, was gibberish to the public. (Milton Babbitt's article "Who Cares if you Listen?" didn't help matters.) The most extreme examples of this sort of sandbox entertainment (for the composers) can be found in certain articles in the august periodical *Perspectives of New Music*. One of my favorite examples is located in an arcane, abstruse article by Philip Batstone on 'multiple order functions' (Batstone p. 92). This stuff has lost the listening public completely, not to mention it has a repulsive impact on the better composers (surprisingly?) addressed herein. We in the audience simply can't *hear* permutations of integer values taken to the eleventh power. We don't want to have to try, either.

Works so composed belong in the private setting of the university. The best of today's advanced work, though, is contrastingly vibrant, as I hope to show in this book.

Other approaches worked to doom music within the realm of the old modernism. Some are gimmicky, having been born of poorly considered goals, and even more poorly executed models. Worse, some work in poor taste (e.g., the destruction of musical instruments) fed the public desire to walk away, and also fed the formerly modernist composers' desire to revise their approach. The composer of post-modern music found a new way to compose. That way was to relax the tension and the corresponding dissonances and revitalize access to the audience. But is this necessarily the best (or only) way to address the problem, the only way to readdress the concerns of the audience? (Julio Estrada, the advanced Mexican theorist/composer, expressed a need for caution against reliance on the sedative effects that these more relaxed approaches may impart to the listener, if taken to the exclusion of other, more challenging music.)

The unfortunate and unwitting victims of the post-modernism alignment with the public are the serious craftsmen who are the best practitioners of the finest music the new modernism offers. These are the composers who have brought consideration and care for the public mind into their craft, those who have taken the time, and who have made the effort to address the public need for a pleasurable experience couched within the goal of expanding one's mind (that is, the engagement of a full and fulfilling musical experience). Post-modernism and the new modernism are very different in focus. The former tries to engage the public at an instinctual level (focusing mainly on the emotional component). The latter can do that while expanding the mind and enhancing the resources needed to provide a greater listening model (the teaching and progressive components). It is the goal of this book to refocus public attention toward what is viable in the new modernism. This is not to reject much good work in the post-modern era, but to offer additional avenues by which to seek joy in music.

Such a goal is realizable only within a necessarily selective framework. Not all composers are included, nor can they be. Much fine work by very conservative composers such as Giacomo Puccini, Richard Strauss, Jean Sibelius, and Sergei Rachmaninov is excluded from the discussion, as it simply isn't part of my focus. Additionally, some of the more venturesome composers of the so-called 'neo-classicism' are not considered here either, even though their gifts exhibit a certain pungency, sometimes erroneously characterized as 'modernist'. The best works of Albert Roussel, Sergei Prokofiev, Arthur Honegger, Alfredo Casella, and others are strong, but don't fit into our crucible. Finally, I needed to be selective even amongst the group that seems to fit the strict definition of sound-based composition. Without diverging aimlessly into territory best left for later, I only say that many composers fall into the so-called 'cluster' camp of composition. For the sake of expediency, I selected but one representative (Witold Lutosławski) for extended consideration, as he seems to stand out from the rest. None of these exclusions is meant to imply that any of their works lack beauty.

We should be grateful for the gifts of those composers whom we most cherish: those whose art is direct and relieves us from the banalities of everyday life. The works of Ralph Vaughan-Williams, Claude Debussy, Maurice Ravel, Gustav Mahler, Manuel de Falla, Aaron Copland and others offer a mysterious journey out of day-to-day insanity, and toward communion with something that we too rarely choose for company: the seat of our best inspirations and insights--the contemplation of beauty. Also, though, we can be elevated by seemingly unlikely source stimuli: sound worlds that do not as readily yield their fruits, that contain messages not so eager to succumb to our aural scrutiny. These works surrender their prizes much less willingly, but do so forcefully upon reflection by minds schooled in and sensitive to their unique messages. The works to which I allude here are those focusing on the new modernism. Some familiar names are reexamined in this new light, especially Arnold Schönberg, Anton Webern, Béla Bartók, John Cage, and others. Some less familiar composers, who have been unjustly neglected, such as Gian-Francesco Malipiero, Matthisj Vermeulen, Giacinto Scelsi, Iannis Xenakis, and Julio Estrada, (to name a few), are also analyzed and presented as being especially worthy, through their special efforts by clarifying what is meant in music and its very nature and essence.

I offer these words and insights primarily to you, the concertgoer, as a means for discovering new treasures of sound. However, ancillary value can be obtained, as well, by the interested professional, especially by those forward-minded professors and teachers; their students; and, of course, the composers themselves who are in search of new means by which to reinvigorate their arsenal of musical materials.

I invite you to join me in exploring and unlocking these secrets of this mysterious art of music and its divinations. As we gain our epiphanies into the raptures enshrouded within these miracles, I hope that we take joy in our mutual journey. The following words are a listener's insights into a world whose doors that I, through persistence, have managed to open. To convey my delight, I have taken care to try to *infuse* (enthusiasm), not to *confuse*. Missing are the terms pregnant with the mechanical gyrations that are so much a part of the musical jargon of the past modernism. Very little honest-to-goodness analysis is included here. I'll leave that to the musicologists, as is so much their wont. We are dealing here with *listening* experiences. I hope to make you *want* to hear what is, after all, meant to be *heard*. May these creatures of a brilliant new sound world find their way into companionship with you, the discerning listener.

◆◆◆

# Introduction
## Background to Tomorrow's Music

Rather than publishing a complete survey of all trends, I wish to explore, fully and exclusively, the emergence of the real *avant-garde* in 20th century music. Then, those characteristics of modernism's *best* practitioners will be identified to ascertain what makes that music so vibrant. This segment of modern music consists of those composers who, by their works, introduced new sounds and new methods to produce sounds. The encapsulation of new sounds is contained, primarily, in new timbres and new forms. I believe serious listeners can understand and appreciate this modern music, if it is presented, for once, in a clear and approachable fashion. I intend to do this. I want to sell you, the reader/listener on the beguiling magic in this modern music. Our journey will lead from the contributions of composers earlier in this century into the new modernism of today. The binding thread is a concept we discuss next.

## Sound-based composition

The composers, upon whom I concentrate most, comprise a very special subset of this remarkable class of musical sorcerers. They are composers of what Gerard Pape and some technical musicologists call 'sound-based' music. This is music that is created by the manipulation and transformation of raw sound materials from one characteristic state to another. It focuses on the qualities inherent in sound; i.e., composition focused solely on *natural phenomena* that access the very doorways to comprehension by the ear and the mind. Scelsi cites the addition of a third dimension (depth - timbre) to the main constituents of pitch and duration. The third dimension receives concentration in sculpturing 'sound-based' music (Pape "Composition" p. 2 ff.). Formerly, only pitch and duration had undergone intensive, systematic treatment.

The sound-based approach presupposes an understanding of psychoacoustics, or the study of how the human mind perceives sound and the way it evolves. All serious practitioners of sound-based composition are well grounded in this discipline. So, the emphasis is on listeners' perception and not on composers' methods (as in so much serial composition). While sound-based composition does involve algorithms (quasi-formulas or stepwise procedures) specifically designed to shape sounds into coherent entities, these gestures *serve sound*, not the other way around (again, as is the case with much serial music). We explore this in-depth in the concluding chapter, by surveying new methodologies and concepts in this field.

Sound-based composition is a new term for a process that is not new. Although it has not been labeled and codified explicitly, until recently, the techniques that enrich composition via an emphasis on sound and its nature have germinated and evolved since about the time of Janáček. With the passage of time, the methods have become more explicit. This book surveys the development of sound-based music from the time of Janáček to today.

An example of sound-based composition may help to clarify what is meant by the term. Arnold Schönberg, for instance, fostered the early development of the concept by his subtle handling of timbre variation in what he termed '*klangfarbenmelodie*' (tone-color melody) (Vinton p. 397), in which a single pitch is visited in sequence by a succession of different instruments. The different instruments' timbres provide the variety. The evolution of this timbric pattern exudes a 'melody' confined to a single note and defined only by changing tone color!

This method of sound transformation has been refined considerably in the years succeeding Schönberg's seminal work. Karlheinz Stockhausen has investigated the evolution of gradually shifting timbres by very sophisticated procedures. Iannis Xenakis has developed a means of evolving sounds into patterns whose degree of *disorder* (ataxy) varies by complex manipulations of sound screens using logic functions (*PAR* Xenakis p. 63). John Cage systematically incorporated formerly 'unwanted' sounds, even to the point of allowing the invasion of unintended sounds into the otherwise planned soundscape.

While much of the work of composers like Arnold Schönberg, Alban Berg, Anton Webern, and even that of Stockhausen and Pierre Boulez gravitates around a sound-based approach, some of their approach is decidedly beyond that realm. For example, the system of tone ordering known as *serialism* is concerned mostly with fixed, discrete pitch (or, later, duration-value, or intensity) sequencing. Very little serial composition concerns itself with the qualities inherent in sound, and of its transformation, systematic or otherwise (i.e., Cage). So while much of Schönberg's work, a fair portion of Stockhausen's, and a little of Boulez's, Berg's, or Webern's involves sound-based ruminations, much doesn't, so I intentionally limit its focus.

I take license in including certain composers, though, whose work is really only marginally associable with the sound-based concept. Paul Hindemith's work is mostly about melodic and harmonic evolution, but a certain portion is at least parenthetically associated with future developments (for example his traversing through fifths (Machlis p. 206), his early Expressionism, his motoristic rhythms, and his characteristic streamlined sound). Similarly, the work of Darius Milhaud is included. Certainly, a quasi-historical venture of modern music is incomplete without some reference to their work and contributions.

What typifies composers' efforts in sound-based work is mostly frame of reference. Gerard Pape, Director of studio Les Ateliers UPIC, for instance, has insisted that *conception* (rational, abstract ordering procedures, etc.) be made subservient, and conjured subsequent, to interests of *perception* (how people are able to perceive what's being played). So much serial music suffers in the minds of listeners because their interests are not addressed. The complexity of the linear polyphony in serial music does not lend itself well to mental pattern formation. The counterpoint dissolves into fortuitous bands of isolated sounds. Xenakis, in his article, "The Crisis of Serialism" addressed this very problem (Xenakis p. 8 - referencing the "Gravesaner Blätter" article in the 1950s that caused such a stir among the serialists). He devised a stochastic treatment to allow the sounds to be coalesced into overall patterns more susceptible to recognition.

Did Schönberg make a huge mistake in devising his twelve-tone method? It seems to me that his best and most expressive works are the pre-serial, freely atonal ones, from the 19-teens. The serial works immediately following those seem to abandon the once rich and exciting realms of coloration that were so much a part of his earlier work. For much of the '20s we are treated to dry and pedantic-sounding music. After the '30s, though, Schönberg's work recaptures some of the vibrancy it had been lacking, as he became more sure-footed in his new serial system. This goes to corroborate Xenakis' own admission that, at least some serial music is good music. Nonetheless, serialism is only a means of constructing arrays. It cannot create new materials.

The exploration of new sound materials, then, begins with a careful consideration of how humans perceive sound--and what types of sounds--and how their transformations best can serve as soundscapes. Method follows an understanding of the kernels of sounds, themselves: their characteristics, and ways they may best be made to evolve in patterns that the ear can follow.

# A History of models in sound-based conception

Some historical perspective will provide a backdrop against which specific factual analysis may proceed within a composer-by-composer study. Romanticism had concerned itself with gradually evolving harmonic enrichment and melodic sophistication. Composers avoided dissonance, except where it provided variety and transition between distinct patterns. Later, previously well-contained, clear harmonic functions (e.g., in Mozart symphonies) lost some of their freshness and vitality with usage. As harmonies got richer and more complex, modulations appeared and harmonic resolution was frequently delayed. The brew began getting to be too thick and complicated (e.g., in Wagner's operas).

The first piece of modern music, Debussy's ***Prelude to the Afternoon of a Faun*** (1892-4), saw the dawn of an intuitively sound-based music. Debussy consolidated his musical experiences and created an exotic, dreamlike world of sound. Harmony was stripped of its functionality, as sounds rolled through vague patterns. Colors emerged in shifting patterns. There was scant concern over *next-ness*; that is, over whether there ought to be a 'B', now that an 'A' had made its appearance.

Shortly thereafter, Schönberg created a radical, new harmony based on fourths *(First Chamber Symphony* - 1906). Again, Schönberg gave genesis to another new concept, his *klangfarbenmelodie* and correlated free atonality in *Five Pieces for Orchestra* (1909). Special stringed effects emerged in Berg's *String Quartet,* Op. 3 (1910). Stravinsky composed his exotic *Petrouchka* (1911) with its bitonal chord combinations and octatonic scale configurations (van den Toorn p. 32). Webern began isolating single tones in quasi-melodic cells *(Symphonie,* Op. 21 - 1928). Bartók created string quartets that sound orchestrally conceived (his six *Quartets* - 1908-39). Most significantly, Edgard Varèse composed a whole series of percussive works characterized by complete lack of melody, motivic cells that gyrate around sustained tones, and shattering dissonances in evolving densities (*Integrales* (1925), *Ionisation* (1929), and others). His later work in electronic music was even more provocative (*Déserts* - 1950-4).

These works were startling in the brazen new sounds that they revealed. All were highly influential on subsequent work. Olivier Messiaen's work ushered in the period known as the "avant-garde" (all periods can be considered avant-garde, within their time frame. My choice of this term is deliberate and convenient, even if, perhaps, misleading). Messiaen *(Quartet for the End of Time* - 1944) launched his work from Claude Debussy's edifice. With Debussy's work in Impressionism as a foundation, Messiaen systematized Webern's intuitive serialism, but applied it to modal, as well as to chromatic structures. Messiaen also enlarged upon Varèse's concept of static cellular motives that seem to go literally nowhere. Color is everything in Messiaen.

Boulez' main contribution was his utilization of electronic devices and computers to assist him in transforming sonorities gradually. Stockhausen's work is more profoundly significant. By treating timbre and pitch as special cases of rhythmic transformation, Stockhausen constructed works that travel in and out of carefully contrived rhythmic patterns that generate pure tone color (***Kontakte*** - 1960).

The work of Cage is sound-oriented only in a peculiarly default sense. All sounds, intended or not, are fair game for music. This idea, though, should not be considered trivial, as Cage, in cooperation with the radical pianist and electronics engineer--his collaborator, David Tudor--produced a body of work for 'live' electronics (e.g., ***Variations II*** - 1961) that defies description. That piece's confrontational collage of unimaginable timbres renders it an otherworldly cast! His ***4'33"*** (1952) consists solely of ambient sounds in the environment, and silence.

Luigi Nono evolved from being a rigid serialist into becoming a highly original composer of subtle, shifting tone colors. The sounds in his later body of work are delicate and explore, in very systematic fashion, the territory occupied by near silence. The polemical early works decrying the harshness of war and fascism were intensely expressive, highly reminiscent of Schönbergian Expressionism. These harsh, loud, angst-ridden dissonances gave way, in his late works, to quietude in refined, ingenious sounds of ghostly loneliness, punctuated by sudden orchestral outbursts. ***No hay caminos, hay que caminar... Andrei Tarkovskij*** (1987) is exemplary. His work foretold of clearly new avenues for sound quality that are under investigation today, in electronics music studios in Paris and Freiburg, Germany.

Most important work has been that of Iannis Xenakis, who created the studio CEMAMu and that of the Mexican revolutionary, Julio Estrada.

Xenakis' contributions to the aesthetic of sound-based music are legion. His work has traveled the gamut of the musico-philosophical territory embraced by all types of known stochastic and symbolic formalizations. The formal concepts unleashed in Xenakis' works are marshaled from disciplines far removed from traditional musical territory. The concepts he employs are grounded in the very processes of human thought. He considers sound to be a physical phenomenon, subject to the same laws that govern the behavior of particles of matter. Likewise, the mind is a primarily physical entity, and it will understand best what is arrayed into stochastic patterns, those being the most physically characteristic patterns. *Pithoprakta* (1955) is important for its use of sound-clouds in a stochastic environment.

Xenakis resorted to thought experiments (PAR Varga pp. 72-96) to evolve an increasingly systematic formalization of musical genesis. Gradually, free stochastics gave way to symbolic logical patterns, until Xenakis was able to axiomatize and generalize the process of musical composition abstractly and systematically. Concepts of degrees of *disorder* (ataxy, related to increasing entropy in thermodynamics) (Xenakis p. 63) were introduced (*Syrmos* - 1959), so that fluctuations into and out from order would stretch the listener's 'mind's eye' toward heretofore uncharted sound vistas.

Concurrent with his investigations into sound pattern structuring, Xenakis thoroughly investigated the realm of tone-color gradations, first introducing granular sounds (*Bohor I* - 1962), then by using logic screens to control the evolution of sound from one timbre to another. Finally, new scales were derived with the aid of *sieve-theory* (*Herma* - 1960-1 and *Nomos Alpha* - 1966) (Varga p. 93-4), some *non*-periodic (Protheroe - Wergo record) through which he could explore unfamiliar terrain. Even so physical a concept as Brownian movement, and its correlative abstraction, 'arborescences' (a general type of linear tone movement - *Evryali* - 1973) (Varga p. 89), were corralled to guide sound particles in fortuitous walks through sound space, weaving unbidden, jagged patterns.

In addition to his seminal work at CEMAMu, Xenakis invented the UPIC (Pape "Les Ateliers UPIC" website) computer graphic composing module. It was originally intended as a tool for easy teaching of children; it gives direct output from input that circumvents the messy complexities of musical notation. Its results are direct and immediate. For these purposes Xenakis established studio Les Ateliers UPIC, a work studio with electronics equipment including the UPIC. Ultimately Xenakis and others have proven that the UPIC is also a first rate compositional tool. Several highly sophisticated works have been composed using the console, most notably Xenakis' own *Mycenae-Alpha* (1978). Xenakis turned over directorship of the studio in the late 1980s and early 1990s to a variety of people, the most successful of whom is Gerard Pape, so that Xenakis, himself, could concentrate on work in the CEMAMu studio. Pape has held seminars at Les Ateliers UPIC, featuring guest composers, and also has composed a body of his own UPIC works.

Scelsi provided a powerful stimulus for future sound investigation in his seminal work that explored the structure and morphology of the single tone and its interactions. Scelsi's *Quattro Pezzi* (1959) is the culmination of his years of experimentation in sounds and their limitless transformations. Never before, nor since, has the single tone been subjected to such subtle and minute refinements.

The work of Julio Estrada brings us to the present in contemplating the work in this field. Estrada has absorbed certain findings of both Xenakis and Stockhausen and combined them in a fashion unique to his personal goals. He has developed mathematical algorithms that he uses along with his theory of the 'continuum', to help him control pitch, timbre, and expressive inflections separately. By the splitting of staff lines (Pape "Composition... p. 41) into separate sets, for pitch and rhythm, Estrada has removed expressive gradation away from subjective manipulation, and towards rigorous, disciplined control. The resultant scores, requiring each player to read distinct sets of independent staves, simultaneously, have proven daunting, but effective, achieving changes of incredible refinement, otherwise unattainable. *Yuunohui'yei* (1983) began, and *Ishini'ioni* (1984-90) culminated this effort.

Gerard Pape extends Estrada's work by treating chaos as a formal concept (*Weaveworld* 1995).

Some philosophical analysis, included herein, is based upon ideas that have been extracted from two crucially important abstracts: one that is yet-to-be published, *Composition and the Structure of Sound* - 1995 - (publication pending for a projected book in French, *Le Continuum*, written by Gerard Pape); and another, recently published, *Luigi Nono and His Fellow Travellers* (sic) - 1995, also by Pape in the august journal *Contemporary Music Review.*

These recent innovations did not occur in a vacuum, or suddenly. All the recent composers' work has benefited from the solid framework accorded by the masters of the early years of the 20th century. We embark upon our journey now, through the 20th century, to view the flow of this history in greater detail. The book is composed of two main parts addressing first the early, then the last part of the 20th century. The work of Mahler, Debussy and Janácek presages that of Schönberg, Berg, Ravel, Malipiero, Webern, Bartók, Stravinsky, Hindemith and Varèse. Brief glimpses into the work of Ives, Ruggles, Milhaud and Vermeulen follow, closing consideration of the first half of the century. Next, we look at Messiaen, Boulez, Stockhausen, Cage, Xenakis, Lutoslawski, Nono, Scelsi, and Estrada. Finally we look at the present work in studio Les Ateliers UPIC to take the pulse of music and scope out prospects for the future of modern music

♦♦♦

## Historical time-line chart of the development of sound-based composition:

1892 -    **Debussy** - Chords as components of timbre *(Prelude to the Afternoon of a Faun)*

1908 -    **Bartók** - Stringed instrumental effects *(String Quartets)*

1909 -    **Schönberg** - Klangfarbenmelodie (tone-color melody) *(Five Pieces for Orchestra)*

1925 -    **Varèse** - Colliding clusters structured in complex timbral hierarchies *(Integrales)*

1944 -    **Messiaen** - Shifting kaleidoscope of static chords in 'color-harmony' *(Quartet for the End of Time)*

1952 -    **Cage** - Silence and ambient environmen tal noises *(4'33")*

1955 -    **Xenakis** - Clouds of sounds *(Pithoprakta)*

1959 -    **Scelsi** - Oscillating tones in plasma of timbral variations *(Quattro Pezzi)*

1960 -    **Xenakis** - Ataxy: disorder as a formal organizing principle *(Syrmos)*

1960 -        **Stockhausen** - Contact between pitch and timbre with rhythm in varying speeds *(Kontakte)*

1962 -        **Xenakis** - Granular sounds *(Bohor I)*

1960-6 -     **Xenakis** - Sieve theory for generalized formalization of scale construction *(Herma / Nomos Alpha)*

1973 -        **Xenakis** - Arborescences, or branching patterns (diagonal contours) *(Evryali)*

1983 -        **Estrada** - The continuum *(yuunohui'yei)*

1987 -        **Nono** - Nearly inaudible realm of tone spectrum in microtones/special electronics *(No Hay Caminos, Hay Que Caminar...Andrzej Tarkovskij)*

1995 -        **Pape** - Chaos structured in all levels of form *(Weaveworld)*

# Part I

# Leoš Janáček

# (1854-1928)

౿ఌ

Leoš Janáček's birth was very early for a composer who is commonly regarded as 'modern'. The birth of the 20th century musical tradition is temporally set around the mature music of Mahler and Debussy, each of whom was born in the early 1860s. In fact, Janáček's early music was based on Moravian and Czech nationalist folk tradition. In 1877, he befriended Antonin Dvořák, whose own music, no doubt, provided an early formative stimulus. Janáček's early music has a romantic hue that betrays an interest in the very traditional dance and song character of his heritage. There is very little remarkable in this early music to have set Janáček apart from most ordinary composers of his time.

However, after Janáček assimilated a more thorough understanding of the folk inflections into his work, and with the benefit of more formal education, his work took on a radically new quality. By example, it sets a standard for nationalistic composition that is both profoundly thorough, and thoroughly modern. It is this quality that has secured Janáček a place in the modern tradition of the early 20th century.

## • __His Life__

Janáček was born in a small burg in Moravia (Hukvaldy). He was the ninth of fourteen children. His father was the local schoolteacher, and when Janáček was eleven, he was sent to Brno where he sang in a monastery choir. He later returned to the monastery to teach and direct the choir, and he composed some organ works at this time. Janáček moved to Prague to tighten and hone his musical skills and knowledge. There, he trained at the organ school and he developed a taste for a career in music.

After his stay in Prague, Janáček returned to Brno and resumed teaching. There, he was appointed conductor of the Beseda choral society, where, in combination with his monastery choir, he produced large-scale works of Mozart and Beethoven. Included were Mozart's **Requiem** and Beethoven's **Missa Solemnis**. Thereafter he studied composition at the Leipzig Music Conservatoire (1879-80). Then he attended the Vienna Conservatoire, but left after three months following an argument with the authorities.

In 1881 Janáček married his sixteen-year-old piano student, Zdenka Schulzova. He founded an organ school at Brno shortly afterwards. The marriage to Zdena was troubled from the start; the couple separated, but reunited by 1884. Then their son died in 1890, a tragedy that was to increase the strain on an already difficult relationship. Around this time, Janáček founded a music journal *Hudebni listy*.

Janáček's first large-scale work was an opera, **Sarka** (1887). The work explores Czech mythological subjects. Janáček's interest in the Czech and Moravian tradition was heightened as a result of his work on the opera. (Burke website). His schooling also had sharpened his taste for developing a refined cohesion of solid craftsmanship and a thoroughly idiomatic Czech musical phraseology. At the invitation of a fellow teacher at Brno Gymnasium, he collected and notated folk songs in northern Moravia for several years. This became the basis of an intensive study of folk speech patterns and inflections that came to inform his music thereafter.

Janáček's work was slow in coming, primarily because of his painstaking reviews of the materials he had collected in his travels. He began to shape a characteristic phrase structure based on these folk patterns. He termed this "speech-melody" (Burke website), in which native language inflections and rhythms (including hesitations (Lebrecht p. 170)) generate musical contours. These qualities are colorful and lend the music a charming, if somewhat rugged and rough-hewn flavor. Less attention is given to smoothing out phrases and to commonly accepted practices of blending voices. On first hearing, the overall effect seems unpolished and raw, but many hearings reveal the originality lurking in these strange musical waters.

From 1894 to 1903 Janáček labored over the first great masterpiece to bear the stamp of his originality, the opera *Jenufa*. The couple's daughter died around this time, an event that was to deepen the scars in his marriage. (the musical time - R. N.) He was later to meet and correspond with another woman, although his marriage did remain intact, with a surface show of unity. Meantime, *Jenufa* received its Brno premiere in 1904. It wasn't until 1916, though, that it received its critically acclaimed Prague premiere. For the latter premiere, the staging was revised, and it was a brilliant success. The work exudes all the flavors that Janáček so carefully cultivated. The orchestral flavor was rough, but forceful. The orchestra plays a major role in his operas, by helping shape the action, and by molding the phrasing, lending the works a heightened sense of drama.

The typical classic-romantic set-number format gives way to flow dictated more by the action and the inflections inherent in the native speech (Boynick website). If tension is atypically handled, the progress is molded through adroit treatment of repeated patterns punctuated with brass and tympani outbursts, a treatment common in all his subsequent works. These developments reflect Janácek's increasing efforts toward independence from the stifling dominance of Austrian musical and cultural heritage. *Jenufa* received a deeply sympathetic and supportive review by Max Brod, an influential critic. Brod was to become Janáček's biographer and translator of his operas.

*Jenufa's* melodic qualities gradually gave way to more tense atmospheres in Janáček's succeeding operas. Murder and intrigue received treatment in many subsequent operas, themes common in the Expressionistic works appearing on the European musical scene. Janácek met Kamila Stosstova while at a resort, and was very taken by her. He revealed his affection for her through his 700-plus letters. His second string quartet, *Intimate Letters (*1928), reveals the depth of his affair. Another showcase for this relationship was the 1921 opera, *Kat'a Kabanova*, known to have been inspired by her.

Other important works following *Jenufa* include the opera *Mr. Broucek's Excursion to the Moon* (1908-18), *Kat'a Kabanova* (1919-21), *A Cunning Little Vixen* (1921-23), and *The Makropulos Affair* (1923-5). *A Cunning Little Vixen* is the first of a trilogy, joined by T*he Makropulos Affair*, and completed by the very late *From the House of the Dead.* The three-part operatic set reflects on various aspects of nature's cycle of life and death, interestingly reminiscent of Malipiero's great trilogy, *L'Orfeide.* The latter two Janáček works, the brutal *Makropulos Affair,* and the grimly internalized *From the House of the Dead*, are less approachable than anything Janácek had produced up to that time, with their dissonance and rough subject matter.

His whole operatic output is intensely original. The works, although not directly influential upon succeeding composers, mark Janácek as a major contributor to the canon of 20th century art-music. Several of his operas have enjoyed important productions at the Metropolitan Opera.

Janáček was less well known for his purely orchestral work than for his operas. However, two late works shine: *Taras Bulba* (1918), and the Sinfonietta (1926). The *Taras Bulba* is a tone poem dedicated to the struggles of the Czech people after the outbreak of World War I. His characteristic phrasing emerges for the first time in his instrumental work. The conclusion of the work is most remarkable for its brass and tympani peroration in the resplendent climax. This segment, with its short alternating tonic and subdominant two-note motives in brass, punctuated by tympani bursts, is more highly developed in the later *Sinfonietta*.

The *Sinfonietta* also has militaristic roots, having been dedicated to the Czech armed forces. The grand brass, with its nine trumpets in C, three trumpets in F, and two bass trumpets, along with horns, trombones, tuba and tenor tubas is splendid indeed. The opening mottoes unfold in answering motives passed between trumpets and tenor tubas. The work ends with a brilliant declamation reminiscent of the previous *Taras Bulba*.

*The Concertino for Piano and Chamber Ensemble* of 1925 is a much smaller-scale work, but is equally ingenious for its employment of modal and advanced triadic harmony. Once again, the melodic contours follow speech-melodic principles. The *Glagolitic Mass* of 1926 is especially noteworthy. It is a mass in the Czech language with unbridled power in its primitive and spasmodic rhythmic eruptions.

The work is more nationalist than religious. Janáček revealed in a 1928 magazine interview, "I wanted to portray the faith in the certainty of the nation, not on a religious basis but on a basis of moral strength which God takes for witness" (Goodfriend Columbia record). The work is especially powerful in its unfolding of national fervor.

*From the House of the Dead* (1927-8) and the second string quartet *Intimate Letters* (1928) finish the creative output of this remarkable composer. Janácek died in 1928 after catching pneumonia from a chill he contracted searching for Kamila Stosstova's son on a ski slope.

Although it is impossible to trace a definite lineage of influence from Janáček's works through those of subsequent modernists, he was thoroughly original and left his mark on music through compositions that serve as profound models for musicmaking within nationalist idioms. There is no evidence that he or Bartók were profoundly influenced by one another; but Bartók was the only other major composer whose work has been imbued so deeply with a refined and carefully honed folk-based idiom. The two stand as towering models for all other composers working in this direction.

## • <u>His Style</u>

Hallmarks of Janáček's style are grounded in his special treatment of speech-melody and his use of modal harmony. There is some increased use of dissonance in his later operas, in which he abandoned key signatures, but harmony remained basically functional. There is some use of 4ths and 2nds, and occasional appearances of quartal harmony. Modal harmonic schemes are more common, though (Burke website).

Repetition through variation and displacement replace development in the unfolding of his formal designs. A quaint awkwardness informs some of his orchestration. This is not a reflection of a lack of skill; rather, it is an inbred naturalness that he assimilated from his folk-music studies.

Janáček's intensely original style should be appreciated for its honesty through his willingness to remain faithful to his artistic goal in the face of a disinterested academic establishment. This is the quality that earns him his honored place as one of the most respected modernists.

♦♦♦

# • <u>His Major Works</u>

<u>*Operas:*</u>

  *Jenufa*
  *Mr. Broucek's Excursion*
  *The Makropulos Case*
  *A Cunning Little Vixen*
  *From the House of the Dead*
  *Kat'a Kabanova*

<u>*Orchestral and Choral:*</u>

  *Taras Bulba*
  *Sinfonietta*
  *M'sa Glagolskaja*

<u>*Chamber:*</u>

  *First String Quartet (Kreutzer)*
  *Second String Quartet -*
  *(Intimate Letters)*
  *Concertino for Piano and Chamber*
  *Orchestra*

# Claude Debussy
# (1862-1918)

ᘓᕽᘔ

Music in the late 19th century seemed destined to drive headlong toward an impasse. The expansion of tonality into richer textures and chromaticism (the use of tones not in the diatonic scale of the key at hand) in dissonance or modulation clouded the sense of home base. Composers began to delay cadences, using ever more suspensions and cluster chords, until a resolution was finally reached. Literary texts used as a basis for the evolution of a work further distorted the sense of form. Musical discourse became lengthy and verbose, as operas (especially Wagnerian music dramas) and (Richard Straussian) tone poems stretched the ability of audiences to follow the flow. Patience and endurance were tested to the limits. Part of the problem was the continued reliance on classical forms, such as sonata-allegro, theme and variations, rondo, etc. to handle contents too cumbersome for those formal vessels. Tonality based on triadic harmony was also near collapse.

The nature of the dilemma was altered irrevocably by two major tonal experiments proffered by two of music history's most radical revolutionaries: Claude Debussy (Impressionism) and Arnold Schönberg (Expressionism). It is most unusual to encounter a musical period that has undergone so much change as the 20th century, or that has been so profoundly affected by so few individuals. The contribution of Claude Debussy to the musical evolution of the 20th century is hard to overstate.

## • <u>His Life</u>

Debussy entered the Paris Conservatory at age ten, after some preparatory piano lessons. He studied piano with Marmontel, solfège with Lavignac, harmony with Emile Durand, and score reading with Brazille. Debussy was introduced to Mme. Nadezhda von Meck, who had been Tchaikovsky's patroness. Although Debussy was exposed to Tchaikovsky's symphonies through his relationship with Mme. von Meck, he was completely unmoved by them. This seems to have been the first indication that Debussy had no taste for continuing along the lines of hyper-expressive Romanticism as evolving through ever more-tortured distortions of classical forms. Composers were pouring out feelings in novels of lush sounds and dense romantic harmonies. Debussy was uninterested in *pouring out*; he wished to *take in* and *reflect*, thereby allowing the mood to control the form in unpretentious musical gestures. Far more interesting to him was the more exotic music of the Russian nationalist composer, Modest Mussorgsky. The oriental flavor of the strange harmonic idiom, with its pulsations that followed the speech-flow of Mussorgsky's native culture was highly formative for Debussy *(SUM* Slonimsky p. 402).

By the mid-1880s Debussy began to leave an imprint of his own. He composed an orchestral tone poem (ca 1887) with wordless chorus (a concept to which he later returned in the last movement of the **Nocturnes** of 1893-99) (Holmes

p. 27). This early tone poem was destroyed, but it revealed Debussy's growing predilections for conveying a mood, and for using voices and instruments in unconventional ways to evoke, rather than to propound. The piece was atmospheric, his first example of Impressionism, revealing a certain vague (elusive) formal quality. Debussy won the Prix de Rome in 1884 with his cantata ***L'Enfant Prodigue.***

Debussy's stay in Rome was frustrating to him. He ached to return to Paris. By 1886 he did return by special permission of the Prix committee. Debussy was becoming more attuned to currents swirling about Paris in the other arts. He came into contact with the famous Symbolist poet, Stephanie Mallarmé. Many of France's leading cultural intellectuals met every Thursday evening at Mallarmé's home to bandy about new ideas and philosophies of art. Mostly writers and painters attended, many with an inclination to the new Impressionism. Debussy was one of very few musicians to attend. Whistler, Manet, Verlaine, and Valéry were among notable dignitaries who regularly attended. The discussions centered around the Symbolist philosophy as spelled out by the group's leader, Mallarmé: a Symbolist allows him/herself to become a human literary receptacle for stimuli from the outside; he/she should empty him/herself of all else to enhance his or her receptivity. This lesson stayed with Debussy for his whole life *(SUM* Holmes p. 29).

Later in life as Debussy struggled to find a vessel for his musical imagery that could replace the over-worn and unmanageable classical structures inappropriate to his needs, he developed a system of proportion that resembles the contours shaped by the Golden Section (Howat p. 1). However, the seeds for this approach may have been sown by his friendship with another Symbolist, painter Maurice Denis, who had access to the writings of a pedagogue within the movement: Paul Serusier. The latter's *ABC de la peinture* contains several pages devoted to proportion in art, including some on the Golden Section (Howat p. 164 ff.). This relationship was another sign of the potent influence the Symbolist and Impressionist movements had upon Debussy's formative development.

Other influences surged within Debussy at the time. The Wagnerian harmonic freedom, (as opposed to the Wagnerian Germanic philosophical heritage, or the overwrought formal distension in his operas), as well as the Lisztian freedom of expression in tone poems, loomed as compositional models for Debussy for a while. However, soon Debussy's profound hate for anything German, and his aversion to literary imagery and grandiloquence in music, fostered a lifelong attempt to shed the Wagnerian musical mantle. More important and lasting was the experience he absorbed upon hearing the oriental music and gamelan orchestras at the Paris World Exposition in 1889 (Slonimsky p. 402). These exotic sounds, and the influence of Mussorgsky, were the most significant for Debussy. Vocal works such as **Cinq Poèmes de Baudelaire** (1887-9) and **Ariettes Oubliées** (1888) combined Symbolist poetry with exotic music.

In 1890 **Suite Bergamesque** appeared, containing **Clair de Lune.** By 1892, Debussy began work on his most important work for orchestra, **Prelude to the Afternoon of a Faun,** completed in 1894. The free tonality is redolent with musical imagery, heightened by systematic use of modes, getting away from the straitjacket of the major-minor diatonicism that was on the verge of collapse under hyperextension (*PAR* Slonimsky p. 402). Modes were a frequent staple in Debussy's work, as he was to return to them from time to time. His favorites were the Phrygian and Lydian (Emory University website). Even more potently original and influential upon subsequent composers was Debussy's highly radical treatment of chords. In keeping with Symbolist ideology by which the composer would take in sensations, Debussy's work breathed forth the very exotic perfumes that seemed to conjure subtle dreamscapes. Chords followed one another in strange progressions that defied analysis. The harmonic cadences based upon sequences of tonic-dominant resolutions (common in established Germanic tradition) *weren't there.* Chordal movement was made synonymous with color. Functional harmony had been stripped from musical expression.

Debussy worked mostly in miniature forms, thus enabling himself to avoid the German-Romantic symphony, with its cadential harmonic functionality and sonata-development structure. Debussy hated musical formulation that drove melodic substance through programmed patterns. He once confided that what is good once is not necessarily better, said twice. The brevity of the Prelude enabled Debussy to get around the formal pitfall of how to construct a large-scale work that would remain formally coherent. This problem could not be outmaneuvered for long. In later works, notably his opera *Pelleas et Melisande* (1893-95) and his tone poem *La Mer* (1903-5), each containing a minimum of thematic materials and little development, Debussy solved the problem largely through special proportional treatment (Howat p. 156).

Analyst Roy Howat claims (pp. 5, 6, 7, 163) that Debussy *may have* systematically used the Golden Section, employing it to supply formal relationships formerly provided by the now-abandoned classical forms. As evidence Howat painstakingly analyses juncture points that mark changes in musical declamation (e.g. appearance of different instrumental voices, or rhythmic emphases), and climaxes. Additionally, he quotes a letter from Debussy to his publisher saying that a missing measure (*Estampes,* 1903) would "compromise the divine number" (Howat pp. 6-7). The implication is that this number refers to the Golden Section. Although this is speculative, it is interesting to follow his display regarding the proportional formalization of *La Mer.*

This systematization reminds one of another speculative analysis provided by Ernö Lendvai on the proportions in the work of Bèla Bartók, an admirer of Debussy. The Golden Section ratio is a special value achieved by a division of the whole (be it a line segment in math, or a whole movement in music) by way of length or duration, so that the parts assume a specific relationship. The ratio can be approximated by using a numerical sequence *(Fibonacci sequence)* and by providing sizes or durations proportional to neighboring numbers in the sequence. The ratio is so powerful that it has been used since Greek antiquity to provide strong structures in all arts, particularly architecture and structure. Whether Debussy or Bartók actually did the calculations can be debated, but apparently some concrete planning was used to impart structure, and it resembles the Golden Section. The important point is that a viable technique was consciously employed as a substitute for what had been given up by abandonment of classical tonality.

*Pelleas et Melisande* used whole tone scales and parallel fifths and octaves (Slonimsky p. 403). The scales lack a leading tone, giving the piece the flavor of tonal suspension. Parallel fifths had been forbidden treatment since the Renaissance gave way to the Baroque.

*La Mer* was followed by the colorful *Images* (1906-12). During this time, Debussy began to accept conducting engagements. In 1908, he conducted his work in London; in 1910, in Vienna; in 1911, in Turin; in 1913, Moscow and St. Petersburg; and in 1914, Rome, Amsterdam, and The Hague. His style began to see a shift towards tighter harmonies, with 7ths and 9ths (Slonimsky p. 403). Greater degrees of dissonance were employed, especially in his ballet work *Jeux* (1912). This partial change in style was a reaction to the trends of the times. Expressionism arrived through the paintings of Kokoshcka, Kandinsky, and Schönberg. Music reflected that development in works by Schönberg and Berg. The music captured the flavor of newly expressed negative emotions (fear, rage, etc.) in concert with the psychoanalysis of Sigmund Freud.

Debussy was unmoved by the whole Expressionist aesthetic, as it dwelt on angst and negativism. Mahler, Schönberg, and the whole Viennese musical scene seemed not to impress Debussy. Yet he was unable to resist the enrichment of his musical language with the dissonances then being explored by so many others.

Debussy had played piano on tour in 1917, but he had to cancel his American tour when he suffered severe symptoms of colon cancer. Previous surgery had left no hope. Finally, on March 25, 1918, the music world lost one of its most original and remarkable geniuses.

## • <u>His Style</u>

Debussy's style was one of understatement. He preferred to expound less, rather than more. His works contain rich, colorful chords that are non-functionally manipulated. Much of his work includes non-western harmonic practices, including the use of whole tone and pentatonic scales (diatonic, less fourth and seventh degrees). For example, the solo piano work, *Voiles* (1910), is mostly in the whole tone scale; the middle section is pentatonic (Slonimsky p. 403). While the whole tone scale usage did not originate with Debussy, his usage was the most systematic to that time.

For Debussy, tone color--or timbre--is a clarifying dimension in harmonic movement, while non-functional harmony provides an amplification of melodic contour. When harmonic density increased with greater chromaticism, the differentiation between timbres became severely compromised. So Debussy exerted two subtle shifts, one in the use of timbre and one in harmonic elaboration, to resolve the problems associated with what Curtis Roads calls "brown music" (music of suppressed contrasts, especially severely evident in serial music (Pape - *Composition...*- p. 3)).

In timbre, Debussy exploited non-traditional and softer shades in his orchestration than those formerly employed, thus increasing differentiation (and improving clarity). Then, for harmony, he used static chord structures to 'shadow' the melody as it unfolds. This enriched the melodic line without compromising timbral clarity. It also imbued harmonic structures with a 'tone-color' spectrum, thus replacing its classical functionality. With these approaches, orchestration became inseparable from harmonic evolution. These innovations exerted great influence, in revised form, upon Messiaen and Varèse.

More descriptively speaking, string effects such as harmonics are frequently employed. The volume levels are usually hushed, emphasizing stringed and woodwind timbres. Brass is often muted. The combinations are skillfully mixed. The rhythms are shifting and, at times, voluptuous, suggestive of excitement, such as rolling waves. The atmosphere can be sensuous as in **Prelude to the Afternoon of a Faun**, or charged as in **La Mer.** It is always evocative.

Debussy's sense of formal freedom, as well as his coloristic harmonic approach exerted an enormous influence on subsequent composers. Igor Stravinsky was drawn to his fluctuating rhythms reminiscent of the gamelan; Bèla Bartók was attracted to Debussy's sense of proportion; Olivier Messiaen learned from the exotic sounds and scales. Especially, though, the commanding radical, Pierre Boulez, adopted the coloristic textures and refined orchestration, including the gamelan as the pristine moving force of his experimental serialism. A whole host of cluster composers, active in the avant-garde of the 1960s, including György Ligeti, Krzysztof Penderecki, Witold Lutosławski, and Henryk Górecki profited handsomely from Debussy's pioneering effort. To this list, one may add the Italian modernist Bruno Maderna, the sensitive Japanese miniaturist, Toru Takemitsu, and the American master of understatement, George Crumb.

◆◆◆

## • <u>His Major Works</u>

*Suite Bergamesque (w/ Clair de Lune)*
*Prelude to the Afternoon of a Faun*
*La Mer*
*Nocturnes*
*Images*
*Jeux*
*Le Martyrdom de St. Sebastian*
*Pelleas et Melisande*
*Estampes*
*Voiles*

# Gustav Mahler
# (1860-1911)

ℰℐ

It isn't often that one encounters a highly regarded composer who was once condemned and, subsequently, neglected for decades. Gustav Mahler once carried that albatross and with it, scorn, for works that were thought prolix, too long, too loud, and even amateurish. His stature has grown immensely, and what was once thought to be verbosity and inconsistency of expression now is seen, in the light of history, as an epoch-making foundation for the Expressionism that soon would follow his example. Through his music, Mahler seems to have touched a chord in the audience of empathy for the fight of mankind against the injustices of a cruel world. Once thought excessive, the tremendous climaxes sound as a beacon of hope for humanity in its desperate struggle to meet God.

Mahler's work has appealed equally to the musical avant-garde of Vienna in the early 1900s (Schönberg), and to today's avant-garde (Boulez et al). If his work appealed to audiences weary of social strife and frustrated with the human condition of the 1960s, it appeals even more to advanced composers for its copious wealth of new sound materials.

## • <u>His Life</u>

At age fifteen, Mahler entered the Vienna Conservatory. He studied piano with Julius Epstein, harmony with Robert Fuchs, and composition with Franz Krenn. Later, he studied history and philosophy at the University of Vienna. In 1880, he was appointed conductor at the operetta-theater in Hall, Austria. He held various other conducting posts from 1881-1885: Ljubljana (theater - 1881), Olmütz (1882), and Kassel (1885). He became an assistant to the then-renowned Anton Seidl at the Prague Opera where he conducted Richard Wagner's operas. From 1886 he assisted Arthur Nikisch at Leipzig. Other posts included that of Music Director of the Royal Opera in 1888, and directorship of the Budapest Hamburg Opera in 1891. Mahler developed his subsequently famous mastery of the baton during his Hamburg tenure.

He also became familiar with Wagner and the new theories of expression in the orchestral works of Franz Liszt, Hector Berlioz, and Anton Bruckner. Mahler also developed a consummate knowledge of the orchestra and was to become a master orchestrator. In 1897, he was offered the most important position of his life. Mahler, never an unorthodox Jew, had no compunctions about becoming Catholic to win the position of Music Director of the Vienna Court Opera. (Offering the post to a Jew was not possible in that anti-Semitic climate.) Mahler held this conducting position for 10 stormy years, during which he had to overcome personal hostilities and intrigues, as well as enormous resistance to his uncompromising musicality.

Mahler slowly and persistently broke performance barriers that were developed from previous conductors who were grounded a little too much in a legacy of traditional old chestnuts and light works (operettas and the like). Much sloppiness in performing habits was entrenched. It took Mahler's forceful and fearless perseverance to break the bad habits. This cost Mahler dearly with the elderly women who ran the board. As if that weren't enough, Mahler had to fight vigorously on behalf of the new repertoire he was trying to instill. The battle was much tangled in the then-hostile Brahms vs. Wagner controversy raging in Germany and Austria. Finally, Mahler was unashamed to present his own works that were seemingly outlandish in size and expression. Brahms is said to have thought of Mahler as a revolutionary, after having heard the *First Symphony ("Titan")*.

At the end of the day, when all had been said and done, Mahler had succeeded in raising the performance standards, as well as the repertory, to previously unknown heights. This, though, was not enough to prevail over the increasingly vicious attacks from board members and players alike. Ultimately, Mahler was forced to resign (*SUM* Slonimsky p. 1116).

Mahler was a summer composer. Although his tasks as Music Director had become exceedingly demanding, he never neglected the opportunity to compose. The toll on Mahler, never a robust figure, was great. But composing was more important to him even than conducting was. Mahler's *First Symphony ("Titan")* was completed in 1888, and new materials were already apparent. His uses of muted brass and of special string and woodwind effects are prominent. Instruments were scored in extreme registers. This handling was a result of Mahler's penchant for extremes of expression that were to abound by his late works. Mahler also introduced a trait that was to bring him some infamy until the 1960s, when audiences became ready to hear it: he dared juxtapose a lighthearted ditty--the childhood song, "*frère Jacques*"--within a welter of serious, heavy content! Even worse, Mahler distorted the song into a funeral march! This confluence of unrelated materials bothered critics and audiences at the time. However, this distortion of raw materials was to become a trademark of 20th century art-music, and of jazz, in "third-stream" styles.

The *Second Symphony ("Resurrection"),* completed in 1894, was much longer. In it Mahler introduced a new stylistic trait that was to provide a deep impact on future composition. The weight of the climaxes was spread out so that tutti passages occurred less frequently. Mahler never feared high volumes: the audience is not spared the sudden outbursts so common in his work. The power remains, but the instrumentation is used more soloistically, as well as in small groups. There is a new tendency to get away from textural harmonic thickness, by adopting a more linear counterpoint--a trait that had been eschewed largely by major composers since the time of Bach. Also, the melodic line is treated so as to spread its iterations to different instruments. This handling was greatly expanded in the *Fifth, Sixth,* and *Seventh Symphonies.* Also, Mahler's funeral march idea in the First Symphony became very pronounced in his future works with greatly more sophisticated treatments of grotesquerie, especially in the scherzo movements. The third movement (scherzo) of the *Second Symphony* shows some tendencies in this direction.

The *Third Symphony* was completed in 1896. It is a vast canvass written in a polyphony of seemingly conflicting styles. In 1901, the *Fourth Symphony* was completed. At first glance, this work appears to be a reprieve from the size and expression of the previous works. The sounds of sweetness, though, are overtaken by a bitterness that lurks behind the surface fabric. Mahler's work is usually imbued with a disquieting undercurrent of irony and sadness, even when the sounds at certain instants are bright. The scordatura (out-of-tune) fiddle scored in the middle movement yields a haunting (or *haunted*) quality. These isolated sonic thrusts became the seeds of Schönbergian Expressionism very shortly thereafter.

In 1902, Mahler launched a full-scale assault on the traditions of tonal harmonic handling with the completion of his *Fifth Symphony.* Wagner's rich 'endless melody', couched in a dense harmonic language of ever-increasing dissonance via delayed resolutions, was being stretched further in the music of Mahler's contemporary, Richard Strauss. Mahler adopted some striking dissonance, but continued unraveling the harmonic fabric into intricate webs of independent contrapuntal lines. This refinement became a prominent quality in the work of Schönberg and his *Second Vienna School.* The breakdown of tonality was being propelled by a revolutionary *linear* handling of symphonic structure by this avant-gardist.

Other new devices in the *Fifth Symphony* include a pronounced refinement of the passing of melodic motives from one instrument to another. Note the concluding passages in the second movement. The use of tone color had become an element of melody, and a systematic formal device as well. Indeed, Schönberg, who advanced this technique to its limit in his *Five Pieces* for Orchestra, called the technique *Klangfarbenmelodie* (tone-color melody).

With Mahler's *Sixth Symphony* (1903-5), the tonal tradition continued to suffer assault. While Claude Debussy, Mahler's exact contemporary, was revolutionizing tonality by breaking down the major-minor system altogether, having introduced modality and the whole tone scale, Mahler pursued his assault from within the major-minor system. Mahler blurred the distinction between major and minor modes by combining and mixing them systematically, sometimes within the same phrase. Especially noteworthy is the frequent fluctuation of flatted and natural third scale degree in the opening melody of the second movement. This process is handled even more elaborately in the ***Seventh Symphony*** (1906). Non-traditional tonal treatment notwithstanding, the Sixth is a massive, yet tight (for Mahler) structure. It is his greatest symphony, and possibly one of the greatest of history.

Mahler originally subtitled his ***Seventh*** "Song of the Night" (1904-6). The subtitle was later dropped by Mahler to squelch persistent requests for programmatic "explanations" of his works (Mahler felt they needed none); however, the subtitle seems very apropos. The work is highly unconventional and contains much grotesque and eerie sound images. It contains three *Nachtmusik* movements. The three inner movements of this five-movement work shift moods, going from uneasy, phantomlike motives, to harsh irony, to an unsettling repose. The third movement is especially haunting with wraith-like figures, scurriling busily behind tuba and tympani explosions. This scherzo is reminiscent of the troubling one of the ***Sixth***. However, it's even more phantasmagoric, as it virtually recalls Berlioz' Witches' Sabbath in the ***Symphonie Fantastique,*** with its chilling tuba solo and filigree strings.

The ***Eighth Symphony*** (1906-7) is an ultimate expression of Mahler's religious yearning. It was completed in 1907, and it marks the last time Mahler used such vast symphonic forces in a quasi-exalted manner. (He had just received word of his heart condition.) The symphony is sort of an appeal to the Creator, but contains very little new in the use of musical materials.

After the news of his incurable condition, and with his demise as director of the Vienna Opera, Mahler traveled to America to assume the post of Principal Conductor of the Metropolitan Opera, where he conducted Wagner's ***Tristan und Isolde.*** In 1909, Mahler was appointed Conductor of the New York Philharmonic. While both posts were handled successfully by the standards of public and critics alike, the petty political infighting--so much a part of Mahler's professional musical life--engulfed him once again. Mahler was forced to resign both organizations and to return to Vienna. He had been experiencing the pangs of sorrow at the prospect of an early earthly leave-taking. These feelings came out in his last two major works, the symphonic song-cycle *Das Lied von der Erde* (1909), and the enigmatic *Ninth Symphony* (1910). The sense of sadness deepens with each work *(SUM* Slonimsky p. 1116).

*Das Lied von der Erde* is remarkable for its expanded song form. It incorporates an extended sonata-allegro form that is associated, more usually, with a symphony than with a traditional song-cycle. This fact has led to speculation that Mahler constructed a song-*symphony* to which he was reluctant to affix a number, in the superstitious fear that the fateful number nine would ensnare him, as it had Beethoven, Schubert, and Bruckner. The music is new in that it marks the first time Mahler employed an unusual scale. The pentatonic scale is employed in some of its movements. This provides an interesting comparison to the music of Debussy, especially for his use of the pentatonic scale in his *Voiles* (1907). The common ground for the two composers ends there, except for the fact that both were influential revolutionaries. *Das Lied von der Erde* is perhaps Mahler's ultimate testament in music, a masterpiece on the scale of his *Sixth Symphony.*

The *Ninth Symphony* (1909-10) of Mahler has been dubbed by the radical theologian/composer/analyst, Dieter Schnebel, as "the first work of new music" (Vinton p. 445). I believe that is something of an overstatement in that it skips other important works around that time, not least of all Arnold Schönberg's *First Chamber Symphony* (1906), and Claude Debussy's *Prelude to the Afternoon of a Faun* (1892-4). Still, it reveals the deep impression the work has left on the radical avant-garde in Germany. The work is most notable for its revolutionary treatment of thematic material in the opening movement. Here, Mahler has developed the tone-color melodic process completely. The initial fragment is handed from horn to plucked-string to muted horn within just a few notes. Tympani take up short fragmentary motives, also (very unconventional for those used to drum-rolls!). Webern was to profit considerably by this example in his use of single-tone motives.

Although Mahler completed sketches for a *Tenth Symphony*, the piecing together of the fragments to create a symphonic whole, accomplished by various musicologists, leaves an unsatisfying impression. The fully completed *Adagio*, though, is magnificent, if dark and foreboding. Much high dissonance and unusual instrumental treatment inhabit this remarkable movement. This ominous work was suppressed until the 1960s because of its intensely personal utterances, both musical and poetic (sprinkled liberally throughout the manuscript). Even though Alma relented in the 1960s, allowing the first movement to be performed, many conductors continue to avoid performing it (most notably the avant-gardist, Pierre Boulez, in spite of its prophetic style).

Mahler died of pneumonia and complications associated with his heart condition in 1911. The loss was felt most by his dedicated wife, Alma, and by his friend, the pioneering composer, Arnold Schönberg.


• **His Style**


Most of the stylistic elements in Mahler's music, pertaining to each work under consideration, have been discussed already. Most noteworthy are the special use of instruments in a soloistic, or contrapuntal fashion; the muted brass; the added dissonance; the unusual mixture of major and minor modes; and the emphasis on linear, rather than vertical, combinations. But one last point bears scrutiny. Mahler was perhaps the first of the Expressionists. Sigmund Freud was active in Mahler's time, and Mahler consulted Freud. The emotional horizon was being widened to allow for expressions of less pleasant emotions: fear; hate; and anger. These dark emotions combine with an abiding sadness that lurks as a constant undercurrent in Mahler's work to lend a somewhat depressing color to his music.

This quality is a part of all the Viennese composers' works of the first half of the century. But it is the newness of the *materials* brought into play by these composers, in order to faithfully capture the charged atmosphere of their subject matter, that was to influence music making, profoundly, throughout the balance of the 20th century. Boulez and Stockhausen, in addition to Schönberg, Berg, and Webern, owe a debt to Mahler's example.

◆◆◆

## • His Major Works

*Symphony #1 ("Titan")*
*Symphony#2 ("Resurrection")*
*Symphony#3*
*Symphony #4*
*Symphony #5*
*Symphony #6 ("Tragic")*
*Symphony #7 ("Song of the Night")*
*Symphony#8 ("Symphony of a Thousand")*
*Symphony #9*
*Symphony #10 - Adagio (Incomplete)*
*Das Lied von der Erde*
*Songs of a Wayfarer*
*Kindertotenlieder*
*Des Knaben Wunderhorn*
*Rückertlieder*

# Maurice Ravel
## (1875-1937)

☙

Most major composers of the 20th century are well known for their radical innovations in harmony and rhythm. The most prominent examples are Schönberg, Berg, and Webern (tonality/harmony), Stravinsky and Bartók (rhythm). Varèse achieved fame somewhat later (form). Innovations in orchestration are usually more acceptable to audiences than are innovations in harmony or form, because they seem less audacious and less combative. It was the particular gift of Ravel that he commanded such technical mastery over the orchestra, so his really new sounds are widely accepted as standard practice today. The command, that was effortless for him, has been unmatched by any other composer before or since. He was aware of this gift and took great pleasure in showcasing his skill through astonishingly refined orchestrations of his own piano works, and of the piano works of others (Davies p. 5).

It is a mistake, though, to overlook his other major -- if less apparent -- achievements and contributions, particularly in the field of harmony. His excursions in this arena may seem less spectacular than those of Schönberg and Berg, or even those of Bartók and Stravinsky; however, it is his particularly adroit handling of dissonant chords to make them sound *right* (*consonant*), that makes Ravel so particularly important, and so intriguing. Only by understanding his background is it possible to appreciate how he came to conquer these skills completely and convincingly.

- ### His Life

Undoubtedly, Ravel's predilection for technical mastery was traceable to his father's engineering background, and to Ravel's, and his father's, Swiss heritage. On the flip side, his mother was Basque, a culture known for its native dances and folk music (somewhat reminiscent of Spanish nationalism). Those influences informed Ravel's musicality equally. These disparate and not so familiar aspects of French culture combined with the more customary French backdrop of Paris, to which he relocated in his infancy, to mold his many-sided musical personality.

Ravel began to study piano at age seven with Henri Ghis. He studied harmony with Charles-René at age twelve. In 1889, he entered the Paris Conservatory. His studies there included piano (Eugène Anthiôme and Charles de Beriot) and harmony (Emile Pessard). After leaving the conservatory in 1895 for a brief period, during which time he wrote some piano works (including **Menuet antique**), he returned to the conservatory to study composition under the great French master, Gabriel Faurè (1897). His early piano music revealed his originality in the use of Spanish-flavored phrases and of the old church modes. These characteristics would remain a part of his music and serve him well in his later creative life; however, they would serve him poorly in his later relationships at the conservatory (*SUM* Slonimsky p. 1481).

Ravel is usually associated with Debussy as an Impressionist. The qualities of Impressionism oppose those of Expressionism. The latter evokes states of mind and invokes whatever musical materials will succeed in the creation of the associated ambience. Impressionism is a quality achieved largely through the capturing of a mood or scene. But the harsh sounds and psychological underpinnings redolent in Expressionistic art have no place in Impressionistic art.

The qualities in Impressionism are gentler, more generally serene. Ravel's music to the late 19-teens seems to follow this formula, but the customary linkage with Debussy is misleading. For one thing, Ravel used the whole tone scale so favored by Debussy only once (**Sheherezade Overture**, a youthful work) (Davies p. 11). Other, more subtle differences abound, as well. His studies under Fauré were more important to his mètier. The *ambience* in Ravel's music is similar to that in Debussy, but the *means* and *methods* were more nearly classical, with more traditional chords (extended by Ravel), and formal schemes (Baroque dance forms --gavotte-- etc.). These early studies, along with Ravel's coolness, aloof Swiss heritage, and his leaning to the colorful Basque flavors so encouraged by his mother, set the tone for the later, subtle Ravel musical personality and technical schemata.

After his conservatory studies were completed, Ravel applied for the Prix de Rome several times. Although he did capture the second Prix (his cantata **Myrrha**), he never won the grand prize. After the first two attempts were unsuccessful, he was barred from competing further on a technicality based on age. Several second rate composers won in his stead. A scandal ensued with charges of favoritism flourishing. Some speculation has it that Ravel's unconventional harmonic settings (PAR Davies p. 9) were to blame: he favored the less classical modes than those generally encouraged by the conservatory teaching hierarchy, biasing the judging against Ravel. The events so embittered Ravel that he brought the matter to public light in a periodical, *Mercure de France*, causing a crisis at the conservatory. Its Director, Théodore Dubois, was forced to resign and Faurè took his place (*SUM* Slonimsky p. 1481). Ravel's bitterness even led to his eventual refusal to accept France's highest prize, the Legion of Honor!

During the late 1890s, Ravel frequently visited the Paris World Exhibitions and was strongly impressed by the Javanese gamelan music that featured many colorful and subtle percussion instruments. He also came into contact with Nicolai Rimsky-Korsakov, whose musical orientalism may have impressed Ravel, even if the influence was not pronounced. He also became aware of contemporary music through attendance of concerts. His own work was transforming, as he adopted--and to some degree anticipated-- more modern techniques.

Several more works ensued. Most of the orchestral works of the time were preceded by versions for piano and, at this time, Ravel developed his taste for orchestrating such works. But the result is unique among other composers. For Ravel, the mastery of orchestration was so complete that phrases seemingly *right* for the piano were made equally *right* for the particular orchestral instrument assigned in the ensuing version. It almost seems as though there are two distinct works! The challenge of orchestration was so keen and attractive to Ravel that he relished the act of transforming his own works. He studied important new scores of others, (especially Stravinsky's) (Davies p. 5), but also Widor's treatise 'Technique de l'Orchestre moderne' (Davies p. 6). Ravel wanted to be a technician and this approach enabled him to succeed.

*Une Barque sur l'ocean* (1906), **Rhapsodie Espagnol** (1908), **Pavane pour une Infante Defunte** (1910), and

**Valses Nobles et Sentimentales** (1912) round out the early period, except for two impressive ballets. Later, **Ma Mère l'Oye** (1911) was turned into the orchestral suite by which it is known best today. It was followed by the sumptuously orchestrated **Daphnis et Chloe** (1909-12), the only collaboration between the composer and the famous impresario, Sergei Diaghilev. These works are very colorful, with harmonies that are often triadic. As he progressed, however, Ravel became bolder, stretching chord structures to higher complexities: ninths were common, and elevenths and even thirteenths were explored. Such chords contain most of the notes in the diatonic scale. However, through his adroit interval spacing, the 'crunch' generally associated with clusters (closely spaced notes), is made smooth and serene. Here is an example of more traditional tonal functions subjected to atraditional treatment. The chords are highly unusual, yet atmospheric. The sensual sounds reflect Ravel's harmonic mastery and ingenuity.

Ravel's music has a curious side that bears some attention. Late in this 'first' (quasi-romantic, sensual) phase, two works appeared that reveal his penchant for evoking a seeming superficial, artificial abstraction of the 'real thing'. The **Alborada del Gracioso** (1919) is imbued with clever, subtle orchestral effects (i.e., trombone glissandi!) and harmonic effects. **Le Tombeau de Couperin** (1920) is more interesting yet. It is a stylized mimic of older Baroque dance forms carefully draped within a modernist garb. But Ravel treats these old styles at arms' length (Davies p. 7), as though not to become too intimate with the authentic format. Old forms are modified, curiously with a sophisticated modern technique that belies their historical roots. Complex chords invade the quasi-classical structure to impart a surprisingly fresh sound. Ravel was fond of disguising his subject at hand so as not to provide a too-ready window to reveal his soul.

Ravel never married, and real intimacy was difficult for him. This tendency for artifice is even more apparent in the next work, **La Valse,** a waltz in Viennese style that is twisted and distorted to become a caricature of itself. The rich harmonies become acidic and dissonant. Ravel steps beyond the evocative here, as he enters a phase with a more chiseled classicism with its tighter formal focus. This style stayed with him for the balance of his career. His vocal music in the earlier 19-teens is of interest, particularly **Trois Poemes de Stephanie Mallarmé** (1913), which contains his closest brush with Schönbergian atonality. (Of all French masters, Ravel, alone, seemed affected by Schönbergian Expressionism. **Pierrot Lunaire** held a curious attraction for him.) Ravel's later song cycle **Chansons Madacasse** (1926) was even more venturesome, with cluster sounds in dissonant combinations. However, Ravel never abandoned tonality altogether.

His artificiality--or artifice, in the best sense of the word--should never be mistaken for insincerity, though. It reveals Ravel's penchant for unlocking unforeseen secrets within the more superficial veneer of the original. His handling of all this is highly ingenious. Malipiero had a similar quality that may remind one in a distant way of Ravel. It is a recurring thread in the history of 20th century music that composers seek the not-so-obvious flip side of what is taken for granted. Ravel's special gift for adroit manipulation of modern materials reveals him as a potent practitioner of this high art (artifice) *(PAR* Davies p. 8).

Ravel's late works, particularly the song cycles, have a poignant sadness, nearing tragedy (especially **Don Quichotte à Dulcinée** - 1933, his last major work). This quality seemed powerfully present in the works of both Mahler and Malipiero. It may have been that he was becoming acutely aware of the tragic malady that afflicted him from the 1920s onward, ultimately resulting in his death.

He had a rare brain disease, Multiple Apraxia (shrinkage of the brain). It robbed him of his creative powers at what should have been the height of his career. By the late 1920s, composition became painfully slow for him. Every melodic gesture had to be worked out arduously; by **Don Quichotte à Dulcinée's** appearance, it would take weeks to polish a melody to his satisfaction.

Ravel underwent unsuccessful brain surgery in December of 1937. He died nine days later. His tragic illness and early death robbed music of one of its most sophisticated practitioners. Stravinsky called Ravel a "Swiss watchmaker". Until recently, his contributions were largely overshadowed by Stravinsky, Bartók, and Schönberg. He is finally reaping his due measure of musical and historical honor.

## • __His Style__

The hallmarks of Ravel's style are primarily in his superb orchestral invention. Special effects are used to keep otherwise complex patterns clear. Angular intervals in La Valse, and extreme string divisi in Le Tombeau de Couperin and La Valse, influenced subsequent French composers (Davies p. 39). New sounds include trombone glissandi, trumpet fluttertonguing (Piano Concerto in G - 1929-31), jazz effects (same piece), harmonics, and other effects.

In matters of harmony, his use of very high-level chords (thirteenths, etc) is exemplary. These chords are handled functionally, not just coloristically. His rhythms were less aggressive than those of either Bartók or Stravinsky, but are remarkable for their shifting accents, and they achieve a slightly primitive sound in the later works. His melodies make frequent use of modality, and Basque folk-like contours.

Ravel's influence is less dramatic than that of Debussy. Most of the musical avant-garde has shied away from groupings of intervals built on thirds. Debussy's whole tone scale, Schönberg's fourths and sevenths, and Bartók's seconds get more emphasis. Still, Ravel exerted some influence on some composers whose works exhibit a predilection for precision and color. György Ligeti and Pierre Boulez have profited by his example.

♦♦♦

## • His Major Works

(Both versions - piano and orchestral - are inferred, as applicable)

*Alborada del Gracioso*
*Rhapsodie Espagnol*
*Bolero*
*Pavane pour Infant Defunte*
*Daphnis et Chloe*
    *(Complete)*
*La Valse*
*Trois Poemes de Stephanie Mallarmé*
*Chansons adacasse*
*Piano Concerto for Left Hand (D)*
*Piano Concerto in G*
*Ma Mère l'Oye Suite*
*Le Tombeau de Couperin*
*Valses Nobles et Sentimantales*

# Gian-Francesco Malipiero
# (1882-1973)

❧

I have never understood the level of neglect accorded to this great master. I don't believe it's simply a case of Malipiero's work being inherently unapproachable, despite the fact that his work is thornier than that of his more popular contemporary rival, Ottorino Respighi. Still, there are varying levels by which one may approach this admittedly enigmatic figure's music, sometimes in fairly straightforward fashion. It is altogether true that in order to experience the impact of his musical discourse, it does help to understand his philosophy and musical and personal background.

## • __His Life__

Malipiero was born in 1882 into a musical family. His grandfather, Francesco Malipiero, was an operatic composer. His father, Luigi, was a conductor. His schooling included study at the Vienna Conservatory and Liceo Musicale "B. Marcello", These experiences thoroughly grounded him in formal theory and compositional techniques, especially in Italian musical history. Around 1902, his studies led him to some old music manuscripts by Italian composers. He was soon to begin the efforts that won him recognition as one of the leading musicologists of the 20th century, as well as the foremost expert on Italian music literature. (He copied and transcribed the complete works of Claudio Monteverdi and many works each of Giovanni Bassani, Emilio del Cavalieri, Alessandro Stradella, Giuseppe Tartini, Antonio Vivaldi, and others) (Randel pp. 544-5).

Malipiero's interest in the manuscripts was intense. Consequently, he absorbed stylistic traits of the old masters into his own compositions, including the modal and contrapuntal techniques that were to become trademarks of his compositions from that time forward (Ewen p. 461-2). As well, his works from this time were imbued with the peculiarly Italian, plaintive nostalgia that is so characteristic of, and associated with, his work. At the time, though, in the early 1900s, his work seemed to be overly derivative to some (himself included!). His musical gestures were too reminiscent of older methods. Malipiero felt he was out of step, somehow, with current trends; somehow too closeted with the older ways. Several works of this time are bathed in this aesthetic; notable are three early Sinfonie (plural for Sinfonia, an older Italian form of music in a suite-like structure, unrelated to the later classic-romantic Austro-Germanic Symphony with its pattern of repetition and development of thematic materials. Malipiero preferred the Italian nomenclature to make that distinction clear in his own work). Malipiero felt that the three works: *Sinfonia degli Eroi* (Sinfonia of Love - 1905), *Sinfonia del Mare* (Sinfonia of the Sea - 1906), and *Sinfonie del Silenzio e de la Morte* (Sinfonias of Silence and Death - 1908), were too narrow, expressively, and were out of sync with a more forward looking idealism that was just beginning to inform the European compositional landscape. So he isolated these works, as well as several other early works, and repudiated them in various interesting ways. Although Malipiero (ultimately) was to support the *Sinfonia del Mare*, the instrumental Impressioni dal vero (composed in 3 parts: 1913; 1917; and 1923) were more revelatory of his subsequent development.

In 1913 Malipiero went to Paris where he was to absorb a multitude of fresh and stimulating new musical experiences, not the least of which was a performance of Igor Stravinsky's *Le Sacre du Printemps* (The Rite of Spring). In the process, Malipiero came into contact with Claude Debussy, Gabriel Fauré, Maurice Ravel, Manuel de Falla, and Stravinsky himself. These interludes were very influential in helping Malipiero establish a new formal approach, if not an entirely new aesthetic. That is to say, he did not completely discard his entire musical métier. Some of the modality and contrapuntalism were refitted with more modern sounding chordal structures including some more aggressive dissonances (not overly so, when one contemplates some of the stuff put forth by such luminaries as Arnold Schönberg, Igor Stravinsky, Béla Bartók, and Edgard Varèse). But Malipiero was smart enough not to entirely discard his peculiar nostalgia for the older Italian sensibility and sonorities that were uniquely his: he retained his sense of personal expression. One of the ways was to couch the musical discourse in a series of contemplations internal to the architecture (Waterhouse Cyclopedia p. 1318). The main attribute of this new style is a formal series of musical 'panels' (Waterhouse Cyclopedia p. 1317) delineating separate musical episodes, seemingly unrelated, but reflectively interactive towards one another in the manner of a dialogue (somehow reminiscent of Messiaen's "aspects"). The most prominent work in this new approach is his *Pause del Silenzio I* (1917).

After the *Pause del Silenzio I*, Malipiero began to tackle not only other large-scale instrumental pieces, but also opera, albeit cast in an entirely new garb. Malipiero's work proceeded in two directions: first, with his Italian peers, Ottorino Respighi, Alfredo Casella, and Ildebrando Pizzetti, he tried to reestablish the preeminence of the purely instrumental work in Italian art music that had been lost since the Renaissance; second, he was to invigorate the then-stale Italian operatic tradition by turning away from the overexposed 'verismo' styles (i.e. realism) that had dominated Italian opera for decades. The revolution Malipiero wrought in both forms was accomplished through his expressionistic 'paneling' and contemplative schemes (*PAR* Waterhouse Cyclopedia p. 1318). In his instrumental works he turned away from repetitive content and formalism (German Romanticism) toward a free flow of discourse. He was to say later "the Italian Sinfonia is a free kind of poem in several sections which follow one another capriciously, only obeying those mysterious laws that instinct recognizes." (Waterhouse Cyclopedia p. 1318).

In the 1920's and 1930's, Malipiero held several teaching posts, including a professorial post at the Parma Conservatory. Malipiero retired after World War II to his countryside home in Asolo to compose and teach. As a teacher, he was of great influence on the future of the Italian avantgarde, numbering among his students, Bruno Maderna and Luigi Nono. His philosophy and music also inspired Luigi Dallapiccola and Sylvano Bussotti. Bussotti, a major Italian theatrical composer, has sponsored several productions of Malipiero's work in Italy (Waterhouse 8.223603 p. 2). In the 1930's, Malipiero was Codirector, along with Alfredo Casella, of the Maggio Musicale, a series of concert productions devoted to the performance of modern music.

## • <u>His Philosophy</u>

The formal content of Malipiero's instrumental works is intuitive and cumulative, revealing itself fully to the listener's consciousness only as it progresses to the end of the work. Musicologist John C. G. Waterhouse attributes the conductor, Ernest Ansermet, to having remarked that rather than the structure of the work shaping the content as in the classic-romantic Austro-Germanic symphonic tradition, in Malipiero's work, the content shapes the plan (PAR Waterhouse 8.223602 p. 5-6). And what is the content? In Malipiero's work, emphasis is on the philosophical and contemplative, rather than on the pictorial, literary, or event/action. The listener is invited to reflect and turn over often seemingly opposite musical qualities, and to follow the composer's resolution, somewhat as though the musical discourse is made into a dialogue between opposing concepts.

These qualities reside in no smaller degree in Malipiero's operas also, wherein expressive content is focused upon commentary among ancient philosophers--some imaginary--often drawing distinct contrasts between, and parallels to, today's thought (*PAR* Tahra notes). The opposing tendencies are frequently treated instructionally and the panels are presented symbolically. Certainly, for anyone accustomed to a lot of action, this sort of treatment may be unsettling at first exposure! Commonly, Malipiero's focus in his operas is upon man's various states of mind, including thoughts on death, silence, love, as well as many others (*PAR* Waterhouse Cyclopedia p. 1316-7). The sort of operatic treatment required to pull this off differs from the aria-recitative and set numbers common in traditional opera. His operas employ many very unusual formal schemes.

• **His Style**

In general, Malipiero's work is intuitive, presented through a formal technique that builds and accumulates expressive material. Like Debussy, a composer he greatly admired throughout his artistic life, Malipiero distrusted the packaged forms (sonata-allegro, rondo, etc.) of the German Romantic tradition with their emphasis on repetition and development. Malipiero was more fond of freer sonic discourse that enabled a more secretive plan, one that would require greater attention to the exposition, and less to the shell. As a result, one encounters several melodies, sometimes just fragments, which play in the unfolding process. Malipiero's unique sense of variation determines just how this reveals itself. Frequently, fragments appear for no formally traceable reason, seemingly only for whim. There are intuitive designs at work, but their secrets often remain with the composer!

Unlike the classical symphony, the different movements of his Sinfonias often do not contain repeated thematic materials, or materials drawn from previous movements within the same work. Additionally, movements begin in one key and end in another, when key signatures are used (PAR Waterhouse 8.223602 p. 6). The result is often a craggy texture that, for these very reasons, can imbue the whole of the work with considerable charm. The non-symphonic (or non-sinfonic, as the case really is) poems, like **Pause del Silenzio I**, or **Notturno di Canti e Balli**, are usually in separate movements (Notturno), or in 'panels' of action (Pause) held together by means of short interludes of a single theme. These interludes, though thematically common, are varied by means of tempo, rhythm, orchestration, or otherwise upon each appearance. The materials in the main panels are usually unrelated to those in previous panels. These formal expressions signify that it is incorrect, even sloppy analysis to label Malipiero's work 'neo-classical', simply because there exist works with the label "symphony" or "sinfonia". There is no standard patterning here.

Melodically and harmonically, Malipiero's mature work (post 1915) is generally divisible into three overall stylistic periods. The first lasted from about 1915 through the late 1920s, and it was characterized by dissonant sequences of short melodic statement that were then in vogue (Bartók, Stravinsky, et al). The second lasted through the 1930s and 1940s, and was characterized by softer, more relaxed melodic and harmonic treatment. The third lasted through the 1950s and 1960s, and saw the composer's work become very terse and expressionist, and even atonal (though he claimed never to have used serial procedures).

Through all these periods, though, Malipiero retained that signature quasi-modal, plaintive nostalgia. Even in his expressionist works of the late 1950s one hears the poignancy of his earlier works. Schönberg, Berg, and Bartók opened up the musical display of aggressive Expressionism, with its predilection for harsh emotive discourse. Malipiero, even in such works as the ***Sinfonia per Antigenida*** with its dissonances and frenetic syncopations, reveals an expression of a subtler, more mysterious cast, whose logic is not easily revealed.

It is hard to do justice to such an elusive, idiosyncratic, many-sided figure in a brief essay. I hope that the reader will be inspired to experience the primary art of this remarkable composer in a primary way--through listening. The old master reluctantly yields his secrets, but those secrets, once carefully explored in a sensitive way, bear generous fruits, not the least of which are lessons about ourselves and the way we perceive things.

◆◆◆

- ## His Major Works

| Symphonies/ Sinfonias | String Quartets | Miscellaneous |
|---|---|---|
| Sinfonia del Mare | Rispetti e Strombatti (#1) | Dialogue No. 1 (con Manuel de Falla) |
| Symphony No. 2 'elegiaca' | Stornelli e Ballate (#2) | Notturno di Canti e Balli |
| Symphony No. 3 'delle campane' | Cantari alla madrigalesca (#3) | PauseDel Silenzio |
| Symphony No. 4 'In Memoriam' | String Quartet No. 4 | Grottesco (a.k.a. 'I Selvaggi') |
| Symphony No. 5 'Concertante' | dei capricci (Qt No. 5) | Fantasie di Ogni Giorno |
| Sinfonia in un tempo | L'arca di Noè (No. 6) | Sette Invenzioni |
| Sinfonia dello zodiaco | String Quartet No. 7 | Dialogue No. 4 for Wind Instruments |

| | | |
|---|---|---|
| *Sinfonia per Anti-genida* | *String Quarte No. 8* | *Dialogue No. 7* |
| *Sympony No. 9 'dell'ahimè'* | | *PianoConcert-No.3* |
| *Symphony No. 11 'della cornamuse'* | | |

### Opera
*L'Orfeide - Operatic trilogy*
- *La Mort des Masques*
- *Sette Canzoni*
- *Orpheus*

# Paul Hindemith
## (1895-1963)

☙

Paul Hindemith started his composing career as a blazing radical, securing a reputation for instigating musical change and innovation on a par with those of the other major masters of the 20th century: Igor Stravinsky, Béla Bartók, and Arnold Schönberg. He closed his career as one of the stabilizing influences in the middle of the century, having accomplished a tremendous, if puzzling, stylistic transformation towards conservatism. From early in his career through its zenith, Hindemith was a master craftsman, regardless of his style. That he grew in compositional acumen, as his style was growing less innovative, is remarkable for how it reflects on Hindemith's lofty place in the history of musical creativity

## • <u>His Life</u>

During Hindemith's early years, Germany was enjoying relative prosperity, and the social scene was fairly calm as well. The climate seemed conducive to a steadycreative life. Hindemith's father strongly encouraged his three children in their artistic studies and efforts. Hindemith's father,

Robert, was a menial laborer and somewhat unimaginative, but worked very hard. Robert's only musical activity consisted of playing zither. The family would play as a group occasionally, with Paul on the violin.

Despite the family's trying financial straits, Paul Hindemith studied violin with Anna Hegner, who led a local (Frankfurt, Germany) string quartet. No matter the hardship, Hindemith's father faithfully supported musical education. Hindemith then studied with Adolf Rebner, a conservative teacher at Hoch Conservatory in Frankfurt. Hindemith was assigned to play second violin in Rebner's quartet. Hindemith became an exceptional violinist and by the age of fourteen he played portions of Mozart's *D Major K. 218 Violin Concerto* and Bach's "Chaconne" from the *Solo Partita in D Minor BWV 1004*. Paul and his brother Rudolf helped the family financially by playing concert duos for money.

From 1911-12, Hindemith would compose in secret to avoid critical comments of the conservatory staff. In 1913, while still at Hoch, he studied composition from Bernhard Sekles, a strict pedagogue. Sekles' highly disciplined approach was instrumental in the later solidification of Hindemith's own carefully crafted method of composition *(SUM* Rickards p. 16-26). Additionally, his study of Bach helped orient Hindemith in a contrapuntal style.

His father was killed in the war, so Hindemith joined the Frankfurt Opera Orchestra as Concertmaster in order to keep the family afloat. He completed his first major work, the *Lustige Sinfonietta* (Lusty Symphony) in 1916. The Germany of post-World War I was suffering from financial and social crises. The arts reflected the unstable state of affairs, as the rise of Expressionism marked literature, painting (significantly Oscar Kokoschka), and music. Arnold Schönberg and Alban Berg were writing atonal works that reflected new socially acceptable expressions of emotional states heretofore considered forbidden (hate, fear, anger, etc.) (*SUM* Rickards 33-9). Also, Sigmund Freud's psychological theories were being put into practice.

Hindemith was not immune to this trend--far from it. He drew upon his innate rebellious nature to issue new works of savage violence. In 1919, he composed *Mörder, Hoffnung der Frauen*, (Murder, Hope of Women). This extremely expressionist work was a very short opera (as were the early monodramas of Schönberg). Hindemith quickly decided to compose two more short operas as companions, so that all three could be presented as a set for a single evening's fare. The two companion operas were the marionette opera *Das Nusch-Nuschi* (1921), about a philanderer who is sentenced to castration for his indiscretions, and *Sanctus Susanna* (1922), about the sexual fantasies of a young nun (*SUM* Rickards 46-7). Needless to say, this operatic trio's subject matter alone would cause concern even today, let alone in Germany in the 1920s. The music was appropriately harsh, with Hindemith's established trademark heavy-footed rhythms a bulwark for music that explored extremes of register. The dissonant counterpoint would generate block-like, harsh chords. Hindemith had arrived a real bad-boy of music! (*SUM* Rickards pp. 40-47).

Although Hindemith was in vogue, he may have been in the wrong country for his experimentalism. This trio of operas was soon to be the source of grave regrets for Hindemith, in his interface with the soon-to-come Nazi regime. In the meantime, though, he composed with ease, turning out many important new ensemble pieces, especially for the instruments of his expertise--the violin and viola. The works explored the full range of technique in a typically uncompromising idiom. Speed and extreme register were stylistic hallmarks of these works (Rickards p. 50). Few, except Hindemith, of course, could master the technical problems in these sonatas. He made contact with the forward-look-ing conductor, Wilhelm Furtwängler, and the even more avant-garde Conductor, Herman Scherchen, at this time. These contacts seemed to solidify Hindemith's position as a sensational modernist.

During the decade of the 1920s, Hindemith contin-ued to explore new territory. For the 1926 Donaueschingen music festival, he composed *Triadic Ballet* for piano rolls. He used the trautonium, a rudimentary electronic instru-ment, in *Konzertstücke* (1926). He even wrote a palindro-mic opera, *Hin und Zurück* (There and Back - 1927), in which music and plot unfold, then reverse (Rickards p. 59). The main subplot, as was the case for most of Hindemith's operatic work up through 1933, centered on murder. Hin-demith developed a new instrumental musical form in his aggressive *Concerto for Orchestra* (1925). His 1929 opera *Neues vom Tage* (News of the Day) was one of his last ex-pressionistic works, marking the virtual end of his experi-mentalism.

However, interspersed with these experiments, sev-eral seminal works appeared that were to show the way of Hindemith's future, more relaxed composing style. *Das Marienleben* (1923), on poetry by Rilke, reveals a contem-plative seriousness not previously heard in Hindemith's work. The work's atmosphere contains many ecclesiastical qualities and serene moments. It is well crafted, with the nervousness of other works taking a breather. This style was to find fuller expression in the opera *Mathis der Maler* (Mathias the Painter - 1934) and the ballet *Nobilissima Vi-sione* (1938). Additionally, *Cardillac* (1926), an opera--al-though it includes murder in the plot--is remarkable for the skillfully crafted matching of action and musical expres-sion. These elements deeply informed some of Hindemith's later works.

Hindemith was appointed Professor of Graduate Composition at the Hochschule for Music in Berlin in 1927. The seriousness of his new position gave Hindemith pause to consider his place in the music world, and how he was to impart knowledge and method to a youth eager to learn. Out of concern for the unorthodoxies in his personal musical education, Hindemith carefully and painstakingly detailed the requirements of the craft of musical composition and of its teaching. These efforts were to bear considerable fruit in the landmark treatise he would publish, *The Craft of Musical Composition.*

In this work, the whole framework for his future was spelled out. From first principals, he developed a solid foundation for harmonic movement including transformations and modulations of key. Hindemith's system encompassed motion between keys (often in fifths) (Machlis p. 201) in which related keys are close by. Modulation to remote keys would follow the closer-related modulations and would be subjected to a methodical treatment. Harmonic function could be retained while vastly freeing the use of dissonance from its classical methodology. The method enabled Hindemith to maintain a firm tonal center, and to move away from the grip of his youthful Expressionism. Bach's works provided a model for his style of exploring tonalities in the works that followed. Hindemith's peculiar system of harmony included simultaneous movement of unrelated chord structures in what Machlis calls "harmonic polyphony" (*PAR* Machlis p. 201).

Meanwhile, the incoming Nazi regime was deeply affronted with what had been Hindemith's modernism. Hitler attended a performance of ***Neues vom Tage***, and left disturbed (Rickards p. 65). The news of a revival of Hindemith's operatic trio of 1921 didn't help matters. Hindemith was in critical trouble. Eventually, he immigrated to Switzerland and, later, to the US.

Concurrent with his work on his method of composition, he composed many simple sonatas to provide learning tools for amateur musicians. This work is sometimes called *Gebrauchsmusik* (music for use). It revealed his growing concern that music not be out of the reach of its audience and practitioners.

In 1932, as discussed previously, Hindemith wrote a major operatic masterpiece, **Mathis der Maler**, on the life and works of the Renaissance painter, Matthias Grünwald. The paintings in the Isenheim Altar provide the basis for the plot. An operatic symphony from thematic materials in the opera was also published. Three tableaux provide most of the central focus: The Concert of Angels; The Entombment of Christ, and the Temptation of St. Anthony. The music is moving, even serene--most assuredly strong. Both forms of this piece are landmarks. The dissonant tonality is most revealing of his new style.

Nearly of equal importance was the **Nobilissima Visione** (1938). This work, a ballet centered on St. Francis, is also very moving. The concert suite, drawn from materials in the ballet, contains some of Hindemith's finest music. The serene opening, which unfolds to an equivocal close in the opening movement, precedes two lovely movements, the last of which proceeds unremittingly to a satisfying climax of controlled power and beauty.

Two more major works bear mention. The first was a highly ingenious set of variations on four separate melodies from four obscure works by Carl Maria von Weber, the **Symphonic Metamorphoses on Themes of Weber** (1943). This work is particularly noteworthy in view of Hindemith's adroit use of rhythmic patterns and dissonant harmonies within a completely tonal context. Finally, the sumptuous opera, and its attendant operatic symphony **Die Harmonie·der Welt** (The Harmony of the Universe – 1950-53) appeared. This rich, post-baroque work rounds out Hindemith's major work.

Hindemith held a post at the Berkshire Music Center at Tanglewood in 1940, and was professor at Yale University from 1940-53. Hindemith traveled widely, conducting his own works. He received many awards and continued turning out music until his death in 1963.

• **His Style**

Hindemith's music is fairly consistent within either of his distinct stylistic periods, the Expressionism from 1915-1930, or his later modernist neo-Baroque / Romanticism. The melody is basically lean, within strongly linear contrapuntal lines. The melodies move freely within a set of related keys. The harmony is block-like, with dissonance from the coming together of independent moving lines. The rhythm is sometimes heavy-footed and plodding, but at its best, motoristic, imparting a streamlined feel to the sound.

There is not a great deal new in later Hindemith. Other composers completed the major tonal and rhythmic revolutions. However, he did enforce the evolution of expanded tonal and expressive methods by the force of his personality and craftsmanship.

◆◆◆

- ## His Major Works

  *Mathis der Maler (Opera & Symphony)*
  *Symphonic Metamorphoses on Weber Themes*
  *Concert Music for Strings and Brass*
  *Violin Concerto Nobilissima Visione*
  *The Four Temperaments*
        *(Theme and Variations)*
  *Concerto for Orchestra*
  *Die Harmonie der Welt (Opera & Symph.)*
  *Das Marienleben*
  *Philharmonic Concerto*

# Igor Stravinsky
# (1882-1971)

☙

A single figure rarely dominates the musical consciousness of a whole century as Igor Stravinsky has. Although much of this honor is justified, the disproportionately high adulation accorded Stravinsky seems excessive--particularly when a multitude of composers of high talent and originality inhabits the landscape (especially Arnold Schönberg, Béla Bartók, Alban Berg, and Paul Hindemith, not to mention the isolated geniuses, Anton Webern and Edgard Varèse). Nonetheless, there can be no disputing the remarkable and influential innovations that profoundly undergird such landmark works as *Petrouchka* and *The Rite of Spring (Le Sacre du Printemps)*. The freshness of the rhythmic invention, and of the peculiar bitonal, polytonal, and polar harmonic writing still seems striking with each new listening experience. Many of the devices Stravinsky employed in these sensational ballet-sound-pieces are the stuff of musicians' shelves, handy for access and use by composers worldwide.

## • __His Life__

Stravinsky was born into an artistic environment. His father was a Russian operatic bass. He studied piano early, under Snetkova, a one-time student of Anton Rubenstein. Later, from 1900-1903, he studied theory under Akamenko and Kalafati. Stravinsky was a slow developer. He never entered a conservatory or graduated from a university music school, although he took an 8-semester course at St. Petersburg University. He met two of Nicolai Rimsky-Korsakov's sons during his student years, eventually befriending one, Andrei. That association enabled the young Stravinsky to meet the elder Rimsky-Korsakov. Stravinsky guest-attended many of Rimsky-Korsakov's St. Petersburg classes. Rimsky-Korsakov then taught Stravinsky the art of orchestration privately. Stravinsky's early work, composed while studying with the master, showed little of the polish and consistency that was to mark his later work. Other early works reveal the imprint of Impressionism, then in vogue, especially with Claude Debussy's work. Stravinsky's first notable work, an orchestral fantasy *Fireworks* (1908), was composed for a wedding. Rimsky-Korsakov died days later. Stravinsky was deeply grieved by the departure of his teacher and composed a funeral song, with wind accompaniment, in Rimsky-Korsakov's memory.

By 1910 Stravinsky's composing style had matured greatly, prompting a commission for a ballet from Serge Diaghilev, the famous impresario associated with *Ballet Russes*. The ballet was to become Stravinsky's first masterpiece: *The Firebird* hit the scene in 1910, and was staged in Paris on June 25, 1910. This work reveals the brilliance of orchestration, harmony, and tone color long associated with Stravinsky's teacher, Rimsky-Korsakov. The lessons wore well with Stravinsky. Several original devices emerged in his work, including the use of glissando patterns (trombone), string harmonics, and the great rhythmic variety and vitality that would become characteristic of all of Stravinsky's later music. The asymmetry of the rhythmic structure would be enhanced further in subsequent works. The harmonies and orchestral colors evoke Russian folklore. The scoring is lavish (as was that of his teacher) in keeping with the post-Romantic tradition of the day (*PAR*. Slonimsky p. 1807).

Diaghilev maintained his working relationship with Stravinsky, hoping to capitalize on the great success of *The Firebird*. Stravinsky moved to Paris in 1911 for the purpose of close work with Diaghilev. This venture paid off shortly with a second masterpiece, the ballet *Petrouchka* (1911). Stravinsky's orchestration, rhythmic treatment and tonal management became ever more original. Stravinsky shocked the world by introducing two superimposed triads, in themselves diatonic, built from root tones a tritone apart (the tritone interval is an augmented fourth, such as C natural and F#) (van den Toorn p. 31-2). That interval has a non-consonant, unsettled quality. It perfectly fit the atmosphere of tension Stravinsky desired for *Petrouchka*. The two chords taken together (they appear simultaneously) form a partial scale that is built on alternating half and whole step intervals, as opposed to the seven-tone diatonic scale that contains just two half-step intervals (van den Toorn p xv & p. 5).

This scale is called "octatonic", by analysts, (especially Arthur Berger and Pieter van den Toorn), because it contains eight notes. It also lacks a firm leading-tone tendency inherent in the diatonic scale. This provides a vast flexibility in modulating from one tonality to another. The common nomenclature for this sort of congealing of triads is 'bitonality' (later 'polytonality', when added triadic combinations are superimposed). Stravinsky analysts tend to avoid this term, for even though it's a handy name for ease of understanding by the concert-going public, it really implies that the triads retain their classical functions (as in *functional* harmony, or harmony in which chords progress or resolve by patterns to control form). Stravinsky's chords do not behave that way (van den Toorn p. xiv & xv). They are often coloristic or are disguised as they explore seemingly unrelated keys. So van den Toorn, in particular, refers to this combination as non-classical octatonicism or octatonic/diatonic treatment mixtures. Suffice it to say that these technical processes greatly enriched the harmonic texture to which Stravinsky availed himself.

The rhythms in *Petrouchka* are explosive and more abrupt than those even in *The Firebird.* This advance in rhythmic techniques was to reach its peak, in subsequent works, especially in *The Rite of Spring (Le Sacre du Printemps* - 1913), and, differently, in *L'Histoire du Soldat* (1918).

Of special note, the piano is added to the orchestra, rich and lavish as it was in *The Firebird.* The piano as orchestral member became common technique in the 20th century, enhancing its role as a percussive, rather than a stringed, instrument. Works by Bartók, Malipiero, and Martinů exhibit this usage.

The next major work was also a ballet under Diaghilev's auspices, *The Rite of Spring*--a monument in modern music, both for its exploration of new harmonies, and for its driving, violent, constantly changing rhythms. The rhythms frequently shift from one meter to another (e.g., 3/4-4/4-2/4 or 3/16-5/16-3/16) (Machlis p. 177), often in the span of a couple of measures. Whereas Bartók employed driving rhythms in irregular meters (e.g., 5/4), he shifted meters less suddenly, choosing to shift accents from one beat to another. Stravinsky shifts accents *and* meters in rapid succession. The patterns developed by Stravinsky are not arbitrary, but follow a formal plan of transformation, a characteristic that would greatly influence the subsequent works of the post-Webern serialists, Pierre Boulez and Olivier Messiaen.

The orchestration of The Rite of Spring is lavish, calling upon a huge orchestra, the last such work in Stravinsky's canon.

The harmonies employed for ***The Rite of Spring*** are much more dense and complex than those for any previous work by Stravinsky. There are significant passages containing chord progressions with moving parallel major seventh intervals. This treatment gives a very dissonant quality to the work. Its harsh character results from the dense harmonies and violent rhythms that were used to evoke pagan Russia. The work's first performance (1913) in Paris caused a riot.

The outbreak of World War I wrought a tightening of economic conditions common throughout Europe. Most composers responded by significantly paring down the size of the orchestras required in their works. More intimate compositions, from symphonies to operas (notably Richard Strauss' ***Ariadne auf Naxos***), came to be penned. Stravinsky participated in this trend with an abrupt and pronounced about-face in style. Following the lead of other composers in the development of 'neo-classicism', Stravinsky took aim at creating works that were less emotionally dense. He largely eschewed Russian nationalistic subjects and sound flavors in favor of a dry, brittle, biting style. (Also, Stravinsky was unhappy with the turn in Russia towards communism. He abandoned his Russian connections just as Russia ostracized him for his 'bourgeoisie methods'.) The harmonies became leaner and simpler, although the harmonic *treatment* continued to employ devices deliberately constructed to disguise tonal functionality, including the expansion of the use of the tonally ambiguous octatonic scale.

The major works that followed this transformation include ***L'Histoire du Soldat*** (1918), ***Les Noces*** (1917), ***Pulcinella*** (1919-20), and the ***Octet*** (1922-3) for winds. Stravinsky's next masterpiece was the ***Symphony of Psalms*** (1930), an austere, intensely religious work. Stravinsky's turn toward conservative classical models was now complete, and it coincided with communist Russia completely cutting off Stravinsky's access to his estate (McAllister. p. 2181). The works were even more economical and diatonic than those of the '20s. Other works of the '30s include ***Oedipus Rex***, and the ***Violin Concerto***. This music seems stripped to its barest essentials in orchestral economy. The 1940s showed a gradual return to more aggressive harmonic dissonance and rhythmic aggressiveness. The end of World War II brought several jubilant works of celebration, including Stravinsky's own ***Symphony in Three Movements*** (1945).

As though to confound his critics and admirers alike, Stravinsky did one more stylistic about-face. In the early 1950s--significantly, after Schönberg's death--he adopted serialism, a device he had deplored (much as he deplored its founder, Schönberg). Although, the particular brand of serialism Stravinsky used was based more on Webern's system, with its canonic counterpoint, than on Schönberg's. Retaining his characteristic austerity, Stravinsky wrote many works in the style, most notably, his ***Agon*** (1953) ballet with orchestra.

In 1962, the USSR Composers' Union honored the master for his 80th birthday with concerts in Moscow and Leningrad. This occasion was the only time Stravinsky ever returned to his native Russia after 1914.

After composing, and enduring a major conducting regimen with many major orchestras, he died in New York, in 1971.

## • <u>His Style</u>

Stravinsky's work evolved from the nationalism of the 19-teens. Its lavish orchestral style and pounding rhythms then gave way to an austere classical economy of style, which lasted through his 'neo-classical' years and his serial years until the end of his life.

Stravinsky's early Russian period, with its rhythmic and tonal innovations, and the late serial period, were the most influential upon works of post-Webern serialists. The systemic use of non-tonally-oriented scales in the early work interested Messiaen. His dissonance interested Boulez. Stravinsky's rhythmic ingenuity in his Russian period, with its systematically conceived structures, provided a crucial stimulus for Boulez and Messiaen in their own works. His later adoption of serialism lent Schönberg's harshly criticized method a certain aura of legitimacy that most attracted American academic serialists, such as Milton Babbitt, Benjamin Boretz, and Arthur Berger, a noted Stravinsky analyst.

Stravinsky's rich orchestral scoring in his early work has many admirers and imitators, while his later austerity, both orchestral and harmonic, has had major impact on several American composers who had studied with Nadia Boulanger, a renowned teacher and pedagogue active in Paris. These composers, especially Aaron Copland and Samuel Barber, developed individual 'neo-classical' idioms of their own.

Unfortunately, Stravinsky's own close relationship with Boulanger linked Stravinsky's later work too closely with the 'neo-classical' movement (a term I consider appropriately pejorative). Stravinsky has become an icon for those who wish to compose 'moderately modern' music in a style that is shopworn and cliche-ridden. Consequently, in my opinion, Stravinsky's reputation suffers somewhat by this association.

Most of Stravinsky's work *after Le Sacre du Printemps* shows *adoption* of stylistic methods developed previously by *others*, rather than its own composer's originality (as had been the case in his Russian period), be it serialism (a la Schönberg, and Webern), or 'neo-classicism' (a la Ferruccio Busoni and Richard Strauss). That Stravinsky turned such devices to the service of his superior creative power is an oft-cited excuse provided by his musical acolytes. Nevertheless, it is *at least* partly true that Stravinsky *did* apply serial techniques (in his late works) in original ways, so that it would uniquely serve the personal artistic aesthetic he had so carefully cultivated

By any standards, though, much of Stravinsky's output was highly original, influential, and superbly crafted, even if the works of most of his admirers frequently lacked distinction.

◆◆◆

- ## His Major Works

  *The Firebird*
  *Petrouchka*
  *The Rite of Spring*
  *Les Noces*
  *L'Histoire du Soldat*
  *Song of the Nightingale*
  *Symphonies of Wind Instruments*
  *Violin Concerto*
  *Oedipus Rex*
  *Symphony of Psalms*
  *Pulcinella*
  *Symphony In C*
  *Symphony In Three Movements*
  *Agon*
  *Canticum Sacrum*
  *The Flood*
  *Mass*
  *'Dumbarton Oaks' Concerto In Eb*
  *The Rake's Progress*
  *Persephone*
  *Octet*

# Béla Bartók
# (1881-1945)

℃

Béla Bartók remains one of the giants in 20th century music. That he seemed to take a third seat to Schönberg and Stravinsky is a result, largely, of two factors. The first was his seemingly slavish attachment to the Hungarian folk tradition that placed him as a nationalist composer, thereby directing attention away from his impressive contributions to music theory and methodology. The second was his shy demeanor, which, compared to that of the two previously mentioned masters, deflected attention from him. His shyness could not hide the fiery inner musical flame, though, that bestowed upon the world some of the most far-reaching and skillful technical achievements draped within a pulsating, vibrant sound fabric. Indeed, his music is very powerful and expressive.

## • <u>His Life</u>

Bartók exhibited prodigious musical talent very early in life. His mother was an accomplished pianist. Bartók learned piano from her, and gave public recitals by age eleven. After additional student work in piano under László Erkel, son of a then-prominent composer, Bartók studied harmony under Anton Hyrtl. By 1899, he entered the Royal Academy of Music in Budapest. While there, he studied piano with István Thomán and composition with Hans Koessler before graduating in 1903.

Bartók composed some early, highly derivative compositions (including the tone poem *Kossuth* - 1903) that reveal the influences of Franz Liszt, Johannes Brahms, and Richard Strauss. (He had heard the tone poem Also *Sprach Zarathustra,* and had been quite impressed.) Bartók began intensive studies of Hungarian national music for which he and his colleague, Zoltán Kodály, became famous. The two men traveled extensively throughout Hungary and into other eastern European countries (primarily Rumania and Slovakia). They collected and recorded (albeit in rudimentary fashion) native ethnic songs and dance tunes that intimately revealed the peculiar native inflections that Bartók later incorporated into his personal compositional style. This work was published by the two composers and represents one of the most exhaustive and thoroughgoing studies of folk material ever accomplished (*PAR* Slonimsky pp. 115-6).

Bartók's early instrumental music is imbued with a folk-music-like quality, as it contains the melodic phrasing and tonal and rhythmic quality he had absorbed from his studies. Two key points bear emphasis here. Bartók never quoted nor copied folk materials exactly in his compositions (Lesznai p. 56). Although the folk-like nature of his early works sounds convincing and genuinely ethnic, the melodic material is completely Bartók's own invention. Its authenticity is evidence of the thoroughness by which Bartók incorporated the elements of the style into his sound language. It had been made part of the very essence and nature of his musical personality. A second crucial point is that this ethnic music is not the 'gypsy' side of the Hungarian elan that Liszt had so popularized (Lesznai p. 49), but rather the true folk idiom extant throughout the major parts of Hungary and other territories. This is to emphasize its authenticity.

Several early orchestral works bear the stamp of the newly incorporated stylistic traits: powerful, almost primitive sounding rhythms; unusual tonal inflections, revealing ethnic scale patterns; and colorful orchestration. *Hungarian Sketches* (1930s orchestrations of early piano music), *Hungarian Peasant Songs* (1915/1927 orch.), *Two Portraits* (1907-11), and *Deux Images* (1910) are good examples. Piano works of this period include *For Children* (1908-9), and the barbaric *Allegro Barbaro* (1911). These works are generally characterized by a fairly relaxed ease of discourse (the exception is *Allegro Barbaro*), with clever rhythmic syncopation, and a tonal harmony sprinkled with open fifths and other unusual chords. These works also show his growing interest in Impressionism and the music of Claude Debussy. For the most part, the music is fairly low key. Such would not always be the case.

By the mid 19-teens, his musical language--still imbued by basic elements of folk idioms (unusual scales and rhythmic patterns)--turned decidedly more acrid and bitter. The workings of the ethnic scales became studies in exposition of their extreme sound potential. From 1914 through the late 1930s, Bartók's work was in the forefront of modernist exploration. The rhythms were more propulsive and barbaric; the tonality was exceedingly dissonant. Two stage works were characteristic of this style. After the transitional opera_of 1911, *Duke Bluebeard's Castle*, in which harmonies began to turn harsher, *The Wooden Prince* (ballet 1914-1916), and especially *The Miraculous Mandarin* (ballet 1918) marked Bartók's full-fledged excursion into the violent harmonic and rhythmic idioms that Schönberg and Stravinsky were exploring. Expressionism (in the work of Schönberg and Berg) stylistically reflected the thoughts, moods, and artistic styles of the times. Emotions revealed through music were reminiscent of the psychoanalytic revelations of Sigmund Freud. Schönberg's atonal works highlighted the heightened state of musical declamation. Bartók's work, too, seemed to explode with the expressive violence that characterized the day. *Duke Bluebeard's Castle* explores states of mind encountered upon opening the doors to the infamous den of torture. *The Miraculous Mandarin* explores, in mime, a love story that culminates in violence. The music is fittingly violent with many unusual effects and extremes of expression. Most works in this period are relentlessly dissonant. Other important works of this period, and of times slightly later, include the *(2nd) Violin Concerto* (1927), *Music for Strings, Percussion and Celesta* (1936), *Sonata for Two Pianos and Percussion,* (1937 - subsequently rescored by Bartók as a concerto for two pianos and orchestra - 1940-2), *Dance Suite* (1923), the 3rd and 4th of his epochal *String Quartets* (1927/1928) and the first two Piano Concertos (1926/1930-1), all characteristically dissonant and propulsive.

Bartók toured the US and USSR in the late 1920s as a concert pianist. He nonetheless continued his research work in ethnomusicology. In 1940, as war broke out, Bartók immigrated to the US, rather than be first-hand witness to Hungary's cultural downfall. While in the US, he received an honorary Ph.D. His compositions of this period took respite from the harsh, jagged edgedness that had informed his immediately previous work. The *Concerto for Orchestra* (1943) is markedly less tense and harsh, as was the *3rd Pi-*

*ano Concerto* (1945), and the (unfinished) *Viola Concerto*
(1945). Bartók suffered grave financial crises in his last years
and he died poor in 1945. He was always more human, perhaps, than his most severe works would seem to indicate.
He tirelessly worked to express a humanity in music that informs the spirit of all humankind, even in the face of grave
financial (his US years), or cultural (Hungary in the war)
crises. Perhaps his most towering achievement is the set of
six *String Quartets*, which spanned his creative lifetime. In
these, as in perhaps none of his other works, Bartók's humanity is profoundly expressed. That he never let his vision
waver was his legacy for the future.

## • <u>His Style</u>

The dissonance and acrid-sounding tone of Bartók's
work resulted from the confluence of two forces in his musical life. By way of Bartók's ethnological research, scales relatively unknown within traditional musical circles became
available for his use. Most common is the so-called **acoustic**
octave (Lendvai p. 67), with its augmented (raised) 4th and
flatted 7th intervals. Bartók also seems to have created a
certain twelve-tone variant in a different form from that of
Schönberg and the Viennese school. According to the Hungarian musicologist, Ernö Lendvai, Bartók's middle period
near-atonality results from his treatment of tonality as consisting of poles. There are four (each) of tonic, dominant,
and subdominant triadic combinations, with each root tone
located a minor third apart. The triads could be used (apparently) interchangeably (*PAR* Lendvai pp. 1-16). So unusual progressions, rich with dissonance, would ensue. This
peculiar usage of tonality creates a quasi 12-tone system,
inasmuch as all twelve tones are incorporated into the musical discourse. The system differs from that of Schönberg,

however, in that an external ordering device (i.e., serial) is not imposed upon the material. The harmonic language is an extension of functional harmony.

Additionally, Bartók 'invented' chords that contained all roots of the four tonics and of the four dominants (so-called *alpha, beta, delta,* and *gamma* chords) (*PAR* Lendvai pp. 42/44/47), yielding a harmonic flavor of understandable (and unprecedented) density, complexity, and dissonant harshness. Such chords are not arbitrary or fortuitous; rather they were carefully constructed within Bartók's rigorous principles to serve a powerful expressive purpose.

The rhythmic fertility of Bartók's middle period is the result of great syncopation combined with extreme accent on the downbeat, and then on an off-cadence-beat (i.e., alternating the 3rd and 4th beat accent of a 5 beat measure). Bartók's rhythms frequently emphasize patterns of 5 against 4 or 3. They are always highly accented. It should be noted, however, that unlike his contemporary, Igor Stravinsky, Bartók rarely alternated complex rhythmic patterns in continuous fluctuation (such as from 4 to 5 to 7 to 3, etc.). (The complexity is generally homogeneous, stressing unusual, though singular, patterns, such as accented 5s, etc.). Along with Stravinsky, Bartók is considered one of the two profoundly inventive and influential rhythmic innovators in the music of the 20th century.

In matters of form Bartók was just as original. Lendvai claims that Bartók constructed the formal patterns of his pieces according to the proportions guided by the "golden section ratio" (Lendvai p. 17-34). This ratio has its roots in classical antiquity, particularly ancient Greece. The ratio, when used to construct architectural edifices, was found by many sculptors and architects to be particularly strong and stable. Many arches were built using its properties. It is characterized by the inclusion of irrational (as opposed to simple numeric) ratios. It seems that many of Bartók's works exhibit climactic moments at a time proportional to the shape predicted by, indeed controlled by, the ratio. Whole movements seem to bear an overall shape of discourse informed by patterns characteristic of the golden section. This may account for the seeming power of Bartók's formal structure.

Equally revealing is Bartók's employment of formal patterns that bear a distinct resemblance to the 'shape' of an arch (Babbitt Col record). Such usage has been termed by musicologists as "arch" form. This form has a beginning, a mid-section, and a closing that seem roughly even in duration. There appears to be a building up in the early part of the piece, followed by a climactic moment, then by a settling back into material exposited in the early stage of the movement. One should be mindful that golden section and arch forms are not used solely; Bartók also used classical forms at times.

Orchestration in Bartók's work was original, as well. Bearing a certain degree of similarity to usage in Schönberg's music, Bartók was fond of abrasive muted brass. He was also fond of unusual and special effects in the strings, such as harmonics. His percussion usage is exemplary for its innovative quality. Bartók was one of the most important composers in the forceful use of a great percussion apparatus in a number of his works. In this regard he resembles Stravinsky. His piano scoring is especially interesting. The piano is used to create unromantic, harsh clattering chords, often in clusters (closely juxtaposed simultaneities). In this regard, Bartók's pianistic treatment more closely resembles a usage as a percussion instrument, rather than as a stringed instrument.

Bartók's influence on subsequent composers is less direct than that of the other two giants of the first half of the

20th century, Schönberg and Stravinsky. This is due largely to the peculiar unclonability of the very special ethnic qualities within his work. Also, the methodologies of Stravinsky and Schönberg were more readily codifiable. Still, Bartók has exerted a potent influence in the development of the non-serial post-Webern avant-garde, particularly that in Eastern Europe. Of especial interest in this regard are the music works of György Ligeti, a fellow Hungarian, now famous for densely clustered 'micropolyphony'. Even more closely related is the work of György Kurtág, another fellow Hungarian. Although Kurtag is more closely aligned to Webern's aesthetic than to Ligeti's, via his hyperdistilled pointillism, his work more fully incorporates certain Hungarian idioms common in Bartók's music.

Among non-Hungarians, Krzysztof Penderecki of Poland is bluntly Bartókian in his direct, though somewhat crude, block-like structures (at least in his works of the '60s and '70s). Perhaps less coarsely, Witold Lutoslawski, also Polish, has evolved a chain-like structure of intertwining clusters that owe something to Bartók's example. Czechoslovakian composers have profited, too, notably Bohuslav Martinů, Lubor Bàrta, Otmar Macha, and Svatopluk Havelka. Alois Hába was influenced by Bartók's work only peripherally; his work evolved more directly through Schönbergian dodecaphony (12-tone serialism). In passing, one should mention briefly the work of Leoš Janácek. Like Bartók, he developed a tonal language incorporating native speech nuances, patterns, and inflections (only Czech, not Hungarian, as Bartók's). His work was also powerfully expressive and original. However, there is no evidence that either Bartók or Janácek was greatly aware of the other's work, or that either influenced the other directly.

A special case exists in the work of the Greek architect, mathematician, and composer Iannis Xenakis. He uses many special stringed effects that had become common in the music of Bartók, most notably effects of continuity, such as glissandi and massed effects ('clouds') that are not associated with the post-Webern serialism.

Thus, Bartók's influence may have been isolated to certain locales, but it has been significant.

♦♦♦

- ## His Major Works:

*Hungarian Peasant Songs*
*For Children*
*Allegro Barbaro*
*Duke Bluebeard's Castle*   Boulez
*The Wooden Prince*
*Miraculous Mandarin*
*First String Quartet*
*Second String Quartet*
*Third String Quartet*
*Fourth String Quartet*
*Fifth String Quartet*
*Sixth String Quartet*
*Piano Sonata (1926)*
*Mikrokosmos (Piano Solo)*
*Dance Suite (Orchestra)*   boulez
*Contrasts*
*Music for Strings, Percussion and Celesta*  Boulez
*Rhapsody #2 for Violin and Orch*
*Sonata for Two Pianos and Percussion*
*Piano Concerto #1*
*Piano Concerto #2*
*Piano Concerto #3*
*Rhapsody #1 for Piano and Orchestra*
*Concerto for Orchestra*  Boulez
*Violin Concerto (#2)*

# Arnold Schönberg
# (1874-1951)

❦

Arnold Schönberg remains the most controversial composer of the first half of the 20th century. The difficulty in approaching his music is due to audience unfamiliarity with his composing methods and style. Most people find that they can accept his music, though, with repeated exposure.

## • <u>His Life</u>

Schönberg studied violin very early, and began to compose duets for violin and piano. His father died when Schönberg was sixteen, after which Schönberg took a job in banking, but continued to study music. He played in string quartets with friends after teaching himself cello. He studied composition and counterpoint briefly with Alexander von Zemlinsky, one of his fellow quartet players. They were to become close friends. Zemlinsky would slowly gain public recognition, much later, as a solid romantic composer in his own right. Interestingly, this experience provided the only formal musical training Schönberg ever was to receive. The lessons provided a platform which enabled Schönberg to begin composing quartet music and music for various other stringed instrumental combinations.

After having composed pieces for his group to perform--very painstakingly, with help from studying scores from the early masters and from Zemlinsky's teachings--Schönberg began serious composing. By 1899, he completed his first major work, *Verklärte Nacht* (Transfigured Night). The original version is for String Sextet. The work is considered an accomplished masterpiece by almost all who have ever studied or heard it. Its powerfully romantic, expressive musicality is reminiscent of Richard Strauss and Gustav Mahler, two early musical models (not to mention Brahms and Wagner). The most prominent distinguishing feature is the profoundly accomplished contrapuntal mastery exhibited within the work, a trait not generally recognized in Strauss and Mahler. This trait represents a fusion in Schönberg of qualities contained in opposition in the music of Brahms (the traditional Germanic formalism - Schönberg's formalist side) and Wagner (the equally traditional Germanic trait of heightened expressivity - Schönberg's romantic expressive side). The dual characteristics were to co-exist in unusual degree throughout Schönberg's life, whatever his method of composing for a given piece (*SUM* Slonimsky p. 1629).

After other works, large and small, within a Romantic style that became ever more restless and complex (notably *Gürrelieder* - 1900-11 and *Pelleas et Melisande* - 1902-3 for enormous orchestras), Schönberg found that Romanticism within a traditional tonal language had become outmoded. The old way ceased to be fresh; the oft-used sounds, new at one time, began to seem cliche-ridden and tiring. The orchestration became so large it was cumbersome. He explored stretching tonality to the breaking point. By 1906,

Schönberg had reached a critical equipoise in several works that seemed balanced on the verge of suspension of tonality altogether. Several transitional works, most notably the first *Chamber Symphony* (1906), were composed. They were scored using mostly intervals of fourths (Slonimsky p. 1629) to heighten interest recently lost in post-romantic harmonies. The flavor of chords of the fourth-interval has a peculiarly unsettled quality. This chord usage allowed Schönberg a way to avoid tonal-sounding phrases. This style later developed into 'atonality' (literally, without tonality).

In the meantime, Schönberg gathered several pupils around him who were sympathetic to his revolution. The most prominent, Alban Berg and Anton Webern, became major composers in their own right. Soon the works that earned Schönberg his notoriety were composed. They include (completely from his atonal period): *Five Pieces for Orchestra* (1909), *Pierrot Lunaire* (1912), and *Erwartung* (1909) (Nightmares). The style in these works is extreme dissonance combined with extreme 'Expressionism', a musical trait that had contemporary counterparts in painting and literature (with the psychological underpinnings mentioned previously).

The works in that period were necessarily brief, if not in whole, at least in the individual movements. Schönberg felt a large-scale piece would crumble formalistically under its own weight without some unifying principal to replace the abandoned system of tonality. Schönberg became silent thereafter for six years, during which he worked out the organizing system for which he is now famous (or infamous): the 12-tone method. It became an ordering procedure for tones, analogous to the formalization provided by functional harmony in tonal music. This method gave Schönberg the means to organize large atonal works.

The years thereafter saw the composition of several major large-scale works. Most prominent among them were: *Moses und Aron* (biblical opera - 1930-2), the third and fourth string quartets, the *Violin Concerto* (1936), *Piano Concerto* (1942), *Variations for Orchestra* (1928), *Survivor from Warsaw* (1943) for orchestra and sprech-stimme (speech-song narrator). Finally, satisfied that he had accomplished the creation of a successful alternate method for composition, Schönberg began to return to *tonal* composition! The *Kol Nidre* (1938) for orchestra and chorus is a primary example.

Schönberg died before he was able to complete his most impressive masterpiece, the opera *Moses Und Aron*. The first two acts are complete. Only the third, in which Moses confronts Aaron on the meaning in God's statements, is incomplete, lacking music to supplement Schönberg's text. The work stands as a towering revelation for, and guide to, his personal philosophy. It reflects his personal commitment to the development of a radical new system in the face of unremitting public hostility. Thus, his commitment parallels Moses' insistence on purity of thought.

## • **His Style**

The primary characteristics of Schönberg's music that attain listeners' immediate attention are *atonality, serialism*, and resultant extreme dissonance. Among the more subtle qualities that create difficulties for listeners, are unequal and asymmetric phrasing (such as 2 ½- or 6-measure-long melodic or motivic statements as opposed to the customary four) (Berg p. 61-2), and syncopated rhythmic patterns that tend to offset the normally firm sense of downbeat (Berg p. 65). I have found, though, that repeated listening to a given piece yields huge rewards. Listeners find the work powerful, once they get by the formidable-seeming harmonic complexity. They begin to see it as musically pertinent to what Schönberg, after all, is trying to express. What composer asks more?

His work generally slices into four periods. The first, from 1899 to 1906, is a post-romantic period of highly tense, terse, but richly expressive Romanticism. Its main works, *Verklärte Nacht*, *Gürrelieder*, and *Pelleas et Melisande*, recall the large forces and high Romanticism of Richard Strauss and Mahler.

The second period, from 1906 to 1918, is preceded by a transitional phase, in which chords are constructed in fourths, instead of the customary thirds, heightening the tension. Works include the two chamber symphonies, and the first two string quartets. The *Second Quartet* (1908) was especially prophetic, as the last movement, accompanied by a singer, extols the sounds from 'other worlds'. Indeed other worlds were around the corner as 'atonality' was ushered in very quickly. Atonality means literally 'without tonality'. Schönberg objected to that characterization, claiming his music to be "pantonal" instead: that is, inclusive of *all* tonalities simultaneously. Atonal music is dense harmonically, usually consisting of unusual intervals that create a sense of dissonance. In Schönberg's usage, the intervals stressed are the ones furthest removed from tonal-sounding harmonic patterns (Fennelly p. 773-6). Whereas tonality stresses thirds, Schönberg's work stressed fourths, and later, seconds and sevenths. This Expressionism was in tune with the times during which the gamut of human emotion was explored in psychology and the arts. Schönberg felt he required the appropriate harmonic tools for their expression. The *Five Pieces for Orchestra*, *Pierrot Lunaire,* and *Erwartung* characterize this second period, at that point in full bloom.

After the mid 19-teens, Schönberg became silent, exploring ways to add large-scale cohesiveness to a style that seemed at risk to degenerate into chaos. *Serialism* was developed in the 1920s (his third stylistic period, from 1923 to 1933, when he immigrated to the US) to answer that call. This was a system that ordered all twelve tones of the chromatic scale so that each tone would be used once, and not repeated until all twelve were used. This series could be displayed in any order--hence, the term *serialism* (ordered array). Initially, as Schönberg worked the method out, the whole row was a melody. By using devices such as inversion and retrograde (backwards), he achieved melodic variety. The harmonies were crude in the first works of the style. Later, he began to split some notes away from the leading voice, to other voices (partitioning) for variety and clarity of harmony (*PAR* Slonimsky p. 1630).

It became apparent to Schönberg, as well as to Berg and Webern, that a particular tone row could be selected so as to highlight or emphasize a particular quality of sound. That is, certain rows contain certain intervals that sound dissonant (for instance, emphasizing seconds and sevenths) while avoiding tonal-sounding thirds. Schönberg preferred these intervals for three reasons: firstly, to free his listeners from relying on habits and biases towards the 'olden ways' of tonal thirds (thereby emancipating the dissonance by allowing it to reveal itself as a new consonance, given its context); secondly, to express in the most forceful ways the newly expressed (uncomfortable) emotional content in the literature of the day (fear, etc.); and thirdly, to enable him to enrich the interval content. Major works include *Moses Und Aron*, the 3rd and 4th string quartets, the *Variations for Orchestra*, and *Survivor from Warsaw*.

It should be noted that Berg preferred tone rows rich in whole tones and intervals of thirds, a sort of tonal nostalgia within the processes of Expressionism (!). Webern preferred

thirdly & besides not thirds

rows that exhibited patterns of mirroring (repeated intervallic patterns in note-groups of threes and fours).

The fourth period, termed "Schönberg's US period", lasted from 1933 to his death in 1951. This period shows a distinct relaxation of style with a return to tonality. Note the *Kol Nidre* and the *Concerto for String Quartet and Orchestra after Concerto Grosso op. 6 no. 7 by Handel* (1933).

This description should be especially meaningful to the listener, in that it reveals Schönberg to have been a painstakingly careful composer most concerned with artistic choice; not one who carelessly left strange sounds to chance or to the angst of the listener. By this, Schönberg was a master.

Schönberg's work was profoundly influential upon future generations. While some subsequent composers preferred the aesthetic of his pupils in varying degrees, either Berg or Webern, the concepts of atonality and serialism, developed by Schönberg himself, were to be enormously important in the musical work of almost all subsequent composers. For instance, Milton Babbitt and Luigi Nono were instrumental in further work in row usage, and were influenced most directly by Schönberg. However, Karlheinz Stockhausen and Pierre Boulez, both prominent serialists, cite Webern as their primary model. Other composers, such as Luigi Dallapiccola and Karl Amadeus Hartmann, cite Berg. Nevertheless, it was Schönberg who ultimately developed the system they all used (and that Berg and Webern themselves used!). It was Schönberg who single-handedly revolutionized the musical syntax of the 20th century.

With regard to his use of form, Schönberg was fairly traditional in his approach, unlike Webern in his use of miniature canonic forms and their attendant retrogrades and inversions. Schönberg remained partial to the sonata-allegro structures in the music of the original Viennese school (Mozart, Haydn, etc.). This accounts for the support radicals such as Boulez and Stockhausen accorded Webern, but not Schönberg.

The best attack in confronting Schönberg is to concentrate on the wonderfully new and dazzling instrumental effects. The muted brass (new at the time) and extraordinary stringed effects (special pizzicato and bowing) yield a nearly bewildering array of fascinating sounds that create an unforgettable atmosphere and ethos. Listen also for short motives that repeat higher, backwards and inverted (upside down). Soon the harmonic harshness will fade, and the sound world becomes warm and expressive. You will become enraptured by the very romantic world of which Schönberg has always been a part, within the guise of an original language that he, himself, created.

♦♦♦

- ## His Major Works

Verklärte Nacht
Gürrelieder
Pelleas et Melisande
First Chamber Symphony
Pierrot Lunaire
Erwartung
Five Pieces for Orchestra
Moses Und Aron
Violin Concerto
Piano Concerto
Survivor from Warsaw
Second String Quartet
Third String Quartet
Fourth String Quartet
Second Chamber Symphony
Kol Nidre
Concerto for String Quartet and Orchestra after Handel
Begleitungsmusik zu Eider Lichtspielszene (Accompaniment to a Cinematographic Scene)

# Alban Berg
# (1885-1935)

❧

Alban Berg was a great composer in his own right, even though he had also been Arnold Schönberg's most prominent student. Together with Schönberg and fellow student-composer, Anton Webern, the three composers--known as the "second Viennese school" (after Mozart and Haydn who comprised the first)--triggered the furthest reaching, deepest revolution in musical history. Berg's own work, however, shows that his was a totally independent musical personality, with a composing style immediately identifiable as his own.

## • <u>His Life</u>

Alban Berg showed musical promise when very young, composing and playing piano without formal training. Shortly after 1900, he obtained a job as a clerk in a government office in Austria. Shortly thereafter he was to meet Schönberg, an event that was to shape his future work in composition profoundly. From 1904 until 1910, he was a student of Schönberg. The master became Berg's spiritual guide and lifelong friend as well. Berg's early works showed the influence (then common in the music of German and Austrian composers) of Wagner and Mahler. Under Schönberg's guidance, Berg learned to analyze and apply acute self-criticism in the refinement of his innate, more personal style.

Although Schönberg was loathe to promote his own burgeoning ideas involving the dissolution of classical tonality, concentrating instead on encouraging classical analysis of formal procedures and harmonic methods, (Carner p. 10), Berg's personality leaned toward an Expressionism that had something in common with his master's excursions into atonality. Schönberg was able to encourage this tendency in Berg (and Webern), knowing it would not result in a deterioration of musicality or in mere pedantry. The power of Berg's musical personality, already apparent, would insure that Webern and Berg became fast friends as well. Under the three, master and master student composers, the musical landscape altered considerably (*SUM* Slonimsky p. 159).

Before concerts of works of Schönberg and his pupils had been forced into private settings (in 1918), several concerts took place shortly after 1910 that featured works by Mahler, Zemlinsky, Schönberg, Berg, and Webern (Carner p. 26-7). One particular concert in Vienna deserves mention. It took place under Schönberg's directorship in 1913, two months prior to the famous Paris concert of Stravinsky's *Rite of Spring*, in which a riot ensued. An outbreak of similar proportions reportedly broke out during this Vienna concert. Webern's work, the *Six Pieces for Orchestra*, aphoristic in a manner unique to--and wholly characteristic of--Webern, headed the concert. The audience was stunned quickly. By the middle of the next work, Schönberg's *Chamber Symphony* (No. 1), the audience began to protest loudly.

Two of Berg's *Altenberg Lieder* (5 Orchestral Songs) followed. Berg's heavier orchestration and darker tone, with his characteristic balancing act between tonality and atonality, proved to be too much. Disturbances broke out throughout the hall and the concert had to be terminated before completion. Court cases ensued, during which claims were made that the music had caused nervous disorders, among other things (*SUM* Carner p. 27).

Several of Berg's most important works had been composed by this time. The *String Quartet*, op. 3, was composed in 1910, shortly after Schönberg's first atonal works were composed. This work was pivotal, in that it contained Berg's near-mature style. It was his first purely atonal work as well. Important works immediately following the Quartet include the previously mentioned *Five Orchestral Songs to picture postcard texts of Peter Altenberg,* op. 4 (the now famous *Altenberg Lieder* of 1912). This richly orchestrated work has all the trademarks of Berg's characteristic tonal/ atonal dichotomy. It is complex formally, as well. Berg was fond of placing thematic material in the opening sections of his works into later sections through subtle disguises, including inversion, transposition, augmentation, and diminution of durations (*SUM* Carner p. 102). Berg was form-conscious, and very thorough and painstaking in his approach. The *Three Pieces for Large Orchestra* (1914-5), and the monumental opera *Wozzeck* (1914-21) bring this atonal phase to a close.

In 1918, Berg became active with the other two in the Society for Private Musical Performances that was formed by Schönberg to perform, under guaranteed supportive conditions, works that would have been criticized severely under different circumstances. Critics and the general public were excluded. Many works, the performances of which possibly would be terminated by hostilities and demonstration, could be heard uninterrupted in a peaceful setting. Works by Bartók, Stravinsky, Mahler, Ravel, as well as those of the second Viennese school, were presented, many for the first time. This society was terminated in 1922.

Berg became associated with ISCM in 1925. This enabled him to actively continue the support and production of important new works. Berg's work continued to receive performance throughout the 1920s, but by the 1930s, with the political situations in Germany and Austria becoming grave, performances became more rare. A disillusioned Berg wrote letters to Malipiero, whom he had befriended, lamenting his neglect in his native country (Carner p. 81). Malipiero then unsuccessfully attempted to produce Berg's *Lyric Suite* at the Venice Biennale.

Meanwhile, by the late 1920s and early 1930s, Berg had composed a number of crucially important works in the style just developed by his former master, Schönberg: the 12-tone row. Music written in this style is commonly termed 'serialism' as it involves the unfolding of a group of tones in a particular order or series. Berg's unique contribution to this new method is apparent in several works, including at least four major masterpieces: the *Lyric Suite* (1925-6) for string quartet; the *Chamber Concerto* (1923-5) for piano, violin and thirteen wind instruments; the *Violin Concerto* ('In Memory of an Angel" - the angel being Manon Gropius, a Werfel relative whom Berg had befriended - 1935), and finally the opera *Lulu* (1928-35). In 1934, Berg extracted a symphonic suite from *Lulu*.

Several important items of interest surround some of these works. As for the *Lyric Suite*, it is now common knowledge that Berg had had a secret love affair, while married, with Hanna Fuchs-Robettin. Rumors persisted that Berg's *Lyric Suite* had originally been conceived autobiographically with a text--suppressed early--that contained coded references to this affair. In 1976, a Berg biographer found the original manuscript with annotated text. The annotated score includes disguised numerological clues to Berg's relationship. By these clues musicologists have uncovered a wonderfully complex and tightly woven formal scheme binding the work together (*PAR* Slonimsky p. 160). Berg's favorite number was 23. Hanna's was 10. The two numbers are used (sometimes combined) to calculate duration values (e.g., metronome markings: 100=10 squared, etc.), lengths of subjects (138 measures = 6 times 23), etc. This is a high example of Berg's preoccupation with formal devices (*SUM* Carner p. 123).

Also, Berg's **Lulu** had been left unfinished at his untimely death in 1935. The first two of three projected acts had been completed in music and text. Only the third lacked music. Schönberg and Webern both had been asked to complete the music for the third act, and both refused. Berg's widow was reluctant to allow the work to be altered from its state in any way. However, after Berg's widow died in 1976, the work was painstakingly completed by a minor composer/conductor, Friedrich Cerha, from orchestral fragments used by Berg in other settings, notably the symphonic suite (Slonimsky p. 160). Some speculation has it that if a major composer of Schönberg's powerful personality (or Webern's) had undertaken the challenge, the work may have been imbued with those personalities unwittingly, thereby suffering a 'split personality'. That Cerha was able to accomplish this task is testament to his single-mindedness of purpose.

Berg died in 1935, after attending rehearsals of the **Lulu Symphonic Suite**, succumbing to blood poisoning from the abscess he developed from an insect bite.

## • <u>His Style</u>

Berg's composing style is immediately distinguishable from that of his former teacher, Schönberg, or his friend and fellow student, Webern. Whereas Schönberg stressed the use of asymmetric, angular phrases, and of dissonant tonal intervals (2nds, 4ths, and 7ths), Berg laced his atonality with certain nostalgia for the olden, tonal ways. Most Bergian chords are comprised of traditional interval sizes, e.g., 3rds (De Voto p. 74). The texture of Berg's work is homophonic (harmonic with chords) or polyphonic (moving individual lines of counterpoint).

Berg's 12-tone structure is particularly interesting. Berg uses the tone row with great freedom. Unlike Schönberg's or Webern's works in which row procedures are strictly followed, and in which one row only is used, Berg took considerable liberties, incorporating more than one row in a given work (*Lyric Suite*), or deviating from a row to accommodate certain functional chord evolutions (*Lulu*). The tone rows themselves contain characteristics that reveal his unique predilection for tonal-sounding consonances (De Voto p. 74). For instance the row used in the *Violin Concerto* is made of alternating 2nds and 3rds, with a whole-tone segment, to enable the composer to create triads! Also, Berg used some interval-rich rows, such as the 'all-interval' row in the *Lyric Suite* (this row contains all 11 possible intervals) (Fennelly p. 177). This ensured heightened tension.

Berg's formal schematics have been addressed briefly. An interesting fact regarding his use of classical structures is that *Wozzeck*, a basically atonal opera, is ridden with expertly woven classical formal schemes, enabled by Berg's adroit use of quasi-functional harmonic schemes couched in a dissonant external harmonic atmosphere. Ordinary symphonic forms, including a passacaglia (with 21 variations), a rhapsody, and a suite, are contained within this ingenious work (*PAR* Slonimsky p. 159). The subject is one of nearly unmitigated violence, with its accompanying appropriate dissonant texture. But the form is taut and controlled.

Berg's peculiar tonal/atonal duality was not attractive to most avant-garde composers of serial works after Webern. For them, the flexible structures of Webern's rows, with their capability of being subject to segmentation into subsets that are variants of one another was far more attractive. These forms were ready-made prescriptions for radical abstract manipulation. And at least Schönberg's harmonies allowed a complete break from the past. So, for Boulez and Stockhausen, Berg was clearly a figure of the past. (Interestingly, Boulez, nonetheless, frequently conducts much of the body of Berg's work!) Still, Berg has not lacked adherents since his death. The lyric/dramatic qualities that inform his work have found many admirers. Luigi Dallapiccola (lyric) and Karl Amadeus Hartmann (dramatic) have benefited in very divergent stylistic ways from Berg's example. American composers like George Rochberg and George Perle, too, are true Bergians.

◆◆◆

- ## His Major Works

*String Quartet, op. 3*
*Altenberg Lieder*
*Wozzeck*
*Three Pieces for Large Orchestra*   Abbado
*Chamber Concerto*
*Lyric Suite*   Boulez
*Lulu (Opera)*
*Symphonic*
*Suite from 'Lulu'*   Boulez   Abbado
*Der Wein*   Boulez
*Violin Concerto ('In Memory of an Angel')*

# Anton Webern
# (1883-1945)

❧

The first half of the 20th century was a time of social turmoil. A war broke out in the early part of the century. Sigmund Freud had exposed the world to the phenomenon of therapeutic psychoanalysis, thereby releasing hitherto forbidden emotional states to public consciousness and analysis. Composers of classical music were no longer restricted to 'safe' emotional expression in their works. Arnold Schönberg, Béla Bartók, and Alban Berg developed styles later known as *Expressionism*. Characteristically, their music was composed to maximize expression of emotional states, regardless of the emotions involved, or of the potential discomfort the public may have to endure in the listening process. Thus, a revolution in method (in melody, harmony, and rhythm) flowed from the pens of the aforementioned composers.

If Schönberg, Bartók, Stravinsky, and Berg were the most prominent revolutionary composers of the day, their revolution was deemed at best incomplete, at least in some quarters. A more profound change soon was to sweep over the musical landscape, at first quietly. The work of Edgard Varèse and Anton Webern slowly was making itself heard.

Once the music world became fully aware of their work, huge changes in musical composition soon would follow. Only here, not merely melody, harmony, and rhythm would change. The whole concept of phrase, even the very existence of melody, and the face of musical form itself, would change dramatically. Whereas the work of Varèse soon would shatter harmonic conventions, with the introduction of noise (electronics), and of colliding planes of density, the work of Webern quietly tore apart old notions of form and melody. Webern's revolution, based on foundations provided in the work of his master, Arnold Schönberg, was to form the basis of what became the avant-garde.

## • <u>His Life</u>

Webern studied piano from his mother, an amateur pianist, and cello and theory from a local teacher as a teen. In 1902 he attended the University of Vienna. There he studied harmony and counterpoint. Additionally, he attended classes conducted by the renowned musicologist, Guido Adler. Adler was to become known for his analysis of the works of Mahler. Adler had helped formulate rigorous analysis as an integral part of the newly disciplined field of musicology. Webern was to benefit greatly from this study, adapting rigorous methods to his uncommonly disciplined style of composing. Webern ultimately earned a Ph.D. His dissertation was focused on the work of Heinrich Isaac, an obscure Flemish medieval composer of the late 15th century (specifically, Isaac's *Choralis Constantinus* was Webern's topic) (*SUM* Slonimsky p. 2019). This sort of highly intense, meticulous and methodical academic approach was to imbue the whole of Webern's compositional process. Also, this reveals Webern's particular aptitude for absorbing highly complex contrapuntal procedures characteristic in the school of Flanders. These procedures, including moving voices subjected to inversion, crab canon, etc., in a dazzling display of transformation techniques were skillfully adapted by Webern to his later serial compositional work.

By 1904, Webern began to study with a prominent musician whose work was becoming well known and highly controversial in its own right, Arnold Schönberg. Schönberg's work emphasized counterpoint to a depth not known since the time of Bach, so new student (Webern) and master (Schönberg) seemed a perfect fit. Indeed, like Berg had, Webern formed a lifelong friendship with his mentor. Fortuitously, Berg joined in study with Schönberg shortly thereafter. The friendship between Berg and Webern was to be as intense as that of either pupil with the master, Schönberg. Thus was formed one of the most tightly knit three-way relationships ever in music. Most impressively, each of the three contributed music of great originality and expressive power; the work of each was to exert a profound impact on the future course of music history.

Webern soon began to compose his first important works. A *Passacaglia* (1908) reveals his predilection for brevity and counterpoint. The work is one of two that Webern wrote for large orchestra. It is tonal, but contains highly chromatic chord combinations, reminiscent of the Wagner of Tristan. It also reveals a particular affinity for the processes so prevalent in Mahler's music, especially the passing of thematic motives around the various instruments of the orchestra. Although the brass section is hefty, it is muted much of the time, a trait common in Schönberg's work of the time. The language is basically tonal, with distinct leanings toward a freer harmonic idiom that was to come shortly afterwards in his atonal works. One additional tonally inclined work marked the end of this brief phase of Webern's work.

The new approach, signaled by Schönberg in his atonal music of 1907, became a beacon for Webern. Although Webern was basically introverted, his work did have a brief brush with the Expressionism that so imbued the works of Berg and Schönberg at the time. The important, path-breaking works of this period in Webern's career included the *Six Pieces for Orchestra* (highly expressionistic, for very large orchestra: Webern's last such work - 1909), and the sensational *Five Pieces for Orchestra* (1913). The sensation created by the *Five Pieces* was primarily the extreme brevity, even by the standards of the second Viennese school. One piece lasts nineteen seconds. The whole work lasts just over four minutes (Machlis p. 388)! Schönberg was so moved by the concision of these pieces as to remark, "Fine is the mind capable of finding pleasure in things so recondite" (Machlis p. 388), and, "Every glance is a poem, every sigh a novel" (Machlis p. 385). Indeed, the very quality of melody had been distilled to that of single notes! The usual expressionistic devices as muted string harmonics gave this work a ghostly, ephemeral quality. This quality, among others, is what made Webern's work so attractive to the avant-garde serialists, Pierre Boulez and Karlheinz Stockhausen.

Two other works from the atonal period deserve mention: the *Five Movements for String Quartet* (1909), and the *S Bagatelles for String Quartet* (1911-13). Each contains dazzling arrays of special stringed effects so characteristic of Webern's style of this period.

Webern was active as a conductor in Germany and Austria from 1908 to 1914. In 1917-18 he conducted Deutsches Theater in Prague. Webern then taught composition privately until 1922, while he also supervised programs for the Society for Private Musical Performances, organized by Schönberg to promote performances of new music under sympathetic circumstances. Several other conducting posts, including the Vienna Workers' Symphony concerts, and a brief guest stint with the BBC Symphony Orchestra put money on the table, enabling Webern to continue to compose--for him a very slow, painstaking process--and to teach composition privately. After 1933, (his serial period) when Hitler was active in Germany, Webern's work stopped being performed, as it was considered "degenerate art" in Nazi circles (Slonimsky p. 2019).

In 1929, one of the most radical works in the canon of serial art came from Webern's pen: the *Symphony*, op. 21. Several attributes contribute to this work's advanced quality. That Webern adopted serialism (12-tone technique), as had Berg, was not surprising. What was remarkable was the unique way in which Webern employed his serialism. Motives are (characteristically) very brief, and are worked out in an incredibly meticulous fashion. The contrapuntal devices that Webern had mastered so completely (by such dear labor in his musicology studies of Flemish counterpoint under Adler) bore uncommonly refined fruit in this and subsequent serial works. The canons and inversion techniques of the old masters were relentlessly subjected to a highly disciplined serial method peculiarly suited to Webern's aphoristic style. Time seems suspended and distilled as short motives travel around the orchestra. This work and two others comprise the canon of Webern's art that so altered the musical landscape. The *Concerto for 9 Instruments* (1934) and *Variations for Orchestra* (1940) followed.

In 1938, Webern's work was banned from publication altogether, rendering it difficult for him to eke out a living. Webern provided copy work to survive. In 1945, he and his wife moved to Salzburg, hoping to ride out the war. He was shot accidentally by an American soldier; thus ended the career of this withdrawn pioneer, whose work had been created in near isolation (Slonimsky p. 2019).

After Webern's untimely death (and Hitler's defeat), the Darmstadt school of instruction and performance in Germany underwent rapid change. A new and fresh spirit of adventure characterized the institution. Boulez and Stockhausen, two of Olivier Messiaen's pupils, with the help of others, uncovered Webern's scores. They were subjected to intense study. The pointillism and application of serial-like devices to elements other than pitch (e.g., duration, intensity, etc.) were seen as the wave of all future composition. Extensions of this abstract, methodical approach were developed. The style was in vogue throughout the '50s and well into the '60s. Would that this lonely, isolated genius have lived to witness the decade of the '50s become known, in musical circles, as "the age of Webern".

## • <u>His Style</u>

Webern's music is intense, though inordinately quiet, taut, and brief. The extraordinary controls that Webern imposed on the pitch values (12-tone serialism) seem to have been adapted to duration and volume levels (intensity) as well. Although no evidence exists of an overt mechanism (such as pitch serialism) to control these latter elements, they seem to be carefully guided by principals akin to devices common, at least empirically, to serialism, or to other canonic devices such as those used in medieval music. It is this 'methodism' that was to astound later post-Webern serialists.

As was the case in Schönberg's (multi-intervallic music focusing on dissonant intervals), and Berg's (consonant intervals of thirds) conscious choices of tone rows to elaborate specifically desired sonic atmospheres, Webern's choice of rows was deliberate and designed for artistic preference.

They weren't simply arbitrary. Webern desired a rarified atmosphere that allowed the music to vary constantly within certain highly controlled temporal limits. For this purpose, he constructed many of his series so that the twelve notes of the series could be split into four patterns of three notes each. The particular choice of tone order was such that each of the patterns is a replicated variant of the others. That is, one three note set could be taken as the 'original'. The others were, in turn (in transposition), a retrograde (backward), an inversion (upside-down), and a retrograde-inversion (upside-down and backward) of that original, respectively (Fennelly p. 778). The intervals contained in all four patterns were basically replicas treated to variation. This interval handling is termed "intervallic invariance" by some analysts. Only a real student of olden polyphonic treatments could have devised control of this intense degree! Webern's forms mirror his motivic schemata in their reliance upon canonic structures, complete with retrogrades and inversions (unlike his master Schönberg's preference for classic sonata-allegro structures). This (radical) return to Renaissance period formalism garnered considerable attention from the avant-garde, especially Boulez and Stockhausen. Schönberg's formal approach, more traditional, was anathema to them.

Webern's sound was generally much quieter, and less restless than that of either Berg or Schönberg. While Webern, like the other two, had begun as an Expressionist, he, unlike the other two, really didn't remain one for long. Harsh or loud sounds frightened this retiring composer. Although Webern preferred intervals of sevenths and ninths, avoiding, as had Schönberg, tonal-sounding combinations, the dissonances are largely **mitigated** by his adroit separation of most intervals by wide spaces. This quality, and that of his use of special effects and low volumes, give his music an otherworldly sound that is uniquely his own.

◆◆◆

- ## His Major Works

*Passacaglia*
*Six Pieces for Orchestra*
*Five Pieces for Orchestra*
*Symphony*
*Concerto for 9 Instruments*
*Variations for Orchestra*
*Five Movements for String Quartet*
*Variations for Piano*
*Das Augenlicht (Chorus and Orch)*
*Six Bagatelles for String Quartet*
*String Quartet, op. 28*

# Edgard Varèse
# (1883-1965)

Edgard Varèse stands as a truly lonely figure in the history of western classical music. Unlike his three major revolutionary contemporaries, Schönberg, Bartók, and Stravinsky, Varèse's revolution was thorough, completely uprooting all elements in music. Not only were tonality, harmony, and rhythm subjected to severe surgery, as they had been in the other three, but the concepts of formal organization, phrase, and melodic contour were turned upon their heads as well. This composer rewrote the rules for musical revolution and his work represents an iconoclastic beacon for all who follow his example.

- ## His Life

Varèse was born of parents of both French and Italian heritage. His early childhood was lived in Paris and Burgundy, France. In 1892, he went with his parents to Turin, Italy, the land of his father's lineage. There, he studied composition privately with Giovanni Bolzoni. These lessons were provided at no cost to Varèse. Varèsealso played percussion in the school orchestra. After his stay of a decade in Italy, Varèse returned to Paris in 1903. By 1904, Varèse had entered the renowned Schola Cantorum. There he studied composition, counterpoint, and fugue under the tutelage of Albert Roussel. Other scholarly lessons, including history, conducting, and further work in composition were provided under the masterly direction of Charles Bordes, Vincent D'Indy, and Charles-Marie Widor, the headmaster himself.

Varèse spent a brief stint conducting the chorus of the Université Populaire, a group he himself formed. All this provided invaluable background for his future work in organizing a society for the presentation of music by young composers. Shortly after his time with the chorus, he became associated with leading musicians and artists of the avant-garde. This experience provided the impetus for his future composing and conducting efforts as well (*SUM* Slonimsky p. 1941).

This information isn't usually found in print. The usual synopses of Varèse that are found in music history cut short the story of this background. Normally, a cursory summary is provided that tends to omit almost completely Varèse's pre-American background (pre-1915), thus leaving the mistaken impression that he was a far-out musical vagabond or dilettante who was seeking sensational results. The legitimacy of his musical heritage, unfairly, gets short shrift. It is thanks to *Baker's Biographical Dictionary of Musicians,* and to its longtime editor, Nicolas Slonimsky, who tirelessly supported Varèse and his work, that readers and listeners get any feel at all for the depth and legitimacy of Varèse's musical development. The depth of Varèse's understanding of the musical past at first surprised Igor Stravinsky, who had once stumbled across Varèse's partiality toward the (16th century) composers, Ingegneri and Goudimel! (Stravinsky - Col. record liner notes). (Varèse's knowledge of the work of these composers probably was hard won through his early-music history classes under Bordes).

In 1907, Varèse met Debussy, who was interested in his compositional work-to-date (and who crucially influenced Varèse's approach to sound-based composition). Richard Strauss, through correspondence, also showed some interest in Varèse. However, Strauss' influence on Varèse was limited, superficial, and brief. It should be noted that Strauss' efforts were responsible for getting Varèse's early tone poem ***Bourgogne*** (subsequently destroyed) performed (1910).

The most important musical event for Varèse, though, was his meeting with Ferruccio Busoni. Busoni, a noted composer, performer, interpreter, and avant-garde theorist, had published a book containing radical new musical insights, *Sketch of a New Aesthetic of Music*. In this book some discussion had been given to the development of new, as yet unimagined, scales. Additionally, new sound sources, including a proposed *electronically generated* (!) apparatus were posited. This material was to provide invaluable impetus for Varèse's future work (Schwartz and Childs p. 3).

Varèse composed copiously, but nearly all this early work subsequently disappeared under circumstances not well understood. It is known that he later became dissatisfied with the aesthetic in his early works and he did destroy many of them (Slonimsky p. 1941). Varèse worked with the Italian futurist, Luigi Russolo, for a short time, before Varèse became disenchanted with Russolo's focus on sound effects (noise effects) at the expense of musicality (Slonimsky p. 1941). (Russolo was to become infamous for inventing gadgets that squealed and honked, such as his 'intona-rumori') (Griffiths – *Modern* p. 106).

These events reveal a keen awareness of, and search for, new ways to compose, new sound sources to replace a worn-out tradition-based aesthetic that he believed had long outlived its usefulness. This restless search was to be a part of Varèse's musicality throughout his entire life.

In 1915, he emigrated to the U.S. to embark upon a new musical life. To supplement his meager income he took conducting jobs (including Berlioz' *Requiem* in New York). These experiences were not successful. In 1922, he formed a new music group in New York City devoted to the performances of new and unusual music. Meanwhile, through his composing activities he continued to explore new sound sources. Several new works appeared in an entirely new mold, including the pathbreaking *Ameriques* (1918-21) for large orchestra, *Ionisation* (1929-31) for percussion, and *Integrales* (1925) for percussion and wind ensemble.

These works were organized by evolving and transforming densities (with their emphasis on new sounds - a new concept in musical form) and short motives roiling over extremely harsh collisions of chord-like tone clusters They were very radical, and set the tone for music based entirely on sound itself, rather than the external development of phrases. This music has a peculiarly static quality, not unlike its counterpart in cubist painting (Machlis p. 627), as seeds or germ-cells (motives) of three or four notes are subjected to an intuitive set of transformations, much like light through a prism. Phrase and traditional formal exposition are abandoned in favor of the sound content. (Debussy generated an analogous sound-based harmony in which chords are displayed for pure intrinsic beauty rather than for the traditional functions of the tonic-dominant development.) The music unfolds through its own momentum and comes to a stop after the sounds are fully transformed to their secret resting place.

By the '30s, Varèse's search intensified for new *sources* of sound, not just unusual combinations of sound strictly available through standard instruments. He met Leon Theremin, whose device, the Thereminovox, was capable of producing glissandi-like sounds. Although Varèse incorporated some of these sounds via this instrument in a few compositions in the 1930s (e.g., *Ecuatorial* - 1932-4), the limitations of the new soundmaking device dissatisfied him. He fell silent, not unlike Schönberg in the late nineteen teens during his search for the 12-tone organizing principle. Varèse felt that he needed a fully electronic sound device, such as the one discussed in Busoni's book on aesthetics, to fulfill his ideas of "organized sound" (Slonimsky p. 1942). He approached sound studios unsuccessfully, hoping they would agree to help fund research along these lines. None would.

By the late 1940s, compositional work had begun to use tape machines to copy and then to modify sounds so as to create almost alien sound qualities. Pierre Schaeffer had undertaken some rudimentary work with very limited and uneven results. It took someone with a powerful personality, such as Varèse's, to fully realize a profoundly musical outcome using machines. Varèse worked at Schaeffer's studio and generated a tremendously powerful composition *Deserts* in 1953. The energy that Varèse had pent up searching for a seemingly unrealizable dream came unleashed in music of awesome power. The work is for tape sounds and traditional instruments, sometimes together, sometimes separated. Planes of raw discords (results of independently flowing sound masses), collide, and interact, transforming from one to another level of sound density. The scraping, shattering, shuddering, abrasive character of the mixture of sound with noise is reminiscent of America's entry into the industrial age. The pent up power in this piece is unlike anything heard before. Varèse even applied scientific or mathematical terms to his titles. The machine age was the symbol of a new cultural awakening at the time, and Varèse wasted no time in contributing the unique wonder of his own imagination to it.

In 1958, Philips Corporation sponsored a pavilion for the Brussels World's Fair. Revolutionary composer, architect and theorist, Iannis Xenakis, designed the pavilion itself. He was then thirty-six, and worked under the auspices of a French architectural firm headed by renowned architect, Le Corbusier. Xenakis wrote a brief electronic piece for entry to the pavilion. After tremendous battles with Philips' officials, Xenakis and Le Corbusier won for Varèse the honor to compose the mammoth electronic masterpiece that was heard during tourists' excursions through the structure (Russcol p. 62). That piece, the ***Poéme èlectronique*** (1957-8), is fully 'electronic' (more specifically, Concrète, a term devised by Schaeffer to characterize this music as consisting of natural sounds transformed electronically, as opposed to sounds directly generated by electronic means as in other electronic studios). The piece, even today, is considered to be one of the few genuine masterpieces of the medium.

Varèse composed portions of only one later work, ***Nocturnal*** (1961), that was completed by his only pupil, Chou Wen-Chung, a Chinese-born American theorist who devised an extremely subtle array of new instrumental effects reminiscent of the intricate art in ancient Chinese culture. After receiving various awards and honors, not to mention the long overdue recognition so stubbornly denied him, Varèse died peacefully, an honored pioneer of modern music.

## • <u>His Style</u>

Most of Varèse's stylistic characteristics have been discussed already. It is important to note his harsh harmonic

language is not the result of discords intentionally constructed as *harmony*. The sounds are not intended to behave as
chords. Upon careful listening, the listener becomes aware
that the clusters of tones are collections of sounds coming
together and taking on mass. Varèse's was the first music
ever to adopt *density evolution* as an organizing principal! In
this respect he exerted a modest impact on Xenakis' music,
in Xenakis' concepts of disorder.

Varèse's chord structures have avoided scrutiny by
most analysts. The reason for this is a misunderstanding of
the character of timbre. Varèse's chord structures, like those
of Debussy and Messiaen, lack harmonic function. They
operate as spatial and density-contouring devices, as well as
extensions of timbre. Unlike claims to the contrary by most
analysts (especially those much wedded to serial concepts),
Varèse didn't avoid functional harmonic sophistication because he *lacked* understanding. He avoided functional sophistication because he had understanding!

Varèse's whole musical career was focused upon the
meshing of relatively overtone-pure sounds with sounds
rich in noise content (that is, sounds containing non-periodic vibrations). At this level, chords necessarily lose their
harmonic functionality. Varèse knew what function *was*;
he wanted to *avoid* it. He had other uses for chords, especially towards metamorphosizing them into cluster-blocks
to shape density patterns.

Varèse also treats the intervals contained inside clusters
by augmenting and diminishing them. Still, these evolving
intervals function as more than pivots or as layering schemes.
To think otherwise is the basis for deficiencies in prevailing
analyses of Varèse's music. For instance, Varèse knew the
difference between timbral qualities of instruments playing in different registers. He exploited those qualities in
shaping his sound patterns (Pape, Composition... pp.6/ 7).

Varèse adopted a cluster-hierarchy, somewhat analogous to traditional Western harmonic hierarchies. Different clusters were assigned distinct timbral/registral/density combinations. His formal schemes followed a systematic series of transformations from one to another cluster in that scheme. So each cluster contains unique instrumentation, density patterns, and characteristic intervallic content (*SUM* Pape Composition... p. 8).

Thus, 'internal intervallic' content works in conjunction with continuous changes in the color and density schemata to unfold the musical drama. What was the element that held this together in coherent shapes while providing contrast? *Rhythm* (Pape Composition... p. 8). Varèse used his arsenal of sophisticated rhythmic evolutions to weave an intricate web of sound in turmoil, laden with heavy collisions between competing clusters. Instead of a counterpoint of harmonies or melodies we are left with a counterpoint of densities and of timbral variations!

Complex, near-primitive patterns unfold in a dazzling variety of cross rhythms that continually transform during the course of the piece. Varèse used a multitude of percussion instruments in his works. Through these efforts his work influenced a large variety of subsequent composers (mostly American, especially John Cage, but also including Olivier Messiaen). Especially influential upon Messiaen has been Varèse's use of timbre as a quasi-harmonic device. His influence upon the post-Webern serialists (especially Pierre Boulez and Karlheinz Stockhausen) has been peripheral.

The music of this lonely master is approachable, if only through repeated hearings. Its power reflects the enormous, limitless energy unleashed by the depths of its master's profound imagination.

♦♦♦

- ## His Major Works

  *Ameriques (Orchestral)*
  *Arcana (Orchestral)*
  *Ionisation (Percussion)*
  *Integrales (Ensemble)*
  *Octandre (Ensemble)*
  *Offrandes (Ens./Vocal)*
  *Ecuatorial (Ensemble/male Chorus*
  */Theremin)*
  *Deserts (Orch/Electronic)*
  *Poéme èlectronique*
  *Nocturnal (Large Ensemble/Percussion)*

# Part II

# Pathways to the New Music

ఴ

Several distinct trends were discussed in the preceding biographical surveys. The work of Schönberg, Berg, and Webern abandoned previously cherished tonal traditions, favoring a densely dissonant "pantonality", heavily laden with expressionistic devices. Hackneyed melodic patterns, the cliches in much late Romanticism, gave way to taut, driving motivic patterns. Romanticism's increasingly stale harmonies, with their ceaseless modulations, propelled by complex chordal combinations that skirted the very boundaries between consonance and dissonance, were replaced by harsh, restless harmonies anchored by several or no apparent key centers. Besides the "pantonal" ('atonal') excursions in the music of the three Viennese composers, eruptive, barbaric polytonalities emerged in the primitivistic musics of Bartók and early Stravinsky. Propulsive rhythms (Bartók, Stravinsky), motoristic rhythms (Hindemith), and the emergence of noise, with formalized density fluctuations (Varèse), also made their appearance. The music world was poised for an excursion into unknown territory.

These innovations were amalgamated and consolidated by Olivier Messiaen. Then appeared the totally organized serial works of Karlheinz Stockhausen and Pierre Boulez, richly bathed in post-Webernian gestures. The other trends, detailed above, set the tone for the profoundly radical work upon which John Cage (noise, electronics) and Iannis Xenakis (ataxy/discontinuity) were to embark. However, certain additional tendencies need elucidation. For example, some precedence for the disassociation in the works of Cage is inherent in the work of Charles Ives. Also, some of the polymeters and spatial organization characteristic of Stockhausen's work appeared previously in Ives' work.

Other composers besides Ives added innovative sound structures. Carl Ruggles, Darius Milhaud, and Matthisj Vermeulen, together with Ives, left us work that, while not directly influential upon recent pioneering efforts, contributed seed-material to initiate some new methods for the future. The Expressionism of Ruggles, the polytonality of Milhaud, the polyrhythms of Vermeulen, and the discoveries of Ives, all provide an interesting supplement to the preceding picture.

◆◆◆

# Charles Ives
# (1874-1954)

ℰↄ

## • <u>His Life</u>

Ives was born into a musical family in Danbury, Connecticut. His father, George, was a leader of a band with a
distinctly experimental flair. Ives' father was fond of having
his children, including Charles, practice singing by having
one sing in one key, while the others would provide support
in another (Machlis p. 457). Also, George's band rehearsals
encouraged playing one piece by one instrumental section,
with another section simultaneously playing another piece.
However, Charles also received encouragement from his father to study Bach and other classical masters. He was paid
as church organist at age fourteen. By 1894, he composed
his first Psalm settings.

Ives studied at Yale under the American pedagogue
Horatio Parker. These studies led to Ives' *First Symphony*
(1896-8). This piece contains little of the new material to
be found in Ives' later work. His works of this period show
a sure handling of traditional harmony and form, reveal-

ing Ives' firm classical anchoring. Upon graduation from Yale, Ives accepted positions in various financial institutions, including the insurance company he helped form. His insurance career provided him with sufficient financial independence to enable him to compose at ease on the side. This freedom, along with his early experimentation with his father, enabled him to compose freely in untried styles without fear of poverty. His experiments would be unrestricted by financial needs; or to put it Ives' way, his music didn't need to go "ta-ta for money" (Ives' words - Machlis p. 458). Ives was averse to compromising musical integrity for the sake of pragmatism. Would that more composers be so sincere!

Ives would compose many works in the years thereafter, until he burned out around 1926, beyond which he seemed no longer able to compose. The most important works revealed new polyrhythmic and polymetric usages. Also, new dissonances appear that *seem* to have presaged the tonal experiments of Schönberg, Bartók, and Stravinsky. Most importantly, spatial organization was given attention, owing to the early experiments his father pursued in his band. It is easy to claim that recent trends may seem to have been anticipated by Ives' work, only because Ives constantly revised so many of his works. He often incorporated changes, such as added dissonances, throughout his life. Most of the revisions are undated, so it's hard to tell what was new, and if so, exactly when.

This frustrating tendency of Ives' to 'update' works has been challenged recently by some credit-mongers, as examples of Ives trying to appear more original than he deserves to be considered, thereby stealing recognition for innovations more justly accorded them. One such claim, put forward by (erstwhile) Ives admirer Elliott Carter, actually reached the court of public print (Baron p. 24-5). Although the issue of precedence has not been laid to rest, general critical opinion remains that much of Ives' work is still sufficiently original to warrant Ives receiving due credit (Baron p. 51). These kinds of fights (there has been a similar brouhaha regarding credit for Scelsi's work) are not productive, and only serve to intensify the pettiness of the accusers. Musicians ought to show more integrity, and engage in less nasty, puerile infighting!

## • **His Style**

The most important works center around the excursions into polymeters (***Symphony No. 4*** - 1910-16); collage (***Orchestral Set No. 1 'Three Places In New England'*** - 1903-14 - with its separate bands playing simultaneous, distinct pieces reminiscent of two converging parades); discontinuities (***The Unanswered Question*** - 1908); and spatially organized euphony (***From the Churches and Steeples*** - 1913-19 - complete with church bells). All these trends impacted formatively upon the apostle of disconnexity, John Cage. Cage's goal of setting sounds "free to be themselves", unfettered by influence from 'neighboring' tones, recalls Ives' example strongly. In addition, Ives' spatial formulations predate analogous work by two prominent composers of the recent avant-garde, Karlheinz Stockhausen and Henry Brant. The question of Ives' influence upon these latter composers is conjectural.

In terms of style, Ives may seem unpolished and unpredictable at times; at others, his work is informed <u>with</u> a high sophistication in the exploration of pristine material. His melodies often included tunes from hymns and other standard American fare (march tunes, etc.). His particular juxtapositions resulted in collages of independent sound patterns, generating heavy dissonances. Certain works (e.g.,

*Browning Overture* -1911), though, reveal a taste for harsh harmonies for their own sake. All things considered, Ives was an unabashed experimenter.

♦♦♦

- ## His Major Works

  *Symphony #3*
  *Symphony #4*
  *Three Places In New England*
  *Central Park in the Dark*
  *The Unanswered Question*
  *From the Steeples and Mountains*
  *Robert Browning Overture*
  *Orchestral Set #2*
  *Symphony #2*
  *Tone Roads*
  *Symphony #1*
  *Holidays Symphony*
  *Universe Symphony (Fragments)*

# Carl Ruggles
## (1876-1971)

❧

## • <u>His Life</u>

Carl Ruggles is often paired with Charles Ives, the two being prominent examples of American 'rugged individualism'. There is a certain awkwardness in some of Ives' more blatantly experimental works. This quality is less in evidence in the brief catalog of Ruggles' music. Ruggles, rather, represents a refinement of experimental trends in America. He wrote few works, but they are carefully crafted, matured from extensive revision that spanned his lifetime.

Both Ruggles and Ives were representatives of the great American tradition of transcendentalism. Their intellectual leanings had much in common with the leaders of the literature of the times, Henry David Thoreau, Ralph Waldo Emerson, and others. New England, their homeland, with its rural charms counterposed by big city bustle, provided a crucible of imagery from which both composers could draw inspiration for their musical compositions. Infact, Ruggles was a prominent artist, known more for his paintings than for his musical works. He (partly) shared this dual inclination with the European, Arnold Schönberg.

Ruggles was born in East Marion, Massachusetts. He studied violin and played in theater orchestras as a boy. By 1890, he was playing along as a guest with members of the Boston Symphony Orchestra. He studied theory and composition under Joseph Klaus and John Knowles Paine, respectively. Until 1907, he worked as an engraver for a Boston music publisher and gave music lectures. Then he moved to Winona, Minnesota.

During his stay in Minnesota, he taught at the Mar d'Mar Music School. He also put together an orchestra, and the concertmaster taught Ruggles how to conduct (PAR Randel p. 772).

In 1917, Ruggles returned to New England, taking residence in New York City. There, he associated with Charles Ives, Edgard Varèse, and Henry Cowell. Having much in common with Ives, Ruggles befriended him. Ruggles soon composed several chamber and piano solo works, including Toys (1919), *Vox clamans in deserto* (1923), and *Portals* (1925). An early orchestral work, *Men and Angels* (1920-1), was separated into *Men* (Orchestra), and *Angels* (6 muted trumpets) to provide a more satisfying balance. The orchestral work is hardly ever played.

More successful works for orchestra were composed: *Men and Mountains* (1924) and *Sun Treader* (1926) are his most well known. *Organum* (1943 - large orchestra) completes the list of major works. Only a dozen exist. Repelled by what he considered degeneracy in prevailing musical trends, and by rather nasty critical commentary, Ruggles abandoned composition and moved on to painting (Slonimsky p. 1560). His paintings are no more compromising than his musical scores. They are abstractly expressionistic. His paintings were occasionally exhibited at art galleries (especially in New York). He finally went to a nursing home and died, oblivious to an emerging interest in his music. The Boston Symphony and other orchestras and chamber groups performed his music. Much of it was recovered and published.

## • __His Style__

Ruggles' style is more homogeneous than Ives'. There is no real evidence of his having had extensive exposure to the work of the concurrent Viennese school (Schönberg, Berg, and Webern), with which he shares certain stylistic commonalities. His exposure to Varèse, who had been aware of the Viennese composers' works, may or may not have informed Ruggles. Certainly Ruggles' experimentation was heightened by contact with Ives and Varèse.

Ruggles' work shows a tendency toward long phrases that evolve slowly, but that reveal little direct melodic repetition. They are compact and efficient in their declamation, and very expressive (volume and harsh dissonance are common). The restricted repetitive qualities, the retrograde patterns, and other patterns lent an atonal feel to the music *(PAR* Slonimsky p. 1560). Some passages reveal rudimentary groupings of all twelve tones of the chromatic scale, although Ruggles never formally adopted procedural dodecaphony.

His work has a mystical exaltation that never lent it popular accessibility. It is sometimes harshly expressionistic, in the transcendental cast, rather than violent in the idiom of Berg. Although no direct lineage is traceable through his art to recent sound-based compositional tendencies, the integrity of Ruggles, borne throughout his experimental works, place him as a profound contributor to the music of the future.

◆◆◆

- ## His Major Works

    *Sun Treader*
    *Men and Mountains*
    *Portals*
    *Angles*
    *Organum*
    *Vox Clamens in Deserto*
    *Evacations*
    *Exaltation*

# Darius Milhaud
# (1892-1974)

⁊

## • His Life

Darius Milhaud was a composer who exhibited a variety of musical personalities. He was a prominent member of Les Six, a loose-knit group of composers united by the literary figure, Jacques Cocteau. The main aim of the group was to revoke the vague musical imagery spawned by Debussy, under the guise of Impressionism. Because Wagnerism was equally revolting, the composers adopted classical models as their musical ideals. Strict formalism couched in clear melodies replaced the opaque quality redolent in the music of Debussy. Urbane cosmopolitanism was the fashion. Little was hidden. Harmonies were brash, sometimes even harsh. Milhaud was the group's most consistent advocate, as his harmonies were usually the most audacious.

Ordinarily, Milhaud could not be considered seriously as an advocate of the new sound orientation, especially in company with the likes of Varèse and Schönberg, whose works focused a great deal on color as a self-sufficient for-

malizing element. Still, no less harsh a critic than Schönberg, the master himself, cautioned those among his contemporaries who would make the mistake of making light
of Milhaud's harmonic contributions, or of trivializing his
music. He admonished those critics to take Milhaud seriously.

Milhaud was born in Aix-en-Province. His fecundity
as a composer would emerge early: he composed during his
childhood years. He studied at the Paris Conservatory under Leroux, Dukas, Gèdalge, and Widor. Then he went to
the Scola Cantorum to study under d'Indy.

In 1916, he traveled to Brazil and wrote the colorful
*Saudades do Brasil* (1920). The harmony is raucous. After
he returned to Paris, he composed voluminously, lectured,
and conducted his own works. He traveled extensively, and
included the US as a destination. There, he absorbed jazz
influences, culminating in the composition of his most famous piece *La création du monde* (1923). The work is a ballet, accompanied by music replete with pungent harmonies
and jazz idioms, and was composed around the same time
Gershwin composed his famous *Rhapsody In Blue* (1924),
which had a similar focus.

Other highlights of Milhaud's composing career include the five *Little Symphonies* (No. 1 - 1917 - *Le Printemps;* No. 2 - 1918 *Pastorale*, No. 3 - 1921 Sérénade,
No. 4 - 1921 - *Dixtuor à cordes*, No. 5 - 1922 - *Dixtuor
d'instruments à vent*), and twelve full-length symphonies.
Most impressive in the series of *Little Symphonies* are numbers four and five. These are the most abstract of the five,
and concentrate on unusual tonal excursions. The fourth
ends in a fugue in several keys unfolding simultaneously.
Number five is in a boisterous, peppy style, once again containing several tonalities (Darrell record). Polytonality was a
major characteristic in Milhaud. The twelve large sympho-

nies contain much dissonant tonality, especially the middle group (numbers four through seven (1953-56). The full set ranges in completion from 1940-1962. The large symphonies haven't gotten much attention, but reveal an easy mastery of dissonant counterpoint containing deft handling of polytonality.

In passing, a wonderfully colorful score of incidental music to Claudel's *Protée* (1920) deserves mention, as does the very subtle ballet *L'Homme et son désir* (1918). *L'Homme* has deservedly received its fair share of performance. Not so, inexplicably, Protée. Both these early works show contrapuntal mastery in polytonal combinations.

In 1940 Milhaud moved to the US, visiting Paris during alternate years. He continued to teach at the Paris Conservatory and at Aspen, which he co-founded in 1949. He was always encouraging to modern music aspirants. Among his pupils were Pauline Oliveros and Stephen Reich. He retired in 1971 after a long, fruitful career (Randel p. 59).

## • __His Style__

Milhaud's work encompassed a welter of idioms. He never quite fit the mold of neo-classicist. He wrote many large operas that reveal high drama (e.g., *Cristoph Colomb* - 1930). Much of his enormous output exhibits an all-too-facile garden of pieces, composed as though he had turned on a faucet. It's all colorful and frequently pungent. There is much chamber music, symphonic music, and dramatic music.

What is best in Milhaud is his adroit use of polychordal combinations. It is here that he at once escapes the yoke of Impressionism, yet embraces its best characteristic:

harmonic coloration for its own sake. The chords emerge in a radiance attainable in no other way, yet they reveal a quasi-functional role. Milhaud's music should be seen as fulfilling a special, if limited, role in developing new sound concepts.

♦♦♦

## • <u>His Major Works</u>

*Protée Symphonie Suite #2*
*L;Homme et son Desir*
*Les Choëphores*
*Le Carnival d' Aix*
*Saudades do Brasil*
*La Creation du Monde*
*Little Symphony #4 "Dixtuor 'a Cordes"*
*12 Symphonies*
*Symphony #3 "Te Deum"*
*Symphony #1Pacem in Terris (Symphony 13)*
*Le Bœuf sur le toit*
*Symphony #12 "Rurale"*
*Symphony #8 "Rhodanienne"*
*Symphony #7*
*Symphony #9*
*Concerto for Percussion and Small Orchestra*
*Suite Provencal*

# Matthisj Vermeulen
# (1888-1967)

૭

Matthisj Vermeulen is the classic isolated genius. (So many 20th century composers *were:* Webern, Varèse, Ives, Ruggles!) But perhaps Vermeulen, even more than the others, was ostracized, due to matters of his own making. He was a caustic critic who could (and did) burn bridges for those upon whom he depended for recognition in his creative work.

Conversely, his case provided striking proof that music critics could compose. While many past critics have been composers, few have been able to overcome marginal recognition for composing in well-trodden styles. Vermeulen was an inventive creator with a searching mind. He viewed music as a vast avenue for exploration, and he had no patience for composing within pre-established plans. This attitude was borne out by his public criticism of other composers who pandered to popular taste (e.g., in his opinion, Richard Strauss and Igor Stravinsky) (Composers Voice record). He held his own work to the same rigid standards. His work enters territory far removed from that occupied by most composers, as he created an avant-garde idiom that shows little precedence, and is, just now, gaining attention.

## • __His Life__

Vermeulen was born in Holland. As a youth, he was raised for entry into the priesthood. After this effort failed, he left in 1905 for the capital of Dutch musical culture, Amsterdam. There, he studied under Daniël le Lange and Alphons Diepenbrock, whose daughter was to eventually become his second wife. In Amsterdam, Vermeulen attended many concerts produced by the Concertgebouw, under the great Willem Mengelberg. Vermeulen was poor and could not purchase tickets, so he hid behind the auditorium to learn the music of past masters. After much hardship and poor luck, Vermeulen finally found work that would enable him to support himself. He landed some jobs doing music criticism for some local publications, and his flair for stylized writing won him respect (*SUM* Ketting pp. 5-6).

It isn't clear just what about Mengelberg's conducting style repelled Vermeulen, but he indulged in acerbic criticism of Mengelberg's conducting. This caused a rift that would never heal. Most exemplary was Vermeulen's surmise that Gustav Mahler's music would fare better with no performance of his symphonic cycle than to receive the one planned for 1919 under Mengelberg's baton! (Composers Voice record). Understandably, this and like comments did Vermeulen's own creative cause little good. His own works would have to await their premier performances for over twenty years, and never under Mengelberg. Other remarks reveal Vermeulen's severity of judgement. He chastised some prominent composers for mundane offerings, and he had no sympathy for Strauss' association with the rising army of authority in Germany.

Vermeulen held a high distaste for the Germanic artistic tradition, particularly as defined in the art of Richard Wagner, and Wagner's most ardent propagandist, Strauss.

In this, Vermeulen shared a certain bias with Claude Debussy, with whom (besides Maurice Ravel) he also shares his aesthetic orientation. Vermeulen lacked the early discipline of rigid schooling that most important composers bring to the table. He was really a composer "in the raw", so to speak (Ketting p. 7). On the plus side of the ledger, this very lack of restrictive 'guidance' may have contributed significantly to his developing so unique and personal an idiom.

Vermeulen retained positions as a music critic throughout his life, until his retirement in 1956. His most prestigious appointment was as music editor of *De Groene Amsterdammer* in 1947, after having returned to the Netherlands from self-imposed exile to Paris (to escape Mengelberg). During his exile, he lost his son to the war, and then his wife, in 1944. Upon his return to Amsterdam, he married one of Diepenbrock's daughters *(SUM Ketting p. 4-5)*.

• **His Music**

Vermeulen had a strongly developed affinity for musical Impressionism. He greatly admired the music of Debussy and Ravel; but he also strongly admired originality and integrity in any nationality. So, in spite of his opposition to most things German, he guardedly supported the musical creations of Mahler (in spite of Mengelberg's support)! He was profoundly impressed by the radical discoveries of Arnold Schönberg, almost bestowing upon Schönberg the status of an otherworldly creative genius (Composers Voice record). Edgard Varèse, the French-American iconoclast, received Vermeulen's support, as well. The Netherlands composers (e.g., Diepenbrock and Willem Pijper), conductors (Mengelberg et al), and critics lent the Austrians, especially Mahler and Schönberg, great support, and Vermeulen never quite escaped this influence. So the Austrian and French traditions congealed, along with a musico-mysticism based in his strong Catholic background, and a raging thirst for discovery, to mold a highly unusual musical personality.

His *First Symphony*, (*Symphonia Carminum* - 1912-14), was a Romantic work that exhibits certain rudimentary qualities that would blossom in later works (i.e., rhythmic cross currents, and a cantus firmus supporting ground). Vermeulen then produced a work that departed radically from norms that had defined music until then, the *Second Symphony (Prélude à la nouvelle journée* 1919-20). This work is restless, with wildly meandering rhythmic phrases. Multiple combinations of triplets and duplets, as well as other complexities, transpiring simultaneously, generate a sense of cross-play that foreshadows the work of Karlheinz Stockhausen in the 1950s (*Gruppen* - 1955-7 - a work of splitting, shifting patterns that cut to the limits of audience comprehensibility) (Ketting p. 13). Instruments play seemingly independent rhythms that change and shift patterns and speeds. Extreme registers throw the players into ranges they barely can handle. The impression is sometimes one of a mush of bubbling frenzy. This work exudes terrific tension.

If the last comments seem pejorative, it is borne mostly by the lack of polish resulting from Vermeulen's incomplete musical education. Still, one only can admire the creative fecundity unleashed in this untamed sonotron, the *Second Symphony*.

Other works follow the same basic outline: single movement symphonies within roiling, turbulent 'waters'. The *Third Symphony (Thrène et Péan* - 1921-2) is more overtly Impressionistic and relaxed. The *Fourth Symphony (Les Victoires* - 1940-1) is a majestic statement of triumph. It is his most popular symphony. The *Fifth Symphony (Les*

*Lendemains Chantants* - 1941-5) is a longer work, very tense and intense in its driving frenzy. His last two Symphonies (numbers 6 and 7) reveal little that hadn't been revealed previously. Vermeulen's song cycle for voice with piano accompaniment (later rescored for orchestra), *La Veille* (1917), is limpid and Impressionistic. He also wrote orchestral incidental music to *The Flying Dutchman* (an open-air play - 1930).

## • __His Style__

The most prevalent characteristics of this body of work include multiple subdivisions of rhythmic patterns, chord clusters, wide melodic intervals, extreme instrumental ranges, independent phrases unfolding simultaneously that don't seem to converge, and lengthy passages that don't vary much. Some of these tendencies anticipate newer developments by a matter of decades (*PAR* Ketting p. 12).

It's tough to make a claim that any recent avant-garde composers were influenced directly by Vermeulen (for example Stockhausen in his use of crossing rhythmic patterns - 'cross-play'), because it's almost certain that they were completely unaware of Vermeulen's compositions. Everyone else was. Still, his music constitutes an exemplary addition to the body of formative discovery in the first half of the 20th century. As such, it joins the work of Schönberg, Berg, Webern, Varèse, Bartók, and Stravinsky for innovations that helped shape the direction for the future of new music.

## __Summary__

The composers and works surveyed herein provide a black-box template into which only a few highly creative musical minds have been able to peer. This pioneering effort was the foundation upon which to explore the very nature of form, structure, and sound. The genesis contained in these seeds was to foster an explosive energy that would open secrets heretofore unimagined.

The monumental explorations into the budding field of musics of Schönberg (*klangfarbenmelodie,* or 'tone-color' melody), Debussy (Impressionistic dreamscapes), Bartók (polar tonalities), Berg, (violent Expressionism) and Stravinsky (propulsive rhythms), that are founded solely upon the quality of sound ('sound-based' composition as it would become known), generated new-enough sounds and a sonic landscape that would prove fertile for invention within any culture. Yet, it took the arcane alchemy brewed through the structural ruminations of the reclusive figures Varèse and Webern to provide the crucible from which an uncharted world of sound would emerge. The music of the future was about to take shape.

◆◆◆

- **His Major Works**

  *The Flying Dutchman*
  *Symmpnoy #2 "Prélude à la nouvell journée"*
  *Symphony #3 "Thrène et Péan"*
  *Symphony #4 "Les Victoires"*
  ✳ *Symphony #5 "Les Lendemains Chantants"*
  *Le Veille(Piano and Orchestra Versions)*
  *Le Balcon*
  *On ne passe pas*

✳ Gruppen

# The Doorway to the 'New Music'

&#x204B;

Iannis Xenakis said in an interview that there was a vast chasm one needs to cross to accommodate the avant-garde (Bois). This chasm defines a qualitative boundary to cross whereby one must adopt a wholly new perspective and mindset. Even the new materials of Stravinsky, Bartók, Berg and Schönberg are reconstructions within previously traveled sound terrain. However, Webern, with his isolated sound cells, and Varèse, with his noise and density structuring, paved more proximate paths leading towards subsequent developments. These two composers occupy the edge of the chasm over which we will traverse.

The developments that follow lead to work presently being investigated in Iannis Xenakis' studios CEMAMu and Les Ateliers UPIC. Work by Xenakis, Luigi Nono, Giacinto Scelsi, Julio Estrada, John Cage, and Gerard Pape open new possibilities for exploration into the structure of sound itself. New concepts like Indeterminacy (Cage), Symbolic Music and disorder (Xenakis), 'mobile sound' (Nono) and chaos theory (Pape) are promising for their revelations and insights into the way the mind creates and perceives structures of any kind and, especially, musical ones. Recent work by Estrada in the systematization of minute, gradual timbral evolution is fraught with doors to enter unimagined sonic domains.

The previous background provides the foundation for innovations emerging from the pens of today's energetic pioneers. Seminal works of Cage, Nono, Xenakis, Estrada, and Scelsi, as well as those of the serialist pioneers Messiaen, Boulez, and Stockhausen, will be examined carefully for their pregnant nuggets of discovery. What can emerge in this millenium is, of course, the subject of conjecture. But such speculation should be welcomed, because it engages all curious readers, listeners, and composers to create genuine new models for thought.

◆◆◆

# Part III

# Olivier Messiaen
# (1908-1992)

❧

Olivier Messiaen was one of the most revered teacher-composers in history. He represents a musical receptacle into which diverse trends collected. He was also a source of influence from which a wide variety of musical tendencies emerged. Most major European composers found his work a source for new ideas and their developments.

Messiaen was the first major composer to preach the gospel of the revolutionaries. Debussy, Schönberg, Stravinsky, Berg, Bartók, and Webern each received high analytical treatment in his master classes. Even the iconoclast, Edgard Varèse, was accorded devoted recognition. The main legacy Messiaen leaves is a dedication to the world of sound in its diverse structures and guises.

## • <u>His Life</u>

Messiaen was born to artistic parentage: his father was a translator; his mother was a poet. He studied piano when he was eight. In 1919, he entered the Paris Conservatory, where he studied under the organist-composer Marcel Dupré, and the composer, Paul Dukas, among others. He specialized in organ, improvisation, and composition. He graduated in 1930, having earned first prizes in all disciplines.

In 1930, he was appointed organist at the Trinity Church in Paris. From 1936-39 he taught at the Ecole Normale de Musique and at the Schola Cantorum. His first important activity as a composer came when he organized a loose musical alliance with André Jolivet, Ives Baudrier, and Daniel-Lesur. The informal group, known as *La Jeune France* (the Youthful French), had as its collective goal the rejuvenation of idealistic Romanticism in modern French music (*SUM* Slonimsky p. 1205). It was sort of a reaction to the cosmopolitan ribaldry of Les Six, and their neo-classical café style.

Leading up to the late 1930s, Messiaen had composed a few minor pieces, mostly for organ, piano, or orchestra. Most notable are *Les Offrandes oubliées* (1931 - orchestral) and *L'Ascension* (1933 - orchestra and 1934 - organ with revised 3rd movement). The latter is a devotional work, and contains the seeds of his later mystical treatments of harmonic progressions. *Le Banquet céleste* (1928 - organ) and *Pièce pour le tombeau de Paul Dukas* (1935 - piano) round out this early developmental phase.

In 1939, Messiaen was called for military service. He was captured and imprisoned, during which time he wrote a pivotal work, the techniques in which were formative for his subsequent development. The work, entitled *Quatuor pour la fin du temps* (Quartet for the end of time), reveals the establishment of his highly original rhythmic and melodic treatment. Messiaen analyzed this work in his own provocative 1944 treatise, *The Technique of my Musical Language*. This treatise is an orderly exposition and demonstration of the rhythmic, harmonic, and durational formulations that he had used in the composition of certain of his works around then. The treatise is a process-description in the form of a text of guidelines. It shows Messiaen's highly refined sense of composing by gestures (*PAR* Griffiths Messiaen p. 93).

For example, included are Messiaen's derivations of some of his "modes of limited transposition" based on different ways of splitting his characteristic tritone interval. For instance, mode two is implicit in the tritone (augmented fourth) split into two minor thirds; alternatively, the tritone split into a major third and a major second more closely characterizes mode three, (Griffiths Messiaen p. 93). *The Technique of my Musical Language*, then, codifies much of Messiaen's generative system, making the rules explicit. By using these rules, the composer was able to hold the Western traditional formal framework at bay, thereby allowing the music to assume a timeless quality.

Messiaen's aim was to establish a detachment that would enhance the sense of the infinite, unfettered by human spoilage. In order to accomplish this timeless quality, Messiaen had to dispense with the Western norms of formal exposition and development. In his earlier works, Messiaen's intense religious reflection is given full attention in music that is supremely contemplative. Progression is replaced by ecstatic reverie. Messiaen consciously strove to heighten the sense of the infinite by the systematic use of several important rhythmic and harmonic devices (*SUM* Griffiths pp. 15-18).

Messiaen's melodic flow is detached from the classic regularity of square patterns. A motive or cell is transformed by free use of elaborative techniques. Diminution and augmentation force irregular contours, thereby diminishing the sense of beat. Non-regular rhythms are introduced and manipulated according to tables devised from the 120 'deci-talas' collected by Charngadeva (a 13th century theorist). Motives are varied by serial-like manipulations of inversion and retrograde (*PAR* Tremblay p. 476). This handling of harmony and of rhythm, and the separation of phrases into episodes, impart a sense of image or of a 'vision', in differing aspects, to the music.

Messiaen also avoided reliance on the major-minor system. In matters of harmony, Messiaen imposed highly symmetrical modes into the basic composition. This allowed for him to compose a motivic cell and subject it to transformations that return to the original version in a short time. These "modes of limited transposition" emphasize homogeneity of shape and sound, further enhancing a quality of total stasis. Many 'aspects', or contemplations become possible through the use of these variations that remain so nearly alike in sound.

Exemplary for their symmetry are the whole-tone scale--so favored by Debussy--and the octatonic scale, with its alternating whole and half steps. These, and other scales, lack a true leading tone that is so crucial to the tonic-dominant hierarchy in classical diatonic harmony. The modes lack irregularity of note position, so they are perceived as harmonically static, allowing no favored color or sense of progression. The whole tone scale has no half step, so cadence is obliterated. The octatonic scale alternates whole with half steps, so there are four potential tonal pivots, but on weak positions, since a single leading tone is missing (B natural, as in the key of C natural). Also, Messiaen frequently transposed melodic fragments upwards and downwards a tritone - as symmetrical a position within the octave as is possible. Tonality is thereby obliterated even when *consonant-sounding triads* are employed!

The absolute symmetry of the harmony is counterbalanced with the irregularity of the rhythm. The rhythmic devices Messiaen used are designed to avoid an easy balance and steady meter (Griffiths Messiaen p. 16). Thus, he further avoids a progressive feeling in the Western sense. "Non-retrogradable" rhythmic patterns prevent exactly repeatable values. Messiaen employed several devices: fluid rhythms, like in Debussy (constant shifting of emphasis); Indian music (talas); irregular numeric patterns (Tremblay p. 476); augmentation; diminution; "non-retrogradable" patterns; and so on.

*Quatuor pour la fin du temps* was performed in his army unit and created a sensation. The work uses all the devices mentioned above, systematically. This presaged his rigorous treatment of total serialism, a treatment he later formalized.

Upon his release from the army, Messiaen resumed his organ activities at Trinity Church. More importantly, he was appointed Professor of Harmony at the Paris Conservatory. In 1947, he assumed a post at the Conservatory teaching analysis. There, he accumulated a lineage of distinguished disciples who were to form the backbone of total serial ideology. His pupils included Pierre Boulez, Karlheinz Stockhausen, Jean Barraqué, Gilbert Amy, and others. He privately met with and encouraged Iannis Xenakis. In this class, materials of the leading avant-garde composers of the first half of the 20th century were analyzed, including Stravinsky (*Rite of Spring*), Schönberg (*Pierrot Lunaire*), and Berg (*Lyric Suite*). It is reported that, there, Messiaen first bemoaned the lack of serial-like systematic patterns for rhythm and duration in the classic masters' music. Messiaen was to remedy that shortly.

Messiaen's use of rigid rules had a pragmatic basis. By resorting to rigorous methods, certain human habits could be shorn from the exposition. Pure contemplation of the divine, the ecstatic, and the infinite could be interwoven freely into a serene tapestry of sound. The rules did not serve themselves, as they did in so much later serialism. They were servants of Messiaen's mystical Christianity. They enabled him to weave a web of timeless color. The need to expand the vocabulary became intense for Messiaen. During his stint as analysis professor, Messiaen learned to marry the serial ethic (Tremblay p. 476) to the unfolding of colors and musical 'fragrances' as concocted by Debussy.

In 1949, Messiaen completed his groundbreaking work *Mode de valeurs et d'Intensités* for piano. In this work there appears, for the first time, a systematic serial treatment of all musical elements: pitch, duration, and intensity. This work served as a model for Stockhausen, who listened to it repeatedly (Tremblay p. 477), and for Boulez, in their subsequent total serial works.

Messiaen has since adopted the chromatic scale (in addition to his modes) for use with serial treatment. Several important orchestral works followed. The *Turangalî-la-Symphonie* (1946-1948) is a transitional work, a monumental 10-movement fresco on the theme of love, in all its guises. The orchestra is huge. The treatment of themes is typically Messiaenic: broad motives treated in variations of all kinds, with slow, almost Brucknerian climaxes developed gradually. The movements are panels (reminiscent of Malipiero's contemplative paneling, as in *Pause del Silenzio*) or 'aspects', or 'regards', words Messiaen even used in certain of his titles. This segmentation is common in Messiaen, as it is in later Boulez. The movements highlight stylistic isometries, or isolated homogeneous qualities that are subjected to special treatment.

There followed colorful serial works for orchestra: *Chronochromie* (Chromatic colors - 1960 - one of the more successful serial works), *Couleurs de la Cite Celeste* (Colors of the Celestial City - 1964), and *Et expecto resurrectionem mortuorum* (And I await the resurrection after death - 1964). Finally the mammoth fresco in 14 movements, *La Transfiguration de Notre Signeur Jésus-Christ,* appeared in 1969.

Messiaen composed his only opera in 1983, a work over which he toiled for many years, *St. Francois d'Assise.* His last major work was the orchestral *Éclairs sur l'Au-delà...* (1992). There is little really new to distinguish this work stylistically from its predecessors. It may be that stasis, as a basis for composition, provides too little fresh fuel for inspiration. Messiaen's creative watershed is contained in his highwater works of the late '40s through the '60s.

## • __His Style__

Messiaen's music is often long, but introspective. It unfolds in slowly varying patterns. It is very highly colored, sometimes sugary-sweet. For instance, he was fond of the ondes-martenot, an early electronic instrument activated by moving one's hand over a diaphragm (*Turangalîla-Symphonie*). A sweet, wavy vibrato results. Messiaen also used a variegated percussion section, reminiscent of the gamelan favored by Debussy (and, later, by Boulez). Chimes and gongs in many sizes bring to mind oriental flavors. In this respect also, he exerted some influence upon his most famous and faithful pupil, Boulez. Heavy brass against fleeting woodwind skitterings provides a recurrent figuration. Messiaen had long been a member of various ornithological societies. He catalogued a wide variety of bird songs, often using them in his compositions. Wind instruments were used to emulate many of them; the most important usages are contained in *Oiseaux Exotiques* (1956 - Piano, percussion, and two wind instruments).

Melodies unfold in modes that lack a sense of anchor. One is called to lose oneself entirely in slowly emerging ecstasy. Motives are transposed in retrograde and inversion, as if the listener is invited to 'view' the 'image' from a new angle or perspective, always keeping in mind the divine quality of the discourse and its contemplation. Color is supreme. Instrumental timbre and harmony are stripped of any functional role as they play out their mysterious theatrics to tease out ecclesiastical ecstasy.

Messiaen's influence is most important in his non-traditional usage of timbre, and in his treatment of static blocks of chords. The peculiarly consonant flavor of even his most dissonant chords results from the static harmonic environment in which the chords reside. Scales (such as the octatonic), and his "modes of limited transposition", are usually symmetrical and lack a sense of dissonance or of tension-generating gestures. Chords are used for color transformation only, much as in the effect of changing colors in a kaleidoscope. According to Robert Sherlaw Johnson, there are two important chords that act as strong color-generators (Pape Composition... p. 5): the "chord of resonance" from mode 3 (consisting of the fundamental plus all of the odd harmonics up through the 15 th), (Johnson pp. 16-17); and the chord consisting of 4th intervals that includes all tones from mode 5 (Johnson p. 16).

The chord of resonance has the quality of embodying harmony as an element of timbre. Resonances are added sometimes to create extraordinary richness. Messiaen is able to excite the color spectrum further by playing 'resonance' notes against the principal notes of chords, just above or below them. This interaction fosters interesting timbral alterations.

Messiaen expands upon Debussy's method of stringing chords along an unfolding melodic pattern. However,

Messiaen strings out changing chords, rather than the static ones favored by Debussy. Certain chords become consistently associated with certain colors, depending on the qualities peculiar to the specific mode being used. The lack of a sense of dissonance is addressed by resorting to various rhythmic devices to generate contrast (following Varèse's lead) (*SUM* Pape Composition... pp. 5-6).

Messiaen's influence is considerable. He profoundly affected the highly refined work of his French apostle, Boulez. He has also recently attracted a large discipleship among younger composers, including Tristan Murail, and the late Gérard Grisey. He had a less embracing impact on Xenakis and Stockhausen. Still, the idea of chord coloration found its first systematization in his work, as he extended Debussy's concepts well beyond the latter's generic treatment.

◆◆◆

- ## His Major Works

> L'Ascension
> Les Offrandes oubliées
> Le Banquet céleste
> Pièce pour le tombeau de Paul Dukas
> ✓ Quatuor pour la fin du temps
> Mode de valeurs et d'Intensités
> Turangalîla-Symphonie
> ✓ Chronochromie
> ✓ Couleurs de la Cite Celeste
> ✓ Et expecto resurrectionem mortuorum
> → La Transfiguration de Notre Signeur
>    Jésus-Christ
> St. Francois d'Assise
> Éclairs sur l'Au-delà...
> Oiseaux Exotiques

→ Seven Haiki

# Pierre Boulez
# (1925-)
℘

The concept of total serialization had its roots in Webern, who adopted the tone row idea from Arnold
Schönberg, then extended the ordering concept through the
use of canonic forms borrowed from medieval music. This
usage seemed to imply that strict ordering principles could
be applied to all the musical factors: pitch, dynamics, timbre, and duration. Messiaen actualized this tendency by his
use of "non-retrogradable" rhythms and selection from sets
of predetermined permutations. Pierre Boulez was quick to
see the implications in these devices. He became a devoted
servant of the serialist ideology (as had Stockhausen and so
many others). He viewed serialism as the only valid option
for the composer of the future (*PAR* Machlis p. 433). Only
late in life would he realize the restrictive straitjacket serialism bestowed upon the compositional process.

Boulez is a flexible composer who responds well to
changing circumstances. After years of tortuous reworking of
previous work--and attempting to rediscover freshness and
reawaken musicality lost through serialized methodology-

-Boulez has reemerged as a composer of intensely poetic power. Through his recent work in electro-acoustic research he has opened an avenue for composers interested in exploring and refining the rich fabric of timbre.

## • __His Life__

Boulez studied mathematics as a youth; then, after developing an interest in music, he decided to follow this new beacon. He then studied 12-tone theory (1944-5) under René Leibowitz, a pedagogue who had made the first thorough study of the music of Schönberg and his school. In 1945, he completed study in the master classes under Olivier Messiaen. In 1948, he took his first conducting position as a theater conductor in Paris (*SUM* Slonimsky p. 223). This post was the first of many conducting positions he has taken, making him a true 'conductor-composer' in the tradition established so completely by Gustav Mahler.

Several important works appeared along the way. His earliest important work was the cantata *Le Visage Nuptial* (1946). The work is steeped in surrealist poetry against instrumental dialogues in serial-atonal melisma. The work is the first of three important vocal-instrumental treatments. *Les Soleil des Eaux* followed in 1948, along similar lines. These two works underwent extensive revision in succeeding years, a tendency very common in Boulez. His work has become a "work-in-progress" (Hausler p. 96). Works would appear in rough draft, followed by much revision, including new works focusing on certain aspects of the work at hand. 'Spin-off' compositions are common. Many works exist in more than one version; some with and some without electronics support.

In 1951, there appeared a penultimate prototypical serialist work. One of the first of the new totally serial works in Europe, his *Polyphonie X* stands with Stockhausen's *Klavierstücke I-XI* as a prime example of pure abstraction in sounds subjected to uncompromising control. The resultant soundscape was troubling in its fortuity and peculiar lack of fluidity, especially for a composer of such refined sensitivity as Boulez. By 1955, he had begun to explore composing with a freer serial approach, allowing the poetics of a text to revitalize the sonic atmosphere. The third of his seminal vocal-instrumental works appeared in 1955, *Le Marteau sans Maître* (The Hammer Without a Master).

In *Le Marteau sans Maître*, Boulez explored the relationship between poetry and music in a deeply systematic way. The work, which was his most important until then, is set against three poems by the uncompromising French surrealist poet, René Char. Char's poetry has a seething quality overlaid against texts whose literal meanings are largely impenetrable. The meaning seems hidden, locked inside the very words themselves. The poems are replete with imagery ranging from violence to hallucination. Boulez' musical setting, with its quasi-oriental gamelan effects (no doubt recalling Debussy's or Messiaen's examples), its disjointed, nervous rhythmic flow, and its delicately exotic instrumental colors, elucidates the poetry giving the whole work a hypnotic pulse. The style in this strangely beautiful piece is reminiscent of the ghostly Expressionism of Schönberg's *Pierrot Lunaire*, upon which *Le Marteau sans Maître* is partially modeled (*SUM* Machlis p. 437).

The work is split into several movements, each with its unique, but homogeneous 'flavor'. Boulez was to continue to explore segmenting the forms of his works, as a way to regenerate the balance/contrast dichotomy that serialism lost the ability to achieve. This was to be his initial solution to the quandary posed by serialism.

In 1954, a parallel event occurred: Boulez' formation of *Le Domaine Musicale*. This was a chamber group that produced concerts comprising the major avant-garde works of the day. Boulez was to remain its Music Director for over two decades.

Boulez composed much more slowly after 1960. He seemed to have become caught up in the role of conductor. He made several guest appearances with the New York Philharmonic before becoming its Music Director (1971-8). Among the many crucial performances under his baton, the most famous included his performances of part of the symphonic cycle of Gustav Mahler.

Boulez had been known for his particularly French sensibilities. The cool, almost aloof, musicality with a blend of Impressionist leanings, and a penchant for surrealist poetry, revealed a particularly sophisticated, refined taste. His early models were Debussy and Messiaen, with a dash of Webern thrown in. Expansive musical prose, particularly that of the German variety, were anathema for him. He was, like his idol Debussy, an announced anti-Wagnerite early in his career.

Boulez, however, was also an ardent student of music history. He saw the power of the new serial method as developed by Schönberg and Webern. Although he rejected Schönberg's classical formalism in favor of Webern's rhythmic treatment and neo-medieval structuralism (Machlis p. 434), he was deeply drawn to expressionist art and poetry (Klee, Kandinsky, etc.) and to surrealist imagery (Char, Mallarmé, etc.). He also saw the profound linkage between Webern's historical background and that of Wagner. He studied the Wagnerian music drama to glean its musical essence and became an expert Wagnerian as a result (Slonimsky p. 223), much to the dismay of his fellow Frenchmen. His conducting revealed this new inclination as he put on the complete *Ring* cycle in 1976. Although his compositions show few 'Wagnerisms', he couldn't avoid tracing that historic line through his conducting.

His admiration for Mahler was won through a similar process. He has since recorded the later instrumental symphonies of Mahler (including numbers 5, 6, 7, and 9). Boulez has been drawn to their linear polyphony and to their succeeding legacy in the counterpoint of Schönberg and Webern. Boulez' conducting activities remain an important part of his creative life. He has made a lifelong pursuit of establishing the revolutionaries (especially Schönberg, Berg, Webern, Varèse, Bartók, and Stravinsky) as mainstays in the repertoire. His success in achieving this goal has been mixed, at best.

Along with this activity, Boulez was deeply intent on working his way out of the serialist impasse. He has been only too aware of John Cage's missionary efforts on behalf of Indeterminacy in composition, a solution Boulez rejects. Still, Cage's revelation that the sound of serial and chance music is similar tempted the great constructionist, Boulez, to try his hand at allowing performers a limited degree of freedom. Boulez has since abandoned this avenue.

Boulez saw from his early work that working with timbre was one way for him to establish a consistent level of interest in his compositions. He shared a concern for sonority as a formalizing means with Varèse and Debussy. He started research into ways of using electronic sounds to explore subtle gradations in timbre in the late 1950s. Upon completion of his first major electronic work, *Poèsie Pour Pouvoir* (Poetry for Power - 1958), he realized a lot more needed to be done.

The results of *Poèsie* failed to satisfy him completely (Hausler p. 96). This interest, though, did not leave him entirely. He has worked painstakingly since 1960 to establish means to expand the sound continuum to include sounds of hitherto unimagined subtlety. This sort of work has been pursued by several other composers, most notably Iannis Xenakis, albeit with entirely different goals. The methodology of working directly with sounds is referred to as "sound-based" composition. Boulez was an early advocate.

In the early 1970s Boulez reestablished residence in Paris where he has established the *Institut de Recherche et le Coordination Acoustique/Musique* (IRCAM). This research center is well equipped and well funded by the French government. In his work there, Boulez has worked intensively at establishing his goal of refining the materials and methods of composition. He has enlisted the aid of computers to create a means to unify electronics and acoustical sound-forming algorithms (Slonimsky p. 223). His mathematics background serves him well. Several successes have helped put *Poesie's* memory in the distance. His most important composition based upon this studio work was *Rèpons* (1981-8).

Two highly delicate sound forays are especially significant: the orchestral *Rituel: In Memoriam Bruno Maderna* (1973); and the instrumental, tape, computer masterpiece *...explosante-fixe...* (1973-4). The latter is a brilliant culmination of the traversing of uncharted waters of sounds evolving from, to, and between electronic and acoustic timbres. It explores transitions so subtle it's hard to detect the junctures. A halaphone makes its appearance (Slonimsky p. 223). It is a timbre-producing device run by a set of computers.

## • <u>His Style</u>

Boulez' work along these lines continues. His work has an analog in another computer research group in Paris, Xenakis' CEMAMu. The contrasting characteristics of the work in these two studios is reflected by their opposing focus of emphasis. Xenakis' work is involved with formal procedures as well as noise-rich sound genesis, whereas Boulez' involves primarily the territory occupied by the evolution of subtle timbres. Boulez' strong French sensibility tends to rivet his efforts on poetic sounds, as opposed to noise/sound colors.

Boulez' sense of tone color is rich, but usually soft. Harshness is generally allotted to the woodwinds, and is thereby mitigated. There are no confrontational brass masses as in Xenakis, nor much thin linearity as in Stockhausen. His orchestral palette reveals a bias toward strings, woodwinds, and percussion. He makes fair usage of gongs in a large family of sizes, recalling a similar trait in Messiaen. His forms are segmented to isolate homogeneous groups, thereby enhancing the sense of form.

Boulez' studies in timbre constitute his main contribution to the new music. Although he explores the interesting world of sound-based composition in his unique fashion, he is a largely isolated figure in sound-based work. His single-minded emphasis on subtle sound effects limits the field of his contribution to a narrow but important panorama.

♦♦♦

- ### <u>His Major Woks</u>

*Le Marteau sans Maître*
*Figures Doubles Prisms*
*Poèsie Pour Pouvoir*
*Pli Selon Pli*
*Notations I-XII (Piano)*
*Notations I-IV (Orch)*
*Rituel: In Memoriam Bruno Maderna*
*...explosante fixe...*

# Karlheinz Stockhausen
# (1928-2007)

∞

The resurrection of Anton Webern's ghostly figure from obscurity by René Leibowitz, and the arcane teachings of the mystic, Olivier Messiaen, provided stimulus for a flurry of activity in the European musical capitals, France (Paris) and Germany (Bonn, Cologne, Berlin, and Darmstadt). Until 1952, the summer courses in Darmstadt that had focused on the teaching, since the 1920s, of trends in the new music were dominated by the 'classical' (!) serialist leanings of such stalwarts as Bernd Alois Zimmermann and Wolfgang Fortner. Through their efforts, the works of Bartók, Hindemith, Stravinsky, Schönberg, and Berg were discussed as models for the future of new music. Donaueschingen, the other prominent German new music capital, had been sponsoring performances of these composers' works for many years.

By 1952, though, several young radicals--led by Pierre Boulez, Karlheinz Stockhausen, and Bruno Maderna--redirected the focus of the coursework at Darmstadt to foster the development of a 'total' serialism as prophesized by Webern and Messiaen (Pauli p. 36-7). The pitch serialism of Schönberg and Berg was clothed in the olden classic forms (sonata, variation, etc.). Themes, by then dissonant, were nonetheless molded into expansive phrases with romantic expressive intent. The young generation violently rejected this approach, opting instead for a 'pure' counterpoint, with thematic material held subservient to the canonic forms contained in Webern's idiom. In their minds, this approach alone would complete the revolution and purify music's history, as well as its future promise.

Stockhausen developed his own peculiar blend of total control within composer-dominated chance systems.

## • His Life

Stockhausen was born in Mödrath, Germany in 1928. By the Second World War, he was orphaned, but managed to learn the violin, piano, and oboe. Later, 1947-50, he studied piano with Hans Otto Schmidt-Neuhaus. He also studied composition with the leading Swiss dodecaphonist of the day, Frank Martin (1950), at the Cologne Staatliche Hochschule für Musik. Also, he studied form under H. Schröder (1948). He filled out this impressive musical background with studies at the University of Cologne by taking courses in philology, philosophy, and musicology. He studied in Darmstadt, and then participated in the seminars, focusing on the new serialism in 1952. After studies with Messiaen, in Messiaen's master class, Stockhausen became a well-disciplined musician (*SUM* Slonimsky p. 1790).

Soon, a number of highly controversial works began to appear that would mark Stockhausen as one of the leading (with Boulez) serialists and theorists of the day. *Kreuzspiel* ('Crossplay', 1951) was the first of his important works. It displays a remarkable freshness that was to inform his work until the early 1960s. This work is an early example of total serialism. After Schönberg, Berg, and Webern framed the basis of organizing pitch by ordering the twelve tones of the chromatic scale in series, Webern took a further step in subjecting the motivic cells to treatment found in medieval music. This treatment included using retrograde, and inversion (kind of like mirroring - inversion being upside down, retrograde being backward). Webern extended the mirroring concept to create a structural procedure by splitting the tone row into self-reflective parcels.

Other treatments of Webern hinted at serial-like processes. His motives were short, passing the exposition from instrument to instrument. These procedures, although not explicitly serial, *implied* control of all parameters by conscious ordering means. Stockhausen and Boulez made explicit what had been implicit in the work of Webern. All musical elements: pitch, dynamics, timbre, and duration were subjected to rigidly ordered control.

In *Kreuzspiel*, however, Stockhausen went a step further: he displayed a plastic metric patterning process. One instrumental group slows down according to a carefully measured pattern, while another speeds up simultaneously. Hence, the title "crossplay" is apropos. This method recurred in Stockhausen's works throughout the 1950s. Other stylistic gestures also deserve comment. The speeds in some of Stockhausen's passages can become incredible. The complexity of the patterns is devilish, too. With several simultaneous meters subjected to varying, frequently reversing and crossing speeds, the performance difficulty approached human limits.

Stockhausen became aware of the conundrum of complete control and near impossibility of performance realization. In 1953, he joined Dr. Herbert Eimert at the studio of West German Radio in Cologne in seminal investigations into the budding field of electronic sound genesis. The electronics at this studio differed markedly from those pursued by Pierre Schaeffer in France (from 1948). Schaeffer's work involved recording, mixing, and otherwise transforming natural and instrumental sounds. This technique was called *musique concrète*, as opposed to, and distinct from, the 'pure' electronic sounds in the Cologne studio. The studio contained sine-wave ('pure' tones devoid of overtones) generators, along with potentiometers, filters, mixers, and various control boards. Although the functions of these devices have long since been combined, simplified, and refined, this early work was groundbreaking.

The work in this studio, hand-in-hand with Stockhausen's discoveries through coursework in communications theory and phonetics under Werner Meyer-Eppler (1954-6) (Rich p. 2158), was profoundly formative in his development of rigorous serially controlled musical plasma. These sounds could be subjected to tight processes allowing the context to evolve in complexities and speeds far beyond human capabilities. Stockhausen now had an 'instrument' at his control that he could use to liberate sound without physical restrictions (Rich p. 2158). From this theoretical work, he began investigations into the very nature of timbre and its quality of linkage between rhythmic sine-tone pulses and varying speeds. These efforts were to culminate in the monumental electronic score **Kontakte** (1959-60).

Gerard Pape traces the evolution of Stockhausen's exploration. In his article, Pape contends that Stockhausen discovered a continuum of sound perception that results from treatments of amplitude and rhythm. The speeding up and slowing down of rhythms seems to affect the perception of pitch. Very slow speeds reveal discrete rhythmic pulses devoid of pitch, or 'color', or timbre. As speeds are increased gradually, continuous pitch is perceived. Also, Stockhausen claims, a different timbre becomes discernable by varying intensities applied to other pure tones that are marshaled to behave as overtones, in conjunction with rhythmic variations. What is perceived as rhythm at one level is perceived as pitch and timbre at another, with its melodic implications, according to Stockhausen (Pape Composition pp. 11-12). (It should be noted that Xenakis has challenged the notion that overtone-free sounds can combine to create the impression of timbre. See chapter on Xenakis).

Indeed, *Kontakte* explores the full range of this mysterious transitional landscape. Sounds spiral downward while slowing down to split into pulses. They then re-form in a wondrous array of continuity. These studies were important in the formation of the musical aesthetic of the Mexican composer, Julio Estrada, who is exploring the extremes in sound-based composition.

Simultaneous with this work in the electronic studio, Stockhausen continued to bring forth important instrumental works. *Spiel* (1952- for orchestra) was exemplary for its convoluted configurations. This tendency came to a peak in Stockhausen's piano works, culminating in the infamous, and fiendishly difficult, *Klavierstücke I- XI* (1952-3) for solo piano. This work was so tightly organized that it revealed to Stockhausen some of the problems inherent in slavish subservience to serialist dogma. What had seemed promising as a liberating device had become a tyranny of method, stifling the very freedoms it had been designed to proffer.

The impasse encountered in strict serialism became more constricting in succeeding works. The freshness of Stockhausen's ebullient musical personality managed to save some of the works. Such luminescences as *Kontra-Punkte* (1953) for ten instruments, Nr. 5 Zeitmässe (1955-56) for woodwinds, the wonderfully fluid *Gesang der Jünglinge* (electronically treated voices reading disjointed Biblical passages mixed with electronic sounds - 1956), and *Gruppen* (1955-7) for three spatially separated orchestras, are the best of the series. *Gruppen* seems to explore the very limits of comprehensibility. Space as an element of form was explored in Stockhausen's work both for instruments and for electro-generated sounds (especially *Gruppen* and *Kontakte*), as players and/or loudspeakers were placed strategically throughout the performance arena.

Still, the problems of serialism became apparent in the disparity between the concept (complete control) and the perception by the listener. What had been intended as flow became a seemingly fortuitous dispersion of points of sound. The planned linear counterpoint was too complex (at least in the most rigid and least flowing works, like the piano pieces). The problem with total serialism results from its progressive limitation of choices. As the series unfolds, less and less variety remains available until the series is exhausted. This is not the case in classical tonality or in fully statistical music (in the work of Xenakis). Stockhausen and the other serialists became trapped in a method that provided too restrictive a field for developing contrast. Total 'contrast' became total *homogeneity*.

John Cage's lectures at Darmstadt (1958) intensified this realization. He showed that the *sound* of totally controlled serial pieces and that of totally indeterminate works was *not substantially different*. This realization brought a marked change in Stockhausen's approach. He began to incorporate chance into his work thereafter, instilling a curious stylistic dichotomy that also became a cul-de-sac. Stockhausen's attempts to escape incomprehensibility seem to have *enhanced* it. Many works have followed in Stockhausen's confusing evolution, *Stop* (1965) and *Ylem* (1972) for orchestra being among the most interesting, but none as fresh (for many) as those that reflected his studies in sound-based composition and the dynamics of the linkage between pitch, timbre, and rhythm. Stockhausen has become a curious creature whose legacy is unclear, as each succeeding work seems to withdraw more deeply into a strange world inhabited, and inhabitable only, by himself, and related in no clear way to current trends.

## • **His Style**

Stockhausen's early work heightened the pointillism introduced in the work of Webern. Single sounds frequently become isolated, unrelated to the flow of others, in a constant flux. His best works are fresh and exciting. The early works until about 1960 show a precociously musical tendency. The orchestration, though, peculiarly favors thin, stringy textures. When the work gets too complex, the listener starts to flounder helplessly.

The work in chance in the '60s, '70s, and '80s is usually unremarkable and lacks the blazing, pristine edge inherent in Cage's work. There is no clear continuity in it. The commitment and profound philosophical underpinning of Cage's work is absent in Stockhausen's. However, his very recent work ('90s) shows renewed interest in the exploration of new timbral contours that bodes well for the development of a sound-based compositional aesthetic. Nonetheless, his early work always sounds most exciting.

◆◆◆

- **His Major Works**

*Kreuzspiel*
*Kontrapunkte*
*Nr. 5 Zeitmässe*
*Gruppen*
*Gesang der Jünglinge*
*Kontakte*
*Stop*
*Ylem*

# John Cage
# (1912- 1992)

 confusing symbol

John Cage is the figure most associated with chance in musical composition. From a humbling process in his musical education, Cage realized he had only modest skills in the discipline of harmony. Determined, he set out to continue "beating [his] head against that wall" (Kostelanetz p. 53) until he found a way to make his way in music. The 'solution' was a path to the most radical revolution ever achieved in any art.

If Arnold Schönberg presents the image of the most troubling modernist in art music of the first half of the 20th century, John Cage was the most unsettling and disruptive apostle of change in the last half of the 20th century. With the Greek iconoclast, Iannis Xenakis, Cage was one of the two personalities most responsible for directing composition *away* from the 'total control' mechanics enshrined by advocates of serialism (especially Pierre Boulez and Karlheinz Stockhausen, both followers of the canon of Anton Webern).

John Cage has been enshrined as a philosopher who opened our minds and ears to a world of sounds to be heard and perceived as never before. Dieter Schnebel, a radical theologian and composer, advocated crumbling the edifice of music to its very foundations. His mission was incomplete. It took John Cage to complete it, along a path carefully planned to strip away every familiar element of musical composition (melody, harmony, phrase structure, form, etc.). Through his developments in, and use of, chance and Indeterminacy in composition, he was both music's most dangerous threat, and its ultimate savior.

## • **His Life**

John Milton Cage (Jr.) was the son of an inventor, John Milton Cage, Sr. He graduated as class valedictorian from Los Angeles High School in 1928. He studied at Pomona College in Claremont, California, for two years before dropping out. After preliminary lessons on piano with Fannie Dillon, he sailed to Paris (Spring 1930), where he studied piano with Lazarre Lévy and architecture with Goldfinger. While overseas he began to write poetry and music and to paint, three activities that were to stay with him throughout his life.

He returned to the US in autumn of 1931 and resumed composing, writing, and painting. He took odd jobs to support himself. These included work as a gardener, and lecturing to local housewives about modern painting and music. In 1933, he studied composition with Richard Buhlig. While studying, Cage developed a quasi-serial ordering that he incorporated into some of his early works. The patterns involve ordering a set of two 25-note ranges. This method was used in Cage's *Solo with Obbligato Accompaniment of Two Voices in Canon, and Six Short Inventions on the Subjects of the Solo* (1933). He went to New York and studied harmony, contemporary music, and Oriental and folk music under Henry Cowell at New School for Social Research. Then, at Cowell's urging, he studied harmony and composition under Adolph Weiss.

In 1934, Cage's career took a major turn. He returned to California and studied counterpoint and analysis under Arnold Schönberg at University of Southern California. He was one of Schönberg's best pupils and revealed a keen ability to extract many solutions to problems posed in the classes by Schönberg. However, Schönberg noticed a certain awkward sense in Cage's contrapuntal skills, especially in regards to certain treatments of harmony. Reportedly, Schönberg commented to Cage that he had no feel for harmony and would have trouble becoming an effective composer (*PAR* Kostèlanetz p. 53). Cage merely intensified his resolve (*PAR* Snyder p. 36).

## • **His Musical Life and philosophy**

Cage began carefully studying the relationships between structure ("division of parts into a whole"), method ("note-to-note procedure"), and materials ("sounds and silences") (Cage - Composition p. 18). This began his realization that these elements could be split into those relating to matters of the mind as opposed to form ("morphology of a continuity") that is related to matters of the heart. Composition was the process integrating the "rational with the irrational" (especially structure and form). These philosophical concerns are detailed in his lecture 'Composition as Process' (1958) as part of a chronology of the evolution of his musical thought up to the composition of his *Music of Changes* for piano (1951) (*PAR* Cage Composition p. 18).

By making these refined distinctions, Cage was able to view composition from a completely different perspective from that approached by other composers. He was able to set about dissecting the compositional process altogether stepwise in successive works. That ultimately led to the abrogation of formal procedures altogether, through developments in the use of the *I-Ching* (Chinese *Book of Changes*), and ultimately, into Indeterminacy. Schönberg's admonition led to an outcome that exemplifies the law of unintended consequences: Cage's ultimate and systematic rupture of the compositional process!

The first step in the process became apparent from his work in 1937, as composer-accompanist for Bonnie Byrd's classes in dance at the Cornish School. If Cage had modest talents in harmony, he had no lack of talent in rhythm. Piano pieces were constructed using charts with randomly selected numbers that identified certain formal junctures. Progress within the work would involve Cage's moving from chart to chart in a procedure that resembled motion within magic squares (Cage - Composition pp. 20/21 and 25/26). Pitches were devised in quasi-serial manner akin to that used in *Solo with Obbligato.* Then Cage began composing mainly percussion pieces, with refined rhythmic patterns.

At some point, there were insufficient performers to make a full percussion ensemble. Cage responded with his first piece for prepared piano. This instrument is a piano with objects inserted between strings (including spoons, bolts, rubber bands, etc.) at carefully identified locations. The result is a complete alteration of the pitch values associated with the keys on the keyboard. The effect is strangely musical, even delicate, but with some percussive quality and pitch uncertainty added. *Noise* had made its way into music (the element of pitch was made dispensable)!

Noise had found its way into Varèse's work previously, especially in his *Ionisation* (1927) for percussion ensemble, but the results were *intended*; the outcomes were *known* and *planned*. In Cage's prepared piano work, the results are *not* known, even if Cage had some rough idea of the general sound. The concept of 'experimental music' was born (according to Cage, an experiment is "an act the outcome of which is unknown") (Cage - Experimental p. 13). The first prepared piano work was *Bacchanale* (1938). Originally, the piece was constructed to fulfill a need. The 'new instrument' behaved as a percussion orchestra under the control of a single performer. But the seeds for revolution were sown. Here were shades of the inventive capacity that Cage's father had bequeathed to Cage.

There followed a series of remarkable pieces for prepared piano (some with dance accompaniment provided by his close associate, Merce Cunningham), and others for percussion orchestra that revealed a mind wedded to the unforeseen and unpredictable. The most famous works for prepared piano to follow were *Amores* (1943) for three tom-toms and prepared piano, and the exquisite *Sonatas and Interludes for Prepared Piano* (1946-1948). A remarkable work combining the instrument with full orchestra, the *Concerto for Prepared Piano and Chamber Orchestra* appeared in 1951. Seminal percussion works followed: *First Construction In Metal* (1939) featured non-orchestral noise-makers including brake drums. The *Imaginary Landscape No. 1* (1939) incorporates the use of fixed and variable speed turntables (with sounds originally used in audio research) placed in different rooms, and set in motion to churn out noises, mixed centrally, in a partially planned collage. This was a precursor to real electronic music, nine years before the appearance of 'musique concréte' in Pierre Schaeffer's studio.

In 1941, Cage moved to Chicago and taught a class in experimental music at the Chicago Institute of Design (having been invited by László Moholy-Nagy) (Snyder p. 37). By the mid-1940s, Cage immersed himself in Zen Buddhism. From this study he became aware that composing, performing, and listening to a work of art are distinct events that need not be considered inseparable. This realization profoundly altered his view of the process of composition and of the roles of form and structure in music.

Cage taught at Black Mountain College in North Carolina in 1948. In 1949, he met and befriended Pierre Boulez (with whom he broke off relations shortly afterwards when irreconcilable philosophical differences emerged). He also began to utilize the I-Ching in 1950 for making choices in his compositions. The *Concerto for Prepared Piano and Chamber Orchestra*, the *Music of Changes*, and the *Imaginary Landscape No. 4*, all 1951, are seminal works in this direction. In these works, arbitrary numbers from a book are manipulated so that the choosing, although done 'rigorously', is beyond the conscious control of the performer. Form has been dissolved as an element in musical construction.

The *Imaginary Landscape No. 4* is most remarkable and radical. Subject to the whims of the *I-Ching*, the piece is 'constructed' with great precision applied to notation. Sound volumes are given illusory control by dynamical notations intended for performers turning radio control knobs. Other ephemeral notations act as instructions for other performers to tune the station-selector dials. The piece is 'scored' for twelve radios, each using two 'performers' (one on volume, the other on station selection). The twenty-four performers, within the bounds constrained by Cage's notation, conspire to conjure a nightmare of mixed station signals, static and silence, constantly roiling. The result is chance noise under rigid, though unconscious, control, via a disciplined notational system whose outcome is twice removed from aware-ness (composer and performer). The seeming discipline em-ployed by Cage in the compositional process has two goals: one, by careful discipline, Cage prevents sloppiness and habit from creeping into his compositional procedure; two, noise is generated that bears no relationship whatsoever to conventional musicality.

In 1952, Cage composed his most infamous piece, *4' 33"*, for a soloist. The performer walks onstage and sits for the titled duration--divided into three 'movements'--play-ing nothing on the instrument (usually a piano). Audience noises that may range from catcalls to coughs become the sound content of the piece. This work heralded the entry of ambient environmental sounds as aspects of a work (Cage Composition p. 22).

Cage had come close to the fruition of a concept that had been germinating in his mind for many years, and that he soon was to codify explicitly: that music, or any art, need not be something *done to* an audience; it only need be experienced directly. Life was viewed to be part of art, and art of life. The 'prima donna' status accorded to artists needed to be jettisoned in Cage's view. A composer could write something experimentally (unaware of its outcome), not necessarily needing a performance for its elucidation. Independently, a performer could play something conjured by a composer, without becoming distracted unduly by the composer's original 'intention'. A listener could hear some-thing, anything at all, and not need to know who wrote it. For Cage, all life was music!

One last major step remained in the unfolding of Cage's musical evolution: the concept of Indeterminacy was established. For Cage, Indeterminacy in composition was the act of designing a piece not knowing the universe in which he was dealing. All taste, habit, will, and memory were obliterated from the process of composition (Wolff p. 117). The first major work to show signs of this was the **Concert for Piano and Orchestra** (1957-8). A complex new notational system was devised to separate the flow of the piece from conscious intention. The piece also incorporates Indeterminacy as an ingredient in performance, as the piano player is instructed to drop his score and pick up the pages, in whatever order, and play. Instructions accompany the piece to aid the performer in deciphering the notation. The result is chaos. (Note the use of the word "concert" in the title. Cage avoided the 'art'-form term, 'concerto', so as to demystify the performance process).

**Winter Music** (1957) for up to five pianists followed. Pianists perform independent parts (that bear no interrelationship), thereby creating a montage of cacophony. An even more bizarre work, **Cartridge Music** (1960), was composed for objects, including slinkies, phonograph cartridges, tools, etc. Some are attached to amplification devices, so as to pick up the 'small sounds'. The objects are scratched and manipulated according to gestures defined in notation that was devised from abstract drawings on separate pages, invoking imperfections in the paper. This is an early example of Cage's concept of 'live' electronic music; that is, electronic music that isn't frozen in time, but that unfolds from performer creation in real time. This reflects Cage's ongoing concern that music should always bear a relationship to everyday life. The concept of live electronics bore considerable fruit in the subsequent work of the ONCE Festival composers (Robert Ashley, Gordon Mumma, George Cacioppo, Roger Reynolds, Donald Scavarda, and "Blue Gene" Tyranny), and the later Sonic Arts Union (David Behrman, Alvin Lucier, along with former ONCE composers, Mumma and Ashley).

In 1958, Cage traveled once again to Europe. He lectured at the summer courses held annually in Darmstadt,

Germany. The lectures proved to break the iron grip of serialism on the European musical scene.

Until then, radical serialist composers, whose works had their roots in Anton Webern's canon, had dominated the European musical scene. In the late 1950s, young revolutionaries, led by Boulez, Stockhausen, Luciano Berio, Bruno Maderna, Luigi Nono, and Henri Pousseur, assumed leadership in the courses taught at Darmstadt. Serialism, especially the pointillist variety proffered by Webern with his accompanying minimalism and non-classic forms, had become a dogma. Messiaen's master analysis classes had revealed the shadowy figure of the long-neglected Webern to be a prophet. The younger composers churned out any number of works that were totally organized serially. All their works were variations on a theme of sorts, each with a slightly different slant to The Method. The dogma had become entrenched.

Cage had noticed that a totally controlled piece didn't sound dissimilar to a work constructed according to chance principles, as found in his own work. But his approach allowed for more freedom. The impact of Cage's Darmstadt lectures, and of accompanying performances of Cage's pieces (notably *Cartridge Music*, performed by Cage's close friend, David Tudor, a pianist and very radical composer in his own right), created a sensation. Many of the European composers were to later shed the stifling shackles of the serial methods, creating freer pieces. Many of the future pieces would incorporate serialism as a partial device of control, but in a sound context of greater freedom. Cage's influence was definitely seminal in that respect.

Cage's masterpiece for orchestra, *Atlas Eclipticalis* (1961-2), is presently in the Chicago Symphony Orchestra repertory, having been added by conductor James Levine. Not always has it enjoyed such honor. During a performance of this work by the New York Philharmonic in 1964 under Leonard Bernstein's direction, the musicians themselves destroyed the electronic equipment that the work requires! The work calls for an orchestra that varies in size from performance to performance, ranging from small to very large. The larger the orchestra, the shorter is the work's duration. It consists of parts that are derived from star charts contained in an atlas of the (then) visible universe (*SUM* Downes p. 142-4). Blank transparencies were placed on separate pages of the atlas. Notes were inscribed where stars were located. Later, after removing the transparencies from the atlas pages, Cage affixed segments of staff-lines without regard to the placement of the notes. These decisions were made by chance operations. Clef signs (sometimes more than one to a staff-segment!) were affixed, also by chance operations.

The conductor is to stand before the orchestra and rotate his arms so that a full circle coincides with a minute. This rotation continues for the duration of the piece. The conductor acts like a clock for the performers' reference in the unfolding of the mutually unrelated sounds. Sometimes the piece is performed simultaneously with *Cartridge Music* and *Winter Music*. If the players are assigned one page apiece, the piece is short and the orchestra is large. Versions can result from assigning several pages to each player (small ensemble). A long version results. Sometimes, by asking the audience to close their eyes and conjure images of traveling through space, one can ensure a magical experience, in a journey through a musical no-man's land.

After *Atlas*, Cage began to expand the role of theater in his works. Continuing in the tradition he established for 'happenings' while teaching at Black Mountain College, Cage composed many works for multi-media presentation over the next three decades. Among the most famous of these was *HPSCHD* (1969 - 'Harpsichord', less vowels and r's). This work was composed in collaboration with Lejaren Hiller, a noted computer composer. It is programmed for seven harpsichordists, tapes, slides, and films with fifty-two projectors scattered throughout an enormous hall. Snippets of Mozart and other music collide with one another in a montage that unfolds for the audience as it passes through the immense auditorium. This work is computer-controlled. It has had an impact on works of other, less original composers.

Cage had planned a work that would be a companion piece to *Atlas Eclipticalis*, to be performed by large orchestra, outside, with computer-controlled sound and visual effects mimicking a thunderstorm, complete with rain and lightning. The work would include readings from James Joyce's *Finnegan's Wake*. Its anticipated title would have been *Atlas Borealis with the Ten Thunderclaps*. Cage postponed the project, due to the enormity of its scope. He never completed it.

Cage's later work includes several important pieces. Of special significance were two striking works for orchestra: *101* (1989) and *Ryoanji* (1983-5), (the latter existing in both orchestral and ensemble form). *Ryoanji* seems to incite musical monsters to roam the hidden crevices of our minds and souls.

Cage began to work more intensively in poetry by the 1970s. He developed a type of poetry that he calls "mesostics" (from its distant relative 'acrostics'), in which poetic statements are organized so that letters in different words, on different lines, are made to line up vertically to spell famous names or other statements (Slonimsky p. 283). Several of his literary works have been published, including *Silence* (1961), *A Year from Monday* (1967), *Empty Words* (1979), and *X* (1983).

His notation, often graphic, is so striking that it has passed for visual art. Many collections have been exhibited publicly. He also exhibited over 50 paintings unattributable to, and independent from, musical notation.

Cage has been honored with many awards including his election to the American Academy of Arts and Letters (1968) and to the American Academy of Arts and Sciences (1978). He was awarded an Honorary Doctorate of Performing Arts from the California Institute of the Arts in 1986. He served as Charles Eliot Norton Professor of Poetry at Harvard University as well (Slonimsky p. 283).

Cage had planned to travel to Paris to compose a piece on the UPIC graphic computer composing board developed by Iannis Xenakis, the Greek avant-garde composer, architect, and mathematician. However, that was not to be. Cage died after a stroke in New York City in 1992. He had said in 1957, "Until I die, there will be sounds. And they will continue following my death. One need not fear about the future of music." (Newsweek, August 24, 1992). Fitting enough.

## • **His Style**

Cage's stylistic evolution has been detailed already. The early period (1933-1941) is primarily pianistic with 12-tone controls. Later (1941-1951), percussion, metal, and the delicate noise-rich timbres of the prepared piano dominate. After that, what can one really say about 'style' in works that are generated beyond the realms of the composer's imagination?

He exerted a profound influence on the art of our time. Besides those composers (ONCE composers and Sonic Arts

Union composers) mentioned previously, other important composers benefited immensely from his example. These include the European radical apostles of extremes and disparities, Sylvano Bussotti, Mauricio Kagel, and Dieter Schnebel. Several other American composers' works grew out of the seeds of Cagean aesthetics as well, including Earle Brown, Morton Feldman, Christian Wolff, La Monte Young, and David Tudor.

Although music has undergone a reaction against avant-gardism in general, and Cagean experimentalism in particular, it is safe to say that Cage succeeded in forcing audiences and composers alike to rethink their tools, methods and approach to music. By virtue of this rethinking, we avoid traps associated with unquestioning reliance on outworn traditional methods, and sloppy thought processes resulting from careless misuse of chance methods. These bestowments from this unrestrained genius alone are sufficient to make the future of music secure.

◆◆◆

- ### His Major Works

  #### Music:
  *First Construction In Metal*
  *Amores*
  *Imaginary Landscape # 1*
  *Imaginary Landscape # 4*
  *Sonatas and Interludes for Prepared Piano*
  *The Seasons*
  *Concert for Piano and Orchestra*
  *Concerto for Prepared Piano and Chamber Orchestra*
  *Cartridge Music*
  *Winter Music*
  *Music of Changes*
  *Atlas Eclipticalis*
  *HPSCHD (with Lejaren Hiller)*
  *4' 33"*
  *Etudes Borealis*
  *Ryoanji*

  #### Books and Articles:
  *Silence*
  *A Year From Monday*
  *Notations*
  *Empty Words*
  *X*
  *M*

JOHN CAGE

107 BANK STREET • NEW YORK, NEW YORK 10014

MESSAGE

TO: Mr. James A. McNut
38467 Angela Dr.
Sterling Heights, Mich. 48077

DATE: Mar. 27, 1972

Thank you for writing. I think Christian Wolff is an excellent composer. He continually makes discoveries. His work is published by Peters and he teaches now at Dartmouth. I do not teach now (in Kostelanetz' book on my work (Praeger) you'll find information formally

REPLY

of the names of pupils. I do not think of people carrying on my ideas. I hope they make their own discoveries. Cunningham does his own choreography and uses chance operations in a way appropriate to dance (which is different from music, since involved with physical danger). I would be glad to see what it is you've written, though it is not necessary.

Best wishes,
John Cage

SIGNED

---

Thank you for writing. I think Christian Wolff is an excellent composer. He continually makes discoveries. His work is published by Peters and he teaches now at Dartmouth. I do not teach now (in Kostelanetz' book on my work (Praeger) you'll find information about my teaching formally and the names of pupils. I do not think of people carrying on my ideas. I hope they make their own discoveries. Cunningham does his own choreography and uses chance operations in a way appropriate to dance (which is different from music, since involved with physical danger). I would be glad to see what you've written, though it is not necessary.

Best wishes,
John Cage

# Iannis Xenakis
# (1922-2001)

ço

Iannis Xenakis is the single most defiantly original and unconventional composer in history. His influence upon succeeding composers and his contemporaries is uneven; some respond with unrestrained enthusiasm; some with abhorrence. Part of this mixed reaction is traceable to the fact of Xenakis' unorthodox musical background that, in turn, led him to approach musical composition from utterly outside and beyond the discipline as defined by pedagogues. His self-imposed isolation, even *exile*, results from his philosophical contemplations on music as the purest and most abstract of all disciplines. For Xenakis, music exists beyond its customary states of sentimental expression and invokes mental disciplines as disparate as architecture and mathematics.

It is Xenakis' belief that only once one fully understands music's role in the scheme of all intellectual activities, can one return to its perfumes and fragrances to evoke its full flowering. That is: understand the discipline, logic, and rigor that underlies all philosophical enterprise,and then you can unlock the secrets to music's very essence as the center of all intellectual activity.

The freedoms provided by his unconventional musical background enabled Xenakis to explore relationships *between* disciplines, and involve music making in ways hitherto unimagined. These freedoms enabled him to elucidate the whole process of musical composition as being a promulgator, second to none, of intellectual rigor among other more familiar disciplines, including mathematics, science, architecture, and philosophy (Xenakis/Kanach p. 8).

## • **His Life**

Xenakis' background is crucial to understanding his extraordinary journey through discovery in music and other disciplines. "I am a Classical Greek living in the twentieth century." (Matossian p.11). This comment expresses both Xenakis' unquenchable interest in his Greek heritage and his lifelong frustration at being a prisoner of a dull, mundane life in the modern world (*PAR* Matossian p. 18).

Xenakis' father was a businessman of Rumanian heritage, who was to become an agent on behalf of the British Government during World War II (Matossian p. 18). His father was financially successful and frequently worked as long and hard as necessary to make gains in the world, sometimes at the expense of time spent with his children. Xenakis only felt free to exert his personality at certain times, as when the children were asked to display themselves. Xenakis resented this restrictive existence. His fondest memories were of his mother, a woman of Greek parentage, who doted on him, playing and teaching him piano. Xenakis has always felt the presence of his mother as a part of his inner essence. Her early death scarred him. Thereafter, Xenakis was sensitive, and he found it difficult to manage his way through relationships (*SUM* Matossian p. 13).

His father sent him to a boarding school on the island of Spetzai, in Greece, when Xenakis was ten. The atmosphere was unconducive to building friendships, as Xenakis' classmates constantly harassed him for his peculiar accent. He suffered repeated beatings by his classmates; his teachers were harsh, all leading to intensified withdrawal. He found allies, though, in the Greek headmaster in charge of classical literature and philosophy, and, especially, the English headmaster in charge of English literature, Noel Paton, with whom Xenakis maintained correspondence throughout the latter's life. Paton took Xenakis in for evenings of discussions covering a variety of intellectual topics, and especially music. He played Beethoven records, and this helped tap Xenakis' latent interest in music. Xenakis' activities in the choir, and in extracurricular harmony and piano lessons, were unremarkable. Xenakis had poor relationships with his music teachers. This became a lifelong albatross Xenakis was to bear in his musical development (*SUM* Matossian p. 16).

Xenakis' graduated and went to Athens to enter the Athens Polytechnic at age sixteen. After seven interrupted (by war) years of study, Xenakis graduated with work in law, physics, mathematics, and ancient literature. He also had basic studies in music, including piano lessons, harmony, and counterpoint, under Aristotle Kondourov, a Tchaikovsky admirer. Kondourov was able to install in Xenakis a respect for the importance of rigor in the process of composition. This, if nothing else from Xenakis' youthful musical pedantry, served as a plus in his development (*SUM* Matossian pp. 17-18).

Greece's unstable political scene fell to turmoil in Xenakis' teen years. A fascist general managed to convince the king to abandon the constitution. For years thereafter, Greece became vulnerable to attack and occupation by various external forces, not least, the Italian Fascists, the German Nazis, and the British (!). Although the fascist general unexpectedly had repelled the thrust of the Italian Fascists, he collaborated in Greece's own demise by making clandestine arrangements with Greece's own right-wing factions, and with the British, in an attempt to foil the rising Communist resistance movement.

Xenakis initially joined a right-wing resistance group (the resistance movement in Greece was as multi-political as were the official powerbrokers) (Matossian p. 19). Then, becoming more attracted to the seeming purity of the Communist ideal, he switched affiliations and joined a left-wing resistance group (Matossian p. 20). Xenakis became a leader of the movement. Through this activity, he was finally able to impress others favorably in the movement, thus providing himself an antidote to his former timidity at boarding school. He also garnered much attention from the enemy.

After much turmoil, the British--ostensibly an ally of Greece in resisting Nazi intrusion--betrayed the resistance movement by their intervention, on orders from Winston Churchill, demanding the resistance teams to lay down their arms (Matossian pp. 23-24). Churchill had been troubled by the Communist-backed support given to the various groups. Churchill helped reinstall the king and right-wing collaborators. The British helped to quell demonstrations by firing upon the citizenry, often killing innocent, unarmed families. Finally, in 1944, as he was guarding a home, Xenakis suffered shrapnel-induced tearing along the whole left side of his face. The impact burst his left eye and shredded his cheekbone. His father had him spirited to a hospital where he underwent three operations, one without anesthesia, for facial reconstruction (*PAR* Matossian pp. 26-27).

Toward the end of the war, the resistance was fragmented as authorities forcibly conscripted the youth. Some were sent to camps, Xenakis being one of them. He refused to sign a disclaimer of political philosophy, and, by a ruse, left the camp and escaped and went underground. Eventually, his father helped get him smuggled to Paris. Xenakis was without a country, or a face; his idealism, too, had been broken.

## • __His Musical Life and Philosophy__

Through his studies at Athens Polytechnic, Xenakis had assimilated enough mathematics and physics to provide a viable backdrop for work in architecture. His musical interest was at its peak, with his studies in classical literature enriching his aesthetic orientation. As he was illegally in France, he had very few options for survival. He was able to land a position with the famous French architect, Charles-Édouard Jeaneret Le Corbusier. While with Le Corbusier, Xenakis established an astonishing record of designing incredibly original and durable structures. His first famous edifice was the Philips Pavilion for the 1958 Brussels Worlds' Fair. From 1956 to 1958, Xenakis labored over the designs, ultimately deciding upon a concept that produced ruled surfaces emerging by use of rotating straight lines into a hyberbolic paraboloid shell (Matossian p. 114). The design was radical; it was unlike anything conceived until then.

Xenakis came upon the idea of combining architectural thought and musical structure. After all, isn't a musical composition an edifice? And what provides structural integrity in the physical world, thought Xenakis, ought to do corollary functions in music, by analogy. This was the beginning of Xenakis' painstakingly disciplined journey of discovery of the fundamental laws of music making. Following his progress through the philosophy of composition is best understood by following a series of questions that he asked himself throughout the stages in his creative career (in a way analogous to Albert Einstein's thought experiments). These questions imbue the book, *Conversations with Iannis Xenakis* by Bálint András Varga, which consists of extensive interviews between the author and Xenakis.

· How does one explore gradual evolutions between continuity and discontinuity?

*Answer*: Serial permutations of intervals, using glis sandi as analogue to architectural straight lines. *Metastasis*, (1953-4), (*PAR* Varga p. 75).

· Can one control an evolution from noise into sonority?

*Answer*: Stochastic permutation of instrumental effects (e.g., slapping of backs of stringed instru ments to pizzicato to glissandi.) *Pithoprakta*, (1955-56).

Xenakis' article "The Crisis of Serialism" appeared in the periodical *Gravesaner Blätter*. It outlines his aversion to serialism as promulgated by Pierre Boulez and Karlheinz Stockhausen. In it, he maintains that the linear complexity of serial sounds creates a perception of chaos in the minds of the audience. Individual lines get lost. The ear is forced to analyze the texture probabilistically. So why not employ stochastics as the building block from the start? Discontinuity was a tyranny in classical tonality and serialism. Xenakis wished to break the tyranny with a systematic exploration of continuity and allow sounds to travel the gamut between continuity and discontinuity using probabilities (*PAR* Xenakis p. 8).

*Pithoprakta* was a study in massed sounds. In it, Xenakis used free probability distributions to create clouds of sound that are perceived as a massive entity. The sounds were reminiscent of Xenakis' experiences in prison during his resistance movement days as he heard the sounds of crowds (Varga p. 75). The sounds evolve into shapes that the mind can follow. Gradual and sudden changes alike become traceable. The fortuity inherent in serial writing is quashed by controlled Indeterminacy. Serialism treats all outcomes as equal. Classical tonality treats everything as unequal. Stochastic music (from the Greek term *Stochos*, or 'goal') navigates the gradations between the two extremes. Having tamed these stochastic laws, he posed new questions:

· Can there be an evolution of music from a
   minimum of rules acting on raw data that
   generates a musical output from an automaton?
· Can the musical output be made interesting?

*Answer*: Apply a rare event distribution
   (Poisson distribution). ***Achorripsis***, (1956-57),
   (Varga pp. 78-79, p. 81). Xenakis desired an *inter
   esting*, not just *any*, result.

At this point, Xenakis was challenged to ponder and reconsider the role of the composer in general, and himself in particular. He had become aware that his unique contribution to music lay in his use of non-musical ideas to create musical edifices (Varga pp. 78-80). Mathematics mirrors the physical world. The ear and mind are physical, and so by analogy, they will be especially responsive to music carefully constructed using mathematical models.

The use of probability functions with the aid of computers enabled Xenakis to generate a whole family of compositions from a single set of probability formulae (Maxwell-Boltzman kinetic theory of gases - exerting pressure on sound particles and Gaussian bell-curve distributions to shape glissandi) (Xenakis pp. 32-37/Varga p. 16). Works such as ***Atrées (Homage à Pascal)*** (1962) and ***ST 10*** (1962) are members of this family. But he noticed that repeated attempts using the formulae generated different results as well. So he toyed with various outputs to guarantee the most interesting results (Pape Composition p. 14/Varga p. 16). This itself is strong proof that Xenakis' gestures are grounded artistically and that his music is not simply an automated process. The power of the music is established by his choice of *initial* parameters, too. No machine can tell him what instruments and sounds to call upon at a given time. What the math helps him accomplish is an interesting distribution of the sounds: that is, the *timing* of events to guarantee the most perceptually successful outcome.

Two further excursions into stochastic music are noteworthy: the use of biased probability (a probability whose outcomes are dependant upon previous outcomes--probability with a memory); and 'strategic' music, involving the employment of game theory. ***Syrmos*** (1959) is an example of the former, employing 'Markov Chains' (Xenakis pp. 43-109). ***Strategie*** (1959-62), a game for two competing conductors, is an example of the latter (Xenakis p. 110-130).

Xenakis abandoned stochastic music as he began to ponder what could justify what he was doing musically. His contemplation led him to consider the deepest generalized meanings of concepts usually taken for granted in music. For example, what is time? What is pitch? And what are their interrelationships? Some concepts, such as scale and mode, were poorly understood and erroneously considered interchangeable. A scale is always a scale, whether it is written today or tomorrow. A mode results from operations performed upon a scale and can only be perceived as it unfolds through time (*SUM* Varga p. 33). These realizations led Xenakis to conclude that some structures exist 'in' time, and some only 'outside' time.

Xenakis began to construct structures, like scales, according to the most general principles. He resorted to a 'sieve' process, a technique devised by the ancient Greek mathematician, Eratosthenes. This process separates out some steps and generates scales according to the most generalized theoretical methods. That is, it takes a unit interval (such as a half-step, as in the chromatic scale or the Pythagorean comma, the minute pitch differences between the 7th octave and the 'same' tone achieved by the 12th iteration of a perfect 5th). This unit interval is repeated to generate an octave (forming a complete chromatic scale, all equal intervals). New scales are created with uneven spacing, such as the diatonic scale, or Messiaen's octatonic scale, by sieving out certain of the interval positions (Xenakis pp. 196-200 and 268-277). Even *non*-octave repeating, or non-periodic scales, may emanate (as in Xenakis' *Palimpsest* – 1979) (Protheroe).

The sieve is capable of generating any conceivable scale by a generalized algorithm (Xenakis pp. 268-277). This established a means for Xenakis to devise outside-time structures rigorously. He developed various procedures for treating and evolving in-time structures, as well: that is, he created means to operate on the outside-time structures to create specific in-time structures pertinent to the specific piece at hand. For example, two major works are subjected to group transformations (methods borrowed from symbolic algebra, hence his term "symbolic music") and to the geometry of group transformations. The first is *Nomos Alpha* (1966), a tour-de-force for solo cello in which twenty-four elements undergo transformations of the symmetrical vertices of the cube (Varga p. 87). The second is *Akrata*, wherein twelve elements undergo transformations of the symmetries of a tetrahedron (Varga p. 88).

*Nomos Alpha* is bewitching in its twisting embrace of ghostly contours, the likes of which never before have been so enraptured by human pen. *Akrata* is chilling in its brutal portent--so majestic, magnificent, and thoroughly ominous.

Xenakis also employed logic operations, such as union and intersection, in these and earlier works to achieve a plastic form that allows for varying degrees of order (entropy, or ataxy). The use of logic screens assisted in these order transitions (Xenakis pp. 50-79). This recalls Varèse's formal deployment of varying densities, and marks the first time ever that anyone treated *order-disorder* as a *formal* device!

Xenakis branched out to create generalized methods for proceeding from tone-to-tone. In *Formalized Music*, in the section titled "New Proposals In Microsound Structure" (chapter IX), Xenakis envisioned a general means by which he could create a random walk from one position to another. He would create an atmosphere that would apply 'pressure' to a single sound-unit (analogous to the timbre of a conventional tone) through automatic means using high-powered probability distributions. These distributions create a noise-rich unit kernel of sound, as opposed to the thin spaghetti-strand textures that Xenakis loathed; the thin sounds are associated with traditional electronic sound synthesis, and result from the use of simple trigonometric functions (sine waves, etc., that are devoid of overtones). Xenakis claimed that the simple sine-tones (overtone-free) unravel into thin lines, rather than fulfill their intended timbral function. (The timbral role was posited by Stockhausen, who considers timbre a special case of rhythm.)

The 'pressure' forces the sounds to 'walk' randomly through a sound environment, much like Brownian movement (a scientific term for motion of a particle in an elastic medium, like water) (*PAR* Xenakis pp. 246-248). Xenakis devised a spin-off of this procedure, an 'arborescence', or tree-like structure that defies traditional notation. Arborescences obtain continuous transformations not achievable through traditional notation, because such notational attempts would segment the lineage, thereby breaking continuity (*PAR* Varga pp. 89-91).

This procedure enabled Xenakis to create generalized melodic structures, of which *serial structures* would be a special case (Xenakis p.182)! This development marked Xenakis' return to less formidably dissonant and dense sound patterns. Greek modes seem to appear, with consonant sounding intervals (Varga p. 159). Xenakis had come full circle through the most jarring dissonance to a more traditional structure, *but only once he had understood the philosophical underpinnings of his art!*

***Evryali*** (1973) uses arborescences. The full realization of a total random walk (macrostructure) by sound particles under pressure (microstructure), as proposed in the "New Proposals In Microsound Structure" chapter of *Formalized Music* did not come until the 1991 realization of his ***Gendy 3*** computer program. This work is chilling in the very interesting dense sounds achievable by completely computerized input and output.

Lastly, Xenakis has developed a computer tool for use in teaching children to compose graphically by direct input. It is called the UPIC system. It uses a light pen by which one draws certain patterns and shapes into a computer. These patterns can be said to resemble sound structures. In particular, the proposals in micro- and macro-sound structures, as well as the concepts behind the UPIC, had been germinating in Xenakis' mind for decades (since the late 1960s), when Xenakis headed a group of theorists from various intellectual disciplines to investigate the interactions between the arts and sciences. The group was called CE-MAMu (Centre d'Etudes de Mathématique et Automatique Musicales). The group included psychologists, philosophers, mathematicians, and musicians. (UPIC stands for Unité Polyagogique Informatique du CEMAMu--Polyagogique is for 'many' (poly), and ('agogie') is for 'training').

Other important Xenakis works involve musique concrete ('electronic' music using treated taped natural sounds, rather than electro-generated sounds, as in synthesizers). The most powerful and important of these are *Orient-Occident III* (a 1960 UNESCO creation), *Bohor I* (1962) *Kraanerg* (an imaginary 1968 ballet on social violence for instrumental and taped sounds); *Hibiki-Hana Ma* (for the Osaka EXPO '70 consisting of taped and instrumental sounds); *Persepolis* (1969 for laser-light and sound festival along a mountainside outside Persepolis, Iran), and *la Légende d'eer* (1977 light and sound festival for the Diatope designed by Xenakis in the Beaubourg Square in Paris outside the Pompidou Centre). Both *Orient-Occident III* and *Bohor I* are scored exclusively for magnetic tape. These sound structures are atypical electronic works. They are incredibly powerful, as are their accompanying light shows.

Finally, mention should be made of Xenakis' architectural work. His work under Le Corbusier includes the previously mentioned Philips Pavilion for the Brussels Worlds' Fair (1958). Also, he designed the Convent at Tourette and parts of the Parliament and the Secretariat at Chandigarh, India, in the 1950s. After his break with Le Corbusier in 1959, Xenakis finished several formidable edifices: the interior of the French Pavilion (*Polytope de Montreal*) for the Montreal Exposition (1967); light and sound show for Persepolis (1969); the *Polytope de Cluny*; Paris (1972), and the *Diatope in Paris* (1977) are the most prominent. Xenakis also completed a draft design for a 'Cosmic City' in the 1960s, to be built 5000 meters into the sky. The concept was studied as a way to resolve urban overcrowding while avoiding the usual cluttered slum look commonly associated with most urban projects. For further descriptions of these efforts, refer to Matossian (pp. 109-128 and pp. 210-225) and Varga (pp. 22-23).

Xenakis earned a Doctorat d'Etat in 1976 (a Ph.D. issued on the basis of 'standing' works in lieu of a separate dissertation). *Arts/Sciences: Alloys* (Xenakis/Kanach) is Xenakis' published thesis defense.

## • <u>His Style</u>

The sound of Xenakis is unmistakable. Characteristic patterns are the brutal collisions of brass and the swirling glissandi of strings. Very little special effects are used (such as harmonics, or col legno) as Xenakis wants to retain focus on structure. The structures seem bizarre, though. The strange evolving clouds of sound resemble unearthly organisms that travel a terrain thoroughly rugged with extraterrestrial contours. The music folds and twists in continuous contortion and seeming distortion. The dissonance is shattering in his work (until 1990).

After 1990, Xenakis claims to have assimilated the landscape of the mathematical shapes so thoroughly that he no longer needed to resort to formulas in order to conjure his structures (Pape Composition p. 14). As he puts it: "I now work directly with the *left* side of the equation." (As opposed to the right side of, say $f(x)=\int x dx$) (Xenakis - University of Michigan in Ann Arbor, in 1989).

Accordingly, though, his work has become gentler and less densely aggressive. It has musical sounds as he explores the previously verboten territory of Greek modes and vocal folk declamation. I feel the change has not always worked to Xenakis' advantage. The music of his mathematical period was never sterile or stilted. It had real and awesome power, as if Xenakis were uncovering some potent magic *behind* the mathematical veneer. The math doesn't drive the music; it is merely the vessel in which Xenakis brews his concoction. I believe no other musician ever has used mathematics so rigorously and completely (especially such high-powered stuff) in achieving such profoundly powerful music. It's real art.

The matter of influences seriously begs the question: can there be a precedent for such a deeply Renaissance man? I think the answer is that there was no precedent in Xenakis' case. He reset the rules from outside. He then entered the arena and made real music in a powerful, original way. If there can be a composer that one could call a model, one may point to Varèse, in his evolving density patterns and collisions of masses of sound, or to Bartók by way of his stringed instrumental effects. And Messiaen provided some methodological guidance. But these are superficial influences. Xenakis seems not to have had any real model at all.

His work bears surface similarity to works of certain composers of the cluster school, whose works his preceded, especially Krzystof Penderecki and György Ligeti. But their patterns rely on intuition for their formation and for their perception. No extramusical rigor is applied to shape their sonic contours. In fact, many of the recent Poles and Hungarians view Xenakis with distrust and disdain. He is not well regarded by the academic establishment, either, for his background is musically atraditional. His composing methods are even more atraditional. But his approach, with its thought-modeling, will be hard to ignore in the future.

For example, the Mexican composer, Julio Estrada, is carrying Xenakis' ideas to the next logical step, in his careful controls of inflection and timbric evolutions by mathematical means. Some work by composers at Les Ateliers UPIC, a spin-off from CEMAMu, also founded by Xenakis, shows promising tendencies. Such concepts as chaos-driven evolutions have their roots planted firmly in Xenakian discipline.

Xenakis, more than any other composer of our time--or of any time--promises us a view of tomorrow, albeit through a musical landscape of unspeakable power and wonder. His example is a beacon that beckons us to experience beauty, unbidden and yet beguiling in its magic.

♦♦♦

- ## His Major Works

### Music:

| | |
|---|---|
| *Metastasis* | *Pithoprakta* |
| *Achorripsis* | *Akrata* |
| *Nomos Alpha* | *Terretektorh* |
| *Polytope de Montreal* | *Kraanerg* |
| *Atrées (Homage à Pascal)* | *Orient-OccidentIII* |
| *Bohor I* | *Gendy 3* |
| *La Légende d'ee r* | *Persepolis* |
| *Hibiki Hana Ma* | *Aroura* |
| *Synaphai (Connexities)* | *Palimpsest* |
| *Waarg* | *Jonchaies* |
| *Jalons* | *Nomos Alpha* |
| *Antikhthon* | *Echang* |

### Architecture and Light Shows:

*Philips Pavilion*
*Convent (Tourette)*
*Parliament (Chandigarh)*
*Diatope*
*Polytope de Montreal*
*Polytope de Cluny*
*Persepolis*

### Books and Articles:

*The Crisis of Serialism*
*Formalized Music*
*Arts/Sciences: Alloys*
*Musique Architecture*

I. Xenakis
17 R. Victor Massé
Paris 9.

Paris 15 - 4 - 74

Dear Mr. McHard

      I return you the chapter that you wrote on my music with some corrections. I wish we could discuss about these problems at some length. On June 7th I'll be in Connecticut for the première of my organ piece played by Holloway. Could you come there?

      Answers to your letter of Feb. 8th 74:

- I have used the Fisher, Pearson and student formulas without discussing them in Pithoprakta already and also as well. The Maxwell-Boltzmann is the normal distribution.

- Akrata is not discussed but the complex numbers were used in relation with complex transformations of patterns eg. the duration - pitch domain into itself with various transformation functions.

- The relativity theory can with much difficulty be applied or used in Art because of the cosmic scale of the events. Should the scale be far smaller (our every day scale)) the theory is powerless.

- orient-occident was freely composed except for some of the sequences that were made with the help of some distributions.

      thank you for your interest and work

      Yours sincerely

I.Xenakis
17 A. Victor Mame
Paris 9

Paris 15-4-74

Dear Mr. McHard

      I return you the chapter that you wrote on my music with some corrections. I wish we could discuss about these problems at some length. On June 7th I'll be in Connecticut for the world premiere of my organ piece played by Holloway. Could you come there?

Answers to your letter of Feb. 8th 74

-       I have used the Fisher, Pearson and student formulas without discussing them in Pithoprakta already and later as well. The Maxwell-Bolzmann is the normal distribution.
-       Akrata is not discussed but complex numbers were used in relation with complex transformation of patterns eg. Duration – pitch domain onto itself with various transformation functions.
-       The relativity theory can with much difficulty be applied or used in art because of the cosmic scale of the events. Should the scale be far smaller (our everyday scale), the theory is powerless.
-       Orient-Occident was freely composed except for some of the sequences that were made with the help of some distributions.

Thank you for your interest and work

Yours sincerely,
Iannis Xenakis

Note: I approached Xenakis in 1974 about usage of relativity theory in music. He had not included discussion of this topic in the 1971 edition of his book: ***Formalized Music*** as this letter confirms he had not considered it. However, the reader may note that the topic is addressed in the 1992 version of his book (note pp 255-268, Chapter X "Concerning Time, Space and Music").

# Luigi Nono
# (1924-1990)

಄

Throughout his life Luigi Nono remained an unshakable revolutionary. His revolution extended well beyond the boundaries of music. It encompassed every facet of life. For him exploring new territory in music was dishonest and inconsistent if it did not inform every discipline in which one is engaged. Each discipline affected, and mirrored, the others. He believed that one's life is anchored in the experiences that impinge upon one's mind, and that the ear (musical component of life) is affected very strongly by one's mental experiences and by how the mind, in turn, informs the ear. Nono was a complex man and searched for Utopia as a life model--in the real world, as well as in the world inhabitable only by our thoughts. But, after all, our thoughts serve as a template for our external being, so all is interrelated. Nono was an explorer who worked his revolution from the inside out, thus carrying the force of soundly developed philosophical commitment to the focus of his discipline: musical composition.

Nono's goal was not merely to alter the fabric of music (as so many other members of the avant-garde would) and the corelevant process of musicmaking, but to *subvert* the concepts surrounding the whole musical landscape. His goal was to lay awaste the tyrannies associated with the prevailing diatonic, and (even) chromatic, prejudices, so jealously guarded by musical academia. In so doing, he aimed to reestablish the contact, long lost, between the composer and his inner call for freedom. His musical life was a travel to unknown terrains of sound, at the core of his very existence, in a walk that began in the early 1950s with (originally) sophisticated serial composition. These works were wrought with highly polemical and political undercurrents (rife with the dangers he experienced during his worldly travels). Finally, culminating his tortuous walk in his later works, he explored the realms of pure sound, reflecting upon the way we think.

## • <u>His Life</u>

Nono's apprenticeship began with studies at the Venice Conservatory (1941). There, he spent time studying composition, history, and musicology under the august guidance of Gian-Francesco Malipiero. Under Malipiero, from 1943-5, Nono developed sensitivity to Italian music of the Renaissance and Baroque eras, and to the music of the Flemish masters, especially Johannes Ockheghem (*SUM* Kaltnecker). Nono studied a wide-range of early music, including the refinements of such masters as Don Carlo Gesualdo (especially noteworthy in Gesualdo's fascination for chromatic harmonies as an antidote to the rigidities of diatonics), Nicola Vincentino (whose construction of unusual musical instruments --including an 'arcicembalo' --enabled Vincentino to incorporate microintervals in 1561) (Pape - Nono p. 58) and Andrea and Giovanni Gabrieli (spatial music). Other tangential influences involved Thomas Tallis (spatial music), Josquin Des Prez (imitative polyphony for Nono's early, brief, 'Webernistic' compositional style), and Vincenzo Bellini (rigorous use of carefully shaped vocal inflections).

Nono continued his coursework in music in 1946 after obtaining his law degree (also 1946) from the University of Padua. His musical studies resumed with Bruno Maderna. These focused both on early Italian Music and on the music of the 20th century, particularly that of the three Viennese masters, Schönberg, Berg, and Webern, of whom Maderna was an unrelenting champion. Maderna introduced Nono to Ottaviano dei Petrucci's *Harmonice Musices Odhecaton A.* (1501) in which was published Ockeghem's song "Malheur me bat" ("I am struck by misfortune"), quoted in very subtle guise many years later in Nono's ***Fragmente - Stille, an Diotima*** (1979-80), as a memorial tribute to Nono's great mentor, Maderna. (Stenzl).

Nono then studied under Dr. Herman Scherchen, the renegade radical conductor who championed the three Viennese.

In 1952 Nono courageously joined the Italian Communist Party. He was active in the Italian Resistance movement against the Nazis. (Later, in the 1970s, he was to join the Central Committee, eventually assuming the leadership of the Italian branch. He remained a lifelong member) (*SUM* Slonimsky p. 1313). This was an important role for Nono, whose Communism was more philosophical than ideological; for him it meant an idealized pathway toward his Utopian goal of freedom for mankind through breaking the shackles that restrain the mind. This, in turn, set Nono free to explore the mind and its impact upon the ear and, ultimately, to free the ear from the rigidities of academic pedantry, redolent with its biases favoring olden traditions of tonal structuring.

Nono frequently referred to the words of the Italian Marxist Antonio Gramsci as formative upon his own philosophy. Synopsized, the remarks extol the virtues of struggling for a new culture and morality as they reveal a new way of living. A new way of seeing and sensing will emerge through which one forms a resultant mode of creation. A new truth evolves in which possibilities begin to evoke new realities in the arts (Koch). This philosophy served as a model for Nono in his lifelong work. It was this that enabled him to avoid the simplistic art expression so characteristic of other, more 'proletarian' styles (e.g., Prokofiev's and Shostakovich's, or those favored by Communist leaders, drenched in patriotic banalities), and to hold the banner of originality so high.

Nono's early musical maturity dates from the 1950s, with his association with the Darmstadt serialists, Boulez and Stockhausen, and with the appearance of his first musical compositions. Concurrent with his coursework in Darmstadt, and after Boulez, Stockhausen, and Maderna had taken positions as teachers, Nono published his first important works. *Variazioni Canoniche* (1950 - op. 1) concludes in a tone row adopted from Arnold Schönberg's cantata, *Ode to Napoleon*, a political work. The usage of the row is freer than that in the works of Boulez (*Piano Sonata No. 1*) and Stockhausen (*Kreuszpiel*) of the same period, stressing a more lyrical, yet expressionistic mode (*PAR* Kaltnecker). This work reveals several tendencies found in greater elaboration in Nono's later works, especially his use of octaves, something most post-Webern serialists avoided. Harsh sounds are more reminiscent of Schönberg than of Webern, however, sprinkled with some quiet sounds that already reveal Nono's fascination with the nearly inaudible.

Nono rejected the pointillism of Webern, favoring instead the longer lines of Schönbergian melodic structures. These lent themselves more readily to Nono's natural lyricism, in which he could mold his expressive appeals towards a higher artistic goal. The discontinuities of Webern's music seemed to suggest a self-sufficient exclusivity that focused upon a person's lonely existential qualities. These left no room for the community of humankind, only through which one can grow. So for Nono, the isolated sounds did not speak eloquently. Sounds, like people, must have relationship with their surrounding environment (*PAR* Kaltnecker).

Other early works dealing in isolated sounds (***Polifonica, monodia, ritmica*** - 1951- ensemble - and ***Composizione No. 1 per orchestra*** - 1952) soon followed. The nearly total serial work ***Incontri*** (1955) was his last expression within that aesthetic.

The succeeding works, coincided with his work at Darmstadt (1954-60), and his marriage in 1955 to Schönberg's daughter Nuria, by whom he had two daughters. Nuria and her daughters are the heirs of all his belongings and they have established and run the Archivio Luigi Nono. These works reflect his growing inclination towards harsh polemics. Nono wrote music that expresses, as faithfully as possible, the violence and pain associated with the horrors of war and of political imprisonment. He did this in keeping with the Schönbergian style of incorporating sounds that are appropriate to the expressive environment (e.g., the jagged, throbbing renderings associated with negative emotions expressed in Schönberg's ***Erwartung, Pierrot Lunaire,*** and ***Fünf Stucke für Orchestre***). His first great opera ***Intolleranza*** (1960) is an aggressively militant fresco that incorporates texts by Brecht, Eduard, and others. In it, imperialism and social decadence are excoriated in harrowing musical declamation.

Nono adopted a simpler vocal line in the following work, a masterpiece of equal stature, ***Canti di vita e d'amore***

("Sul Ponte di Hiroshima" 1962). This work shows the composer yearning for a higher quality of life, in music with vocalization that expresses an ecstatic fusion of life, love, and freedom (*PAR* Koch). Nono's polished mastery of the voice is grounded in his study of Bellini's vocal usage, and in Nono's own carefully controlled inflections, so subtlely shaped by changes in facial contours. He was to systematize this in his later works (Pape Nono p. 59). The central piece is a song to an Algerian participant who was tortured in the struggle against French colonialism. This theme--assigning a song, sometimes based on poetry, as a tribute to a 'comrade' felled because of work against social tyranny--was common in Nono's work from 1960 to the mid 70s. Nono's 'tributes' contained music of nearly unmitigated intensity. He used the battle against social injustice and oppression (especially neo-Nazism) to justify his use of advanced idioms not normally associated with the music of 'the people' (i.e., from Communist countries).

He polemicized throughout his life in favor of music that best characterized the atrocities against which he actively resisted. Why not, then, resort to Expressionism, with its *angst*, as the most appropriate methodology? This angst, therefore, is a *teaching* tool, not wanton ugliness. His exhortations in defense of this difficult style, contained in many addresses to various Communist committees, usually fell on deaf ears (*PAR* Slonimsky p. 1313).

*Canti* also shows an early sign of motivic handling that would evolve in high sophistication in later works: a block-like structure in which sound patterns coalesce by gradually emerging, then disappearing into the void. (Koch likens this to a wave-like pattern). This was a pivotal work in the Nono canon.

*A Floresta e jovem e cheja de vida* (1966) for tape, three speakers, clarinet, soprano, and noisemakers (metal sheets) culminates this trend, emanating as it does from the Viet Nam War years. Taped propaganda by the US war machinery is colored as imperialist fascist decadence. The propaganda is bathed in accompanying sounds illuminating the extreme pain associated with war. This is one tough listening experience. It is very hard to endure.

*Per Bastiana, Tai-Yang Cheng* ("The day is dawning" - dedicated to his second daughter, Bastiana - 1967) is a work for electronics and orchestral (but not vocal) accompaniment. It was inspired by a text from the song "The East is Red" from the People's Republic of China. Nono worked the score so that the notes are alliteratively related to the poetry (Koch). Special effects reflect Nono's interest in sound for its own sake (*'sound-based'* composition).

Nono used electronics methods throughout this period. Most usages mix voices and concréte sound, such as in *La fabbrica illuminata* (1964), *Per Bastiana,* and *A Floresta....* This method of concréte manipulation culminates with the searing electronics work *Contrappunto Dialettico Alla Mente* (*Contrapuntal Dialectic with the Mind* - 1967). Nono's future work in electronics would incorporate special equipment from Heinrich Strobel's studio in Freiburg, Germany, that enabled Nono to contour and shape sound and inflections in very minute detail.

A powerful eulogy closes this period. The work eulogizes Luciano Cruz, a young Chilean leader of MIR (Movement of Revolutionary Left) killed during the performance of his insurrectionist activities. In the piece, titled *Como Una Ola de Fuerza y Luz* (*Like a Wave of Power and Light* - 1971), the orchestral music unfolds against sounds from an accompanying tape. Piano and taped female choir are included. The work is richly scored, as orchestral passages are quieter and more graduated in their sonic contours than those of Nono's harsher, more expressionistic scores:

this work also requires a soprano. The genesis of this work--his relationship with a fallen revolutionary comrade--bears light on Nono's lifelong activities traveling the world and helping free freedom fighters caught in the grip of oppression. Nono conducted many such activities at great personal risk. Whatever one's feelings toward Nono's politics, no one can deny his consummate courage.

Nono entered a new stylistic phase in 1976 with the transitional work *...Sofferte onde serene...* (...suffered serene waves), a work in which an intricate craftsmanship takes over, invoking subtle sounds surrounded by near-silence. This work is scored for piano and magnetic tape. It features undulating groups of sound that seem to enter and depart from the field of audibility, almost unbidden. It is here that Nono shows his gift for exploring that special existence enshrouded within our minds. The pianist, whom the work specifies, is Maurizio Pollini, with whom Nono had had a special working relationship for decades.

The last phase of Nono's life reveals his transformation towards a style characterized by refined craftsmanship. He moved far away from rigid serialism, using instead, intuitive processes that draw from several of the most advanced methodologies, be they chance, quasi-set-like constructions, or oscillating wave-like patterns in Impressionistic modes. The most qualitatively characteristic work is the strange string quartet *Fragmente - Stille, An Diotima* (Fragments - Stillness, to *Diotima*, heroine of Hölderlin's poem of the same name -1980). Many special effects are marshaled, as Nono slowly travels through the gamut of stringed instrumental expressions. Most sounds are hushed - the dynamics explore the strange territory between *p* and *ppppp*, or the barely audible. This is the first profound revelation of what Nono regarded as the "mysticism of hearing" (Kaltnecker p. 15) by which he became able to open special doorways to the mind.

In *Fragmente...*, scraps of poetry from various works in Hölderlin's catalogue are scattered throughout the score. Nono admonishes that these bits must *not* be quoted in program notes, nor spoken by players, nor read in preface. The players are to mouth them silently, as they play their parts, as though seeking the poetry's inspiration (Stenzl). The scraps invoke mental states, somewhat recalling the very mental states that are emergent in the work of his teacher, Malipiero. Nono has entered a special world, and embarked on a disquieting, silent journey to discover the ultimate. Quiet though these sounds are in this 45-minute excursion, they are not soothing. Often sounding disconsolate, sometimes disturbing, they become a window to the mind of this intrepid explorer. Through them, Nono strives for that "delicate harmony of the inner life" (Stenzl quoting Hölderlin).

Nono's travel through the secrets of his mind left two unsettling masterworks for orchestra: *A Carlo Scarpa, Architetto ai suoi infiniti possibili* (1984), and *No Hay Caminos, Hay Que Caminar ...Andrej Tarkovskij* (1987).

*A Carlo Scarpa* and *No Hay Caminos...* are both dedicated to artists whose influences on Nono's life were profound and formative. They were travelers along a pathway that had no easy goal. *A Carlo Scarpa* shows in full bloom the "mysticism of hearing". The work is darkly somber, much as in the form of a gradually unfolding eulogy. Microtones are explored by Nono, as he discovers what he called a "mobile sound"--the subtle transitions between chromatic and microtonal sounds (Pape Nono p. 62).

There is an inscription in the halls of a 12th century monastery in Toledo, Spain, that is acutely reflective of Nono's life work. It reads, "Caminantes, No hay caminos, hay que caminar"(Wayfarer, there is no path, you must walk on). No more appropriate inscription could have graced the title of this last great work of Nono's. *No Hay Caminos...* is exceedingly quiet, but sprinkled with sudden harsh explosions of sound. The work ranges from p to *pppppppp* (with the occasional *fff* outburst), a late characteristic revelatory of Nono's lonely, haunting, tortuous journey on the way to discovering Utopia. Microtones are evident even more, as though denizens from another world. Luigi Nono had become a real prophet of sound-based composition.

Nono died three years later of a liver ailment in 1990 at age sixty-six.


## • **His Style and Philosophy**


Much of Nono's early style involved harshly dissonant expressions and polemical, ideological music. Nono's later work gradually evolved into a distant, unsettling quietude, as he explored ways to wring minute transformations into a slowly evolving web of sound.

Nono cites Bellini as an important source for his own vocal evolution. Bellini's peculiar use of silence allows, "space, itself, to sound." The silences are not voids. Further, "a silence that permits a dramatic and emotional resonance" has stronger impact than any sound might have. Nono's silence is the "reverberant and resonant characteristic of the space and of music itself that are allowed to sound." The silences are an intensification of the composed sounds (Pape Nono - p. 60).

Nono also was influenced strongly by the Gabrielis and by Tallis, who wrote works uniquely suited to different acoustic settings. Pape details how Nono followed their example by exploring this avenue even further, employing modern day computer technology to create a "mobile sound" in real time. Laurent Feneyrou, the editor of the

French edition of Nono's collected writings *(Ecrits)*, defines ✳ how Nono's spatial settings are brought to life in his (Nono's) later works: "...the space reveals, unveils, discovers, explores, makes live, is read by the sound, in which the space itself becomes music and the music is composed for and with the space (with traces of the Gabrielis and Tallis): the music composes the space." (Pape Nono p. 60 - Feneyrou in "Luigi Nono", *Ecrits*, Christian Bourgois, 1993, page 14).

Nono also viewed these types of settings as multidimensionally overcoming the limitations of the standard concert hall, wherein sound only can issue from one given source, and is thereby restricted. Pape laments that the classical concert hall subjects us to restricted listening possibilities. The concert hall sound settings "...represent one aspect of the acoustic or sonic dimension of the 'Tragedia d'Ascolto'--the 'Tragedy of Listening', which is the subtitle of Nono's last great opera, *Prometeo.* (1984-5)" (Pape - Nono p.61).

As previously indicated, Nono largely abandoned primitive tape manipulations by about 1980, when he gained free access to the Heinrich Strobel Experimental Music Studio in Freiburg, Germany. Its computer tools enabled Nono to experiment with a wide range of sound and time delay means. Some of the investigation involved the exploration of extremely quiet, high sounds, balancing on the precipice separating the audible from the inaudible. Also, he investigated the gamut of microtonal inflections and their transformation by movements of the lips, tongue, teeth, etc. A computer tool, the sonoscope, helped Nono systematize this research by analyzing sound patterns. Nono asserts that this tool may change how we think musically (Pape - Nono p. 61). He claims this sort of fluidity breaks through boundaries defined by the limited tradition of western musical thinking and opens a pathway to a mobile microtonal sound world.

Gesualdo and Vincentino are the precedent-setters here, by way of their explorations of chromatics (Gesualdo and Vincentino) and microtones (Vincentino with his construction of quartertone sound propagators - the 'arcicembalo' and the 'arciorgano'). Nono detailed his attitudes regarding the investigation of a mobile sound in his article "Towards *Prometeo* - Fragments of a Journal at the Edge" (Pape Nono p. 62).

Finally, Nono used many electronic devices to assist in the alteration and the transformation of sounds in real time. Pape recounts Nono's use of harmonizers to obtain microintervals; the halophone (used also by Boulez in *...explosante fixe...*) for programming spatial movement in time; the digital delay to obtain canon-like structures; and band-pass filters to select from the sound space (Pape - Nono p. 62). These and other instrumental devices (especially including vocoders that alter vocal quality) have been employed in Nono's search for a fully systematic "mobile sound". The sounds can be molded so as to generate movement in space and to transform internally, in real time. Thus enabled, Nono carefully explored an extremely gradated dynamic spectrum wrought, through careful transformation, down to the inaudible.

Nono's later style became less outward, moving to the inner spaces of the mind, reminiscent of Varèse, as in his *Déserts*. The sounds in Nono's later work became accordingly softer, although never less disquieting. Nono was forever the 'traveler', the 'pilgrim', a solitary figure who constantly walked the very loneliest of musical terrains. In this journey, he joined Cage, Xenakis, and Scelsi, as one of the profoundly prophetic innovators in the development of music composed using sounds--many very new--within new structures and forms, for their own sakes: 'sound-based' composition, in the extreme, best sense of the term.

◆◆◆

- ### His Major Works

*Variazioni Canoniche*
*Polifonica, monodia, ritmica*
*Intolleranza*
*Canti di vita e d'amore*
*A Floresta e jovem e cheja de vida*
*Per Bastiana, Tai-Yang Cheng*
*La fabbrica illuminata*
*Das Atmende Klarsein*
*Contrappunto Dialettico*
*Alla Mente*
*Prometeo*
*Como Una Ola de Fuerza y Luz*
*A Carlo Scarpa, Architetto*
*...Sofferte onde serene...*
*Fragmente - Stille, An Diotima*
*No Hay Caminos, Hay Que Caminar*

# Witold Lutosławski
# (1913-1994)

⌘

Witold Lutosławski occupies a place in the avant-garde that is singular for the universal honor that is accorded him. He seems to have won unqualified admiration from the general concert-going public, conductors, performers, and fellow avant-garde composers. This special distinction was earned by his very musical handling of even the most advanced techniques. The resulting sound has always seemed borne of the most carefully crafted musicianship. Apparently difficult passages never confront, but rather, emanate with a decidedly hard won musicality.

Lutosławski had been regarded at one time as a lesser figure in the historical emergence of the so-called cluster composers. Early critical commentary places him with Iannis Xenakis, György Ligeti, and his fellow countryman, Krzystof Penderecki, as a pioneer in employing colorful sound textures built upon chord clusters (chords containing dissonant-rich seconds and tritones).Luigi Nono, and another fellow countryman, Henryk Górecki, recently are added to this comparison. Together, they are all treated as co-conspirators of the movement away from the linear polyphony of formal Webernian serialism, and towards anintuitive homophonic (if discordant) cluster composition. This has been shown to be a deceptive oversimplification.

One reason for Lutosławski's relative accessibility is that he based his clustering upon classical root foundations, including specific chord structures that don't rely overtly on serialism for their genesis (perhaps in their combination, but not in their conception). This characteristic separates Lutosławski clearly from his other supposedly like-minded companions. Xenakis really does not belong to this group. His 'cluster' aggregates result from manipulation based upon analogous physical processes. They are borne of extra-musical methods. Ligeti's early 'mikropolyphonie' infused note clusters with great internal movement that is restricted to small-ranging patterns. His conceptions are borne intuitively within strict musical limits. So are Penderecki's, whose crude movements, in massed bands of sound, comprised dense bars spanning whole octaves and moving in unison. Górecki's discordant thicknesses move in quasi-melodic motions. Nono's chords coalesced into, and out from, microtonal combinations. Lutosławski's triadic chords that grow into complexes are unique from the others' patterns. He was the most thoroughgoing in terms of musicality, so he becomes our composer-of-choice to represent this so-called cluster school.

## • <u>His Life</u>

Lutosławski studied piano, learning to play in early childhood. Then he studied violin with Lidia Kmitowa (1926-32). His studies in music theory (1927 onward) under Witold Maliszewski were generative. Maliszewski imparted a sophisticated sense of formal design that Lutoslawski carried with himself throughout his life. Lutoslawski entered the University of Warsaw and was degreed in mathematics (1931-3). He enrolled at the Warsaw Conservatory in 1932, studying composition with Maliszewski and piano with Jerzy Lefeld.

He served in the Polish army in 1937, and remained until 1938. After he was mobilized in 1939, he was made a prisoner of war. Thereafter, he escaped and earned a sparse living doing cafe concerts, and concerts in private homes in seclusion. Finally, some work with the Polish radio (1945) marked his return to society, and his first major works had begun appearing. Among lighter solo works, several important orchestral pieces were to issue forth. The *Symphonic Variations* (1936-8) is an early tonal work. Its flavor reminds one of Bartók, and already Lutoslawski's peculiar chordal evolution is evident. The *First Symphony* (1941-7) and *Little Suite* (1950) continue in this vein. Although more dense and polyphonic than the previous works, the *Concerto for Orchestra* (1950-4) and *Musique Funèbre* (1958 - dedicated to the memory of Béla Bartók) bring this early period to a close (*SUM* Slonimsky p. 1097).

The next stylistic phase was to be crucial to Lutosławski's evolution as a major, mature composer. The change towards serialism was not sudden, but had been germinating in his mind since the *First Symphony.* By 1947, Lutosławski began formulating a systematic method for moving through dense, dissonant chordal structures, that he would construct according to degrees of complexity (*PAR* Rae pp. 49-50). Melodic patterns would emerge from certain tones in the chords. Serialism would be applied mostly vertically (as opposed to linearly), as Lutosławski was put off by the rigid angularity of most total serialized linear polyphony (Rae p. 85 and p. 142).

But, being confined to his native Poland, a Communist country very much in the grip of Stalinist dictates,

Lutoslawski had to withhold his budding originality. The cultural conditions in Russia were felt strongly in Poland. Formalist composition was forbidden; in fact, it was harshly punished, as the cases of Prokofiev, Shostakovich, and Popov revealed. Like every good Communist citizen-composer, Lutosławski had to restrain his more original inclinations. A relaxing of strictures occurred in the late 1950s, resulting in a flood of radical new Polish music.

Still, the *First Symphony* already showed chord constructions combining independent tonal aggregates. Lutoslawski envisioned a music that would navigate by quasi-serial movements through a table of chordal constructs. So he devised such a table as an independent foundation from which his work in future compositions would draw. Chords were classified into two types. One type would consist of certain numbers and types of intervals. Characteristic applications from the table in his pieces were tritone intervals and chords containing all twelve tones of the chromatic scale. The second type involved complex combinations of certain chords with specified characteristics. These combinations were not static. Motion and evolution were employed to create pseudo-melodic paths (Rae pp. 49-50).

Chordal hierarchies first appeared rudimentarily in his *Concerto for Orchestra*. The hierarchical technique was systematized more completely in subsequent years. In the *Concerto* he also revealed a precursive gesture of linking called "chain technique". In the 1970s, Lutosławski's special type of evolutionary harmonic handling gave rise to a concept of independently intertwined strands of sounds that would ultimately coalesce into moving chordal aggregates that formed links, as in chains. Lutosławski called this procedure "chain" composition. (Rae p. 200).

Important stylistic changes would come in the '60s after Lutosławski heard a radio performance of John Cage's

**Concert for Piano and Orchestra.** The **Concert** calls for unrestrained chance performance. Lutosławski had been looking to enliven music that was beginning to seem stifled and choked by the iron-grips of total serialism. Lutosławski sought a freshening, freedom-giving method that would imbue a work with a sense of fluidity. He was very impressed by the method of the Cagean technique, if not by the sound (Rae p. 75). Consequently, Lutosławski incorporated a *controlled* notational system based on limited chance techniques, to be used in combination with his chordal-melodic genesis. In works of the next fifteen years, Lutosławski employed the most radical chance system to be adopted by any European composer.

The first work employing these techniques in sophistication was *Jeux Venetiens* (1961). It received its first complete performance at the then sensational, now famous, Warsaw Autumn Festival. This annual festival showcases new Polish musical compositions by emerging future Polish masters. Major composers whose works open new doors, and have received performance at this festival, include Grazina Bacewicz, Boguslaw Schaeffer, Wladzimierz Serocki, Tadeusz Baird, Krzysztof Meyer, Krzysztof Penderecki, Henryk Górecki, Andrzej Panufnik, Wlodzimierz Kotonski, and, of course, Witold Lutosławski. Among the most sensational works performed there have been Penderecki's **Threnody: To the Victims of Hiroshima**, Górecki's **Scontri Zdrzenia** (Collisions), and Lutosławski's own *Jeux Venetiens*. All three works broke new ground, but *Jeux* may have been the most radical for its time, especially by virtue of its incorporation of (controlled!) chance.

The title signifies that this is a game in chance, and that its first (partial) performance was in Venice. The work is in four movements, each employing chance evolutions in a different way. The first movement unfolds in an episodic form, with refrains (Rae p. 80). This form was employed by

Lutosławski thereafter, especially in *Three Poémes d'Henri Michaux* (1963), and *Livre for Orchestra* (1968). The third and fourth movements are the most radical. The third movement uses an expanding flute solo over a simple piano ostinato-like figuration. Other wind instruments 'shadow' the flute melody and obtain inexact coincidences. Block movement dominates the fourth movement. The blocks have indeterminate internal patterns and are coordinated inexactly. Tritonal harmony is prevalent, along with clashes of twelve-note chords (*SUM* Rae pp. 81-3).

With the *Three Poémes d'Henri Michaux*, angular vocal movement, common in Webernian linear polyphony, is replaced by ad libitum motion framed within harmonic structures. Lutosławski was disenchanted with the sound of serialized choral music (especially that of Boulez) (Rae pp. 86-7). Singing, monotonic recitation, speaking, whispering, and shouting are used. Two conductors conduct from two scores (one each for orchestra and for choir) to maximize a sense of slight inexactitude, in keeping with the controlled chance principle Lutosławski espoused in *Jeux.*

Lutosławski composed *Livre Pour Orchestra* using the same general chance concepts employed previously in *Jeux* and *Poémes.*

Two important works of the 1970s intensify Lutosławski's systematization of moving, evolving chordal aggregates. The process employed evolved into his 'chain' procedure. The first, *Mi-Parti* (1976), reveals a thorough-going sophistication of handling chords and their agglomerations. Increasing numbers of linear strands emerge and join to form a dense polyphony (Rae p. 139-40). Through pairings of notes drawn from the chords, melodic phrases emerge. The movement is intuitive, rather than being tied to serial methodology. The coalescences create 'bundles' of 'local harmonies' (Rae p. 141).

At this time, Lutosławski was bothered by a philosophical issue that later resulted in his formulation of a new stylistic phase in the late 1970s. He had become dissatisfied with his melodic patterns not standing out sufficiently from the dense harmonies from which they grew (Rae p. 142). The solution would come in the form of simpler harmonic patterns (especially in his 'chain' pieces), eschewing the twelve-note aggregates in favor of more translucent eight-note groupings. The second major work, the *Novelette* (1978-9), revealed this shift in rudimentary form. However, Lutosławski retained controlled chance methods, excluding barlines in some cases. The 'chain' structures gained ever more sophistication. Another way of smoothing out the melodic imbalances occurs in what Rae calls 'rhapsodic lines' played over the emerging harmony (Rae p. 143). This paved the way for future refinements.

The 1980s ushered in Lutosławski's final compositional stage. Free, independently emerging 'rhapsodic' interludes helped highlight melodic movement, bringing it out from the background. The less dense harmonies reduced the dissonance, but jagged phrases still issued forth, especially in the three 'chain'-titled compositions that followed: *Chain 1* (chamber ensemble - 1983), *Chain 2* (dialogue for violin and orchestra - 1984-5), and *Chain 3* (Orchestra - 1986). In these works, the chain technique is used in the fashion of rope building, via intertwining strands consisting of more than just two strands at a time. The mingling occurs in fits and bursts (*PAR* Rae p. 210-11), and contains inexactitudes of chords. For example, the brass chords at the conclusion of *Chain 3* are robbed of their intended role of finality by premature emergence of other material geared toward the conclusion (Rae p. 213).

The *Third Symphony* (1981-3) reveals a deep maturation in Lutosławski's handling of independent melody. The harmonies are more relaxed as well. The *Fourth Symphony*

(1988-92) culminates his life work, save for a small duet for violin and piano.

## • <u>His Style</u>

Lutosławski's chords emanate through states of continual flux. They evolve through increasing complexity, and comprise independently moving lines. The resultant coalescence is usually inexact, and forms dense eight- to twelve-note figurations. Serialism is handled intuitively, usually vertically. The chance is controlled so that it doesn't spread over, or interfere with, large sections of the musical landscape. His chord structures emerge from his purely coloristic handling (i.e., non-functional, except for their spawning of melodic tones), and are replete with dissonance. This is real 'sound-based' composition!

Lutosławski was fond of woodwinds. He also showed a preference for strident brass collisions. In his late work, though, cantabile becomes increasingly predominant in his brass handling (Rae p. 210). String sounds range from glissandi to soft cantabile. Percussive effects are important, too.

The influence of Bartók upon Lutosławski's music is profoundly evident. Lutosławski and Ligeti have been the two major heirs to Bartók's stylistic legacy. They were the two primary advocates of Bartókian methodology for sonic genesis in the new music, especially in their handling of chords and stringed instrumental effects.

Lutosławski wasn't the type of composer to generate a 'school', so direct subsequent influence is hard to trace. Nevertheless, his methods are standards from which future composers can profit well.

◆◆◆

- ## His Major Works

*Symphonic Variations*
*Musique Funèbre*
*Concerto for Orchestra*
*Three Poémes d'Henri Michaux*
*Mi-Parti*
*Jeux Venetiens*
*Livre Pour Orchestre*
*Symphony #1*
*Symphony #2*
*Symphony #3*
*Symphony #4*
*Novelette*
*Chain 1*
*Chain 2*
*Chain 3*

# Giacinto Scelsi
# (1905-1988)

ℰↃ

The case of Giacinto Scelsi is the strangest of this past century's music history. He was a shadowy figure throughout his lifetime. He avoided public discussion of himself and his work as much as he possibly could. Our understanding of this man and his music remains elusive. Scelsi transformed from a sophisticated Western aristocrat to a reclusive composer who had nearly completely shed his very identity, and his concept of himself as composer as well. This change evolved through his contact with, and his absorption of, Eastern-style philosophies, music, and existentialism during his many journeys to Africa and the Far East.

His subsequent self-imposed seclusion--combined with his incomplete formal musical education--and his rejection of certain stereotypical procedural solutions (e.g., serialism) to the malaise associated with tonal decadence, accorded Scelsi the status of 'dilettante' in avant-garde music circles. Yet this seclusion engendered hisconcentrated study of the very nature of sound that has greatly affected the history of recent art music.

## • <u>His Life</u>

Little had been known about Scelsi, as he had suppressed details as much as he could. Recently, though, several important articles that accompany the 2 CD set, *Salabert Actuels SCD 8904-5*, appeared. In Adriano Cremonese's article "Giacinto Scelsi", certain sketchy biographical facts are presented. Scelsi was born to an aristocratic family in La Spezia, Italy in 1905. During his youth, he learned to improvise on the piano, a discipline that would serve him well in his 'crisis' period (1940s). He studied piano under Giacinto Sallustio in Rome. He avoided association with the musical establishment, however, a trait that would re-emerge thereafter.

He traveled widely between the world wars, especially to Africa and to Asia. He spent some time in Tibet, assimilating certain cultural tendencies indigent to that land. He also developed an acute religious mysticism, rich in oriental philosophical tradition. He also maintained temporary residence in France and in Switzerland. Then, during a stay in Geneva, Switzerland, Egon Koehler introduced him to Scriabin's composing system. Later, while in Vienna (1935-6), Scelsi studied 12-tone composition under a one-time Schönberg pupil, Walter Klein.

Scelsi became the first Italian composer to adopt dodecaphony, but abandoned the method in the 1940s, because he had become uncomfortable with its excessive controls. He underwent an intense personal crisis in the 1940s that resulted in his suffering a nervous breakdown. During that crisis, he began to contemplate the nature of sound and how its formation could be studied, and the resulting new sounds composed to enrich the flagging European traditions of art music. He also began to assimilate his Eastern philosophy into every fiber of spiritual essence, through meditation.

By the early 1950s, Scelsi reemerged, energized and fresh. From Scelsi's contemplations, sound became the central focus, overshadowing method. He considered himself a medium through which sounds would flow from some transcendental essence. Scelsi, therefore, felt that he was not really a composer. He returned to Rome and began experiments in sound by improvisation on his piano. He also studied using certain oriental instruments he obtained during his Tibetan journeys. What would eventually emerge in 1959 was a sound conception so radically new that it escapes traditional Western classical analytical scrutiny. In the meantime, he did surface briefly to participate as a member of *Nuova Consonanza*, an Italian avant-garde group that included Franco Evangelisti. His activities in this group included organizing contemporary concerts.

Shortly thereafter, though, he secluded himself so completely that he became marginalized and ostracized from the avant-garde musical community at large. His renunciation of all personal considerations became so complete that he even refused to allow his photograph to be taken. His only concession to publicized self-imagery was to allow a large circle, underlined, to represent himself. This is a Zen symbol that has various interpretations, including that of a rising sun. Scelsi also refrained from signing his late poetry, recalling his consideration of himself as a conveyor, rather than a creator, of art (*SUM/PAR* Cremones pp. 22-23).

One major work in the early style deserves special attention: the ***First String Quartet*** (1944), one of only two large-scale works composed before 1950 that Scelsi refrained from destroying. None of the Scelsian obsession with single tones that characterizes his later works is evident here. Significantly, neither is the systematic serialism that he rejected more than half a dozen years previously. The quartet employs rich dissonance in a non-tonal setting. Bi-modality with tritones and thirds is a prominent feature. Scelsi's unusual sound imagery makes even this early work sound as none other before his time (*PAR* Halbreich Five p. 28).

The radical break in style came with his most famous piece, **Quattro Pezzi** (1959), four separate studies on different single tones. An astonishing variety of methods that operate on those single tones is brought to bear. The most complete sound spectrum possible that can accompany a single sound is marshaled for an incredible listening experience. All overtones associated with the given tone are visited, brought forth, and then gradually abandoned. Microtones in flux sometimes break into octaves that seem to amplify the harmonics.

In his article accompanying *CD Accord 200612*, Harry Halbreich states that a large variety of timbres is included, with each instrument emitting a varied array of sounds in contemplation. The Golden Section is employed formally. Unisons unfold into octaves. Microtones and semitonal oscillations at varied rates emanate in a tapestry of kaleidoscopic, reverberant beauty. This is music that concerns itself not at all with a sense of passing time or of progress. There is an infinite essence in the sound *(PAR* Halbreich *Quattro* pp. 23-4).

Orchestral works alternated in appearance with chamber works for the remaining creative period of Scelsi's life. The most important of his chamber works are the string quartets. Like those quartets, **Aion** (1961), for very large orchestra, travels similar sonic territory, except that the scope of attention is expanded to more than just single tones in the four movements. Scelsi's work grows contemplative, and the traversing between tones is very subtle. One becomes lost in the cosmic sonic collisions. Existence stands still as **Aion**'s sonic facets are slowly explored. Unusual percussive bursts interrupt at key points in the first movement. Scelsi calls this work "a contemplation of the life in a day (90,000 earth years) of a Buddhist monk" (Halbreich *AION*). The low brass, one of Scelsi's favorite colors, prominently growls, as though a collection of beasts is unleashed.

The **Second Quartet** (1961) marks a new stylistic phase for Scelsi's stringed instrumental writing. It appeared at nearly the same time as **Aion**. Scelsi uses several different types of string mutes (Halbreich - *Five.*). In addition to the standard mute, metallic ones are used that enable the muting of individual strings. Abrasive sounds are obtained that usually aren't associated with stringed instruments. In the first movement, G is slowly transformed to B-flat at the temporal Golden Section (*PAR* Halbreich *Five* p. 31). Various special effects accompany the pitch as ghostly visitors, shadowing a traveler whose pathway becomes apparent only with each step. This usage of more tones parallels that in **Aion**, and it reflects a maturation and refinement in Scelsi's language. In the second movement, violent sound modules interrupt immobile quietude. But, again, no 'real progress' is detectable. The third movement unfolds in a palindromic pattern. There is real change in the dynamics and the speed in which the sounds evolve, but the peculiar static flavor remains. It is almost as if liveliness is injected into a motionless liquid. It goes nowhere in spurts of high and slow speed, always contemplating the different faces of the sound fabric (Halbreich *Five* p. 31).

These and other very subtle devices emerge in Scelsi's later work. The major orchestral works include **Anahit** (1965), **Konx-om-Pax** (1969), and **Pfhat** (1974). Of these, **Anahit** merits special consideration. It has a subtitle: *Lyrical Poem Dedicated to Venus* (whose Egyptian name is Anahit). There are eighteen players plus solo violin. The violin part is notated for separate staves--one for each string (except for one). The instrument is made able to play the same tone simultaneously on three strings (Halbreich *Quattro* p. 24). The work is a quasi-concerto. The soloist leads the seemingly recalcitrant ensemble through a journey that tortuously traverses octaves. The sounds are many and incredibly varied. Halbreich (*Quattro* p. 25) once again identifies the Golden Section as a formalizing device for junctures in time.

The subsequent masterly, and mysterious, string quartets appeared in 1963 *(Third)*, 1964 *(Fourth)*, and 1984 *(Fifth)*. The final named piece was Scelsi's last.

An interesting controversy developed concerning this already controversial composer. After his death, one of Scelsi's one-time co-writers, Vieri Tosatti, published an article in the *Giornelle della Musica*, claiming he wrote Scelsi's work. After some research into the matter, what emerged was that Scelsi had improvised experimental patterns on the piano, which revealed sounds that never had found satisfactory notation. Tosatti provided notational help. So, Scelsi was the *real* composer after all (this recalls the controversy surrounding precedence in Ives' discoveries) (Slonimsky p. 1601).

Scelsi's work was rarely performed during his lifetime, except during the last half-decade. Most performances had been in France. In 1982, the picture changed dramatically. The Ferienkursen für Neue Musik, in Darmstadt, featured Scelsi's works by performing several of them. Performances multiplied until 1987, when the grand opening at SIMC International festival honored the composer, dedicating that opening to him. Recordings ensued. He has become a cult figure, especially for those fans that immerse themselves in Eastern cultural mysticism.

## • **His Style and Philosophy**

If most music in Western art traditions, even most serial works, are about exploring ways of traversing from note to note, Scelsi's music uniquely encompasses discovering what's inside of, and just around, each note by itself. Melody and rhythm aren't simply made disjointed or subjugated, they have been made irrelevant. They aren't part of the sound fabric. What we have is wavering, vibrating, oscillating patterns of musical plasma.

The evolution of these patterns was extracted through Scelsi's painstaking probing at his piano, and by his working with exotic Eastern percussion instruments. In his visits to Tibet, Scelsi was impressed by the religious aspects of Eastern contemplation, and by mysticism. He also was deeply affected by the evocative sounds of temple bells and Alp horn-like instruments; also by deep vocal chants by monks, that seemed especially suitable for expressing this ritualistic contemplation. Much of Scelsi's music captures the obsessive contemplation of single tones.

Verbal summaries of this music don't seem to suffice. These are experiences that can be obtained solely through inward reflection during the unfolding drama. One must engage one's very soul to discover the music's meaning, in much the same way Cage's work requires listeners to relinquish consciousness itself to discover meaning. This difficulty in comprehension and discussion of Scelsi's work is lamented most expressively in the peculiar article by Jeremy Drake," Quantum Scelsi" (Drake pp. 23-25), the second of three important revelations in this Salabert CD set. For Drake, an epiphany from Scelsi's work simply eludes effective verbal expression. He makes the surprising suggestion that, until we can conjure sufficient musical terminological armor, we ought to resort to scientific jargon in order to capture these magnificent essences. He proposes several new terms to verbally isolate some of Scelsi's parameters. The three most useful would be "orbit" (central tendency), "oscillation" (amplitude of vibrato), and "interference" ("turbulence" leading to unpredictable results) (Drake p. 24).

Drake also borrows some concepts from quantum mechanics to describe a sudden shift that "escapes" from the "field" of one "orbit" into another, while avoiding the space in the gap between the two.

I suppose this is valid up to a point. The trouble with this sort of thing is that the analogy is poor from the standpoint of causality. Physics is teleological, by virtue of tracking events backward to a moment of creation that is unmediated by human interference. Music is not. Electrons behave as waves and oscillate. So far, we have a good analogy. But the electron does this, and undergoes further state transformations, because it *has* to. Scelsi's notes don't. Still, some of these borrowed ideas can be useful, if carefully chosen. For example, Gerard Pape posits the future potential of exploring chaos, in its scientific essence, as a tool to generate real unpredictability in sound-particle movement (Pape Composition p. 27-28). This is a disciplined extension of the Scelsian probing of sounds. Sounds may emerge in surprising and unforeseen patterns by experimental juxtapositions, analogous to Xenakis' excitation of piano strings resulting from brasses blowing into the open strings (*Eonta* - 1963-4).

Drake can be forgiven to a degree for resorting to these partial analogies, though, because his seems to be the first rigorous, and welcome, escape from the pseudo-mystical mumbo-jumbo that usually accompanies discussion of Scelsi's work. Such pseudo-commentary as (hypothetically) 'bathing in the infinite reality' just doesn't cut it. So Drake's work can be helpful in escaping this conundrum.

Drake reveals the unfolding of a kaleidoscopic timbral spectrum, whereby each note probes the dimension of depth. This is an idea that Scelsi previously and explicitly proposed. For example, Pape states that Scelsi complained of music having lacked progress in exploring its three-dimensionality. Painting had captured that essence; not so music. Scelsi stated that "sound was spherical, but that in listening, it seems to us that it possesses only two dimensions: pitch and duration--the third, the depth, we know that it exists, but in a certain sense, it escapes us." (Pape Composition. p.1). Scelsi further remarked that sounds contain more complexity than just that which can be notated for pitch and duration, but the difficulties associated with depth perception accord great notational problems (presumably, precisely why Scelsi enlisted the help of Tosatti and others!).

Scelsi's efforts to find a suitable notation resulted in extreme solutions such as that employed in *Anahit* with the use of special extra staff lines, one for each string of a violin. The innovative pioneer, Julio Estrada, has accomplished further experimental work in this direction. His solution extends this idea to the notation of timbral evolutions by assigning separate staff lines (one for pitch; one for color) for each instrument.

The question is now begged: what musical entities contribute to a sense of depth? This is the real crux of all sound-based compositional investigation, especially that underway at Les Ateliers UPIC. But it also has roots as far back as Debussy, and travels through the work of Schönberg, Nono, Xenakis, and Varèse, et al. Scelsi brought these matters to a head. "He was the first composer to propose a musical universe in continual expansion of its compositional elements, rather than as a combinatorial of fixed elements." (Pape Composition p. 8).

Scelsi employed several devices to help free sounds from traditional restraints. Firstly, he called for oscillating microtones, including variable vibrato (varying in amplitude--pitch fluctuation, volume, and duration of evolution). This freed pitch to explore close confinement in variation. This is what Drake means by orbit, although Scelsi's term "sphere" may be more expressive, as it seems the exploration of the tones comes as much from within as it does from without. Oscillation is especially apropos, as it implies the existence of an 'ether' within which the sphere exists. Secondly, dynamics (related to Scelsi's dimension for duration, only within which it may unfold) are treated systematically. Frequent, independent, multiple dynamics changes unfold simultaneously in much of Scelsi's work. Finally, timbre, the so-called 'depth', or third dimension, is subjected to variation by a plenitude of sophisticated devices, each uniquely applicable to the different instruments. Pape notes that in Scelsi's later music, a *harmonic* dimension is explored. Sound patterns based on the harmonic series evoke consonances that lack functionality, reminiscent of Debussy's and of Messiaen's preliminary work in this area (Pape Composition p. 9).

Transitions between tones and about pitch centers generate a whole new realm of sound-based composition, in which consonance and dissonance are rendered meaningless.

The movement within these timbral centers is explored somewhat in Enzo Restagno's article (the third of these important articles in the Salabert CD set). Restagno notes that explicit or discrete steps are eschewed for coincidences that result from cumulative and continuous oscillations. These conjugations and conjunctions seem to transform the listener to a state of ecstatic reverie. A hard-won emerging unison has an electric impact. In this way the sound becomes a channel for meditation, enabling one to transcend to a higher level; rational speculations are cast aside. (Freely interpreted, but based upon Restagno p. 25-7).

Mystical intuitions aside, Scelsi must be seen as a primary stimulus in the search for a new sound-based music reliant upon nature -- the nature of sound itself. Stockhausen's parallel work in the study of how certain juxtapositions of notes in electronic music excite difference frequencies, along with Scelsi's work in the way sound can be treated spatially, reveal many interesting new possibilities. Estrada and Pape are taking this pathway yet further. Scelsi, the old master, opened a new doorway.

◆◆◆

- ### <u>His Major Works</u>

*Quattro Pezzi*
*Anahit*
*Aion*
*Pfhat*
*Uaxuctum*
*String Quartet No. 1*
*String Quartet No. 2*
*String Quartet No. 3*
*String Quartet No. 4*
*String Quartet No. 5*
*String Trio*
*Khoom*
*Pranam I*
*Pranam II*
*Konx-om-Pax*
*Kya*
*In Nomine Lucis V*
*Antifona*

# Julio Estrada
# (1943- )
## ℰↃ

Julio Estrada is the most thoroughly integrated musician, theorist, and mathematician in today's music world, mainly by his having extended Xenakis' theories. His integration of mathematical with musical concepts is more traditionally musical than Xenakis', though. He has extended the boundaries of sound, of our understanding of the way we perceive sounds, and of the instruments' capabilities to capture new sounds, by the conception of profound theoretical disciplines that burrow to the core of musical philosophy.

Estrada is living in the very midst of a musical counterrevolution that has assaulted the forward progress that he envisions, and that music had partially achieved until the 1970s. This counterrevolution is known today as postmodernism. Estrada rejects its intrusion into today's musical scene as a cop-out; an abrogation of the composer's responsibility to educate the public, as well as musicians, themselves, in the advancements that are needed to complete our understanding of our sound universe.

In an address he gave in the early 1990s, Estrada complains that post-modernism, which encompasses a mixture of styles borrowed from the past, including minimalism, neo-Romanticism, Impressionism, etc., contains "a portion that would have a content excessively conformist...." It becomes "something cynical like saying: Let's leave all things to be the way they were and let's exercise our memory and our pleasure visiting the history and the languages that others have created. In a way, the composition from that view would be similar to a beggar's ways..." who creates things using "little stitches here and there..." thus making a product consisting of "fragmented ideas of languages or contributions of authors of theories or of systems." (Pareyón/Espinosa).

In response to post-modernism's piecemeal rehashing of the past, Estrada implores us to "keep advancing on the musical ideas not as a memory exercise but as a project of a new perception of music." (Pareyón/Espinosa). Estrada concludes by saying that we must understand the impact of new ideas and instrumental resources if we are to advance. My own thinking on this is that the job of a composer is the awakening of our minds to new concepts. This is the way we as a civilization guarantee our very survival. We must not allow the gift of our minds to decay by lack of mental exercise. What better way, then, to use music--the most beautiful of the abstract arts--as the medium for this growth?

## • <u>His Life</u>

Estrada was born in Mexico City in 1943, of parents who were political refugees exiled from Spain two years previously. This background, his parents' Spanish heritage, and his own Mexican residence gave Estrada a unique mesh of two cultures, European and Latin American. He has taken advantage of this crossroads of culture in his work throughout his lifetime.

In the 1950s, Estrada studied piano, then cello. He started composing by the early '60s. His compositional studies were initially completed under Carlos Chávez, and, more importantly, under Julián Orbón. Orbón provided stimulus for Estrada to delve deeply into the newly emergent modernism. Estrada emigrated from Mexico to Europe and lived in Paris from 1965-9 on a French Governmental scholarship.

While in Paris, Estrada studied harmony and counterpoint with Nadia Boulanger (by whose neo-classical prejudices he fortunately managed to remain unmoved!). He studied musical analysis from Max Deutsch and Olivier Messiaen, both in France (as well as composition from Messiaen). While in Paris he attended lectures given by Iannis Xenakis. Advanced studies in acoustics theory, musique concrète, and mathematics-in-music with Jean-Etienne Marie filled out a startling background in music (Warnaby p. 11).

Shortly afterwards, Estrada attended courses in advanced music theory and philosophy under Karlheinz Stockhausen (Kölner Kurse für Neue Musik - Darmstadt, Germany), György Ligeti (Darmstadter Musikferienkurse - Germany), and Iannis Xenakis (Paris) (Slonimsky p. 507). Estrada was to identify most with the theoretical ideas espoused by Ligeti and Xenakis (and somewhat, Stockhausen). Stockhausen marginally assisted in the development of Estrada's groundbreaking theoretical work on the relationships between pitch and timbre (via their being special cases of each other). More formative was Ligeti for the development of Estrada's groundbreaking theoritical work on new ways of harmonic thinking; also, Xenakis' work proved crucial via his excursions into continuity/discontinuity as a formalizing concept (*PAR* Warnaby p.11). In 1980, Estrada extended his association with Xenakis working, working at CEMAMu and produced a UPIC composition, ***Eua'on***.

He followed these studies with electronics and computer courses at Stanford University under John Chowning and Leland Smith.

Also, back during the 1970s, Estrada expanded and deepened his musical activities and associations. He began to absorb the traditions of the Americas. He studied the works of Conlon Nancarrow, Henry Cowell, and Julián Carrillo (a Mexican whose microtonal usages influenced him).

In 1973, he established a compositional seminar at UNAM (Universidad Nacional Autónoma de México). Estrada worked throughout the 1970s and 1980s to integrate pre-Hispanic Indian traditions with very advanced Western musical idioms, by a musical linkage. To this end, he studied anthropological papers dealing with the relationship between music and myth in pre-Hispanic cultures, as far as was possible, for much history had been destroyed in the Spanish conquest.

Additionally, he studied with Kwan Faré Tzé, an American Indian musician at San Juan Pueblo, a reservation in New Mexico. He completed this background by staying for four months with Tzé and with the Hopi Indians, an Arizona tribe that shares a language heritage with the Aztecs. This tribe managed to preserve its traditions because it was unaffected by the Spanish conquest. This enabled Estrada to fully absorb ancient Aztec traditions involving dream and fantasy in the conveyance of myths and cultural traditions. He would incorporate this approach in his later compositional process as a way of creating sound images through fantasy (*SUM* Warnaby p. 12).

In the early 1980s Estrada formulated his theory of the *continuum*, a basis of combining pitch and rhythms continuously. The continuum concept was codified later when he earned his Ph.D. in musicology, with an accompanying thesis entitled *Compositional Theory: Discontinuum-Continuum* (1994 - University of Strasbourg) (Warnaby p. 12). In the meantime, he was also shoring up his mathematical background. Before this, from 1973-6 he and Jorge Gil jointly did research in Finite Groups Theory and Boolean algebra and in their applications to music (Slonimsky p. 507/Estrada e-mail 3-16-00). Estrada continued teaching classes throughout the 1980s, including courses in new directions in microtonal theory, in incorporating indigenous musical conceptions native to Mexico, and in new music research. In that latter course he encouraged his students to create a completely autonomous system using materials of their choice, followed with aural analyses of the results. This mirrors his personal composing method of choosing new raw material for each new work, from fantasies, in an autonomous system (Warnaby p. 12).

He became, and remains, a member of the Institute of Aesthetics, as well as a professor of composition at UNAM. In 1980, he worked at CEMAMu and produced a UPIC composition, *Eua 'on*. Since 1984, he has been associated with, and has participated in seminars at, Les Ateliers UPIC, Xenakis' studio. Through these activities Estrada has molded a multidisciplinary background as composer, musicologist, performer, teacher, aesthetician, and philosopher (reminiscent of Xenakis!).

He also been music director of new-music performing ensembles including the Pro Música Nueva and the Compañía Musical de Repertorio Nuevo - at UNAM and he became, and remains, member of the Institute Aesthetics, as well as a professor of composition at UNAM. Through these activities Estrada has molded multi-disciplinary background, composer, musicologist, performer, teacher, aesthetician, and philosopher.

## • <u>His Musical Life and Philosophy</u>

Estrada's compositional process has developed through three phases. The early works combine some aleatory (chance) gestures, mostly by improvisation. He adopted this from contact with John Cage's music (and also through Cage's influence on Stockhausen). After the early 1970s, Estrada abandoned improvisation, adopting a far tighter method using mathematical concepts that include Finite Groups, Network, and Combinatory theories. This stage continued until the early 1980s. Then, his mathematics and acoustics disciplines intensified, as he began to formulate a theory that would enable him to systematize the process of musical genesis and its associated notation. This resulted in his development and refinement of the continuum theory, forming the basis of his present compositional stage.

In the early 1970s, several very tightly organized compositions appeared under the group-categorical title *Canto* that combined the employment of mathematical organizational procedures with the absorption of the emotive content of the music of the past. These are works founded upon common principles involving the evolution of the musical plasma toward a goal through continuous transformation. The mathematical concepts underlying these works involve the theory of finite groups that he absorbed during his joint research with Gil (a mathematician and engineer). A book, *Música y teoría de grupos finitos,* (Estrada/Gil, Instituto de Investigaciones Estéticas, UNAM, 1984) emerged based on their joint work.

*Canto Oculto* was composed in 1977 for solo violin, prior to his use of what he calls the "imaginary" (a fantasy-imagined note or set of notes that he subsequently notates and develops). Estrada had not yet fully absorbed the ancient Indian ambience, that would imbue his later work thoroughly; nor had he formalized his continuum theory. This work is a set of variations on a small cellular pattern of three, four, or five notes that he combines in the process of pulling the work together. Through intricate notation, figures become split into two voices articulating different, independent, but simultaneous rhythmic phrases. This superimposition of unrelated patterns is exceedingly difficult to perform.

The sense of progress toward a goal becomes revealed as the work unfolds. Eventually the threads merge at the final stage, having transformed through lower registers to very extreme, high ones. Regular and irregular patterns are explored. Double trills are marshaled to create pulsations as lines occasionally intersect (*PAR* Albera). This is an extension into rhythm of concepts analogous to Scelsi's obsessive variation of timbres in single tonal spheres. The central idea is the tone, not the method, as the vehicle for achieving sounds heretofore not imagined. The work commemorates his uncle's death in the Spanish civil war, and also that of a Mexican who died in a road accident (*PAR* Estrada - Salabert p.6). The images burned in Estrada's mind, and they tumble out to assault our perceptions in shards of sound.

Other *Canto* incarnations evolving along similar lines, and using similar processes of variation, include: *Canto Mnémico* (1973 - rev. 1983); *Canto Tejido* (1974) *Canto Naciente* (1975); and *Canto Alterno* (1980).

About 1981, with the inception, and the conception, of *Eolo'oolin*, the theory of the continuum had germinated in Estrada's mind completely. This theory explores the continuum between sound and rhythm. According to his theory, Estrada envisions a common linkage between two ordinarily separately considered musical elements, sound frequency (Estrada's terminology - more commonly referred to as pitch), and rhythm. Following Stockhausen's lead, Estrada refined, expanded, and deepened the concept of linkage. But, instead of just treating sound frequency, rhythm, and their timbral fluctuations as resultant from changing temporal speeds (rhythmic variation), Estrada posited a set of related physical characteristics common to both elements.

Estrada has detailed this intricate process in a seminal article entitled "Focusing on Freedom and Movement in Music: Methods of Transcription inside a Continuum of Rhythm and Sound" (Estrada Website). He begins the analysis with a description of important historical precedents for the theory of discontinuum-continuum as it unfolds in the theoretical work of Carrillo and Alois Hába (in pitch), Cowell and Nancarrow (in rhythm). Estrada's proposal is a rigorous expansion, combination, and explicit formalization of these germinal concepts. He extends his methods to incorporate the concept of the 'imaginary' (Estrada website p.2).

Estrada claims that both the pitch and rhythm elements are comprised of three components, and that the components in one element are analogous to corresponding components in the other element. So pitch contains frequency, intensity (volume), and timbre as components (Pape Composition p. 15). Rhythm contains duration, attack, and micro-rhythmic structure (like vibrato). The pattern is as follows (in a sample tabular representation - my own):

| Pitch: | sound frequency | intensity | timbre |
|---|---|---|---|
| | I | I | I |
| Correspondence: | temporal | amplitudinal | harmonic content |
| | I | I | I |
| Rhythm: | duration | attack | micro-rhythm |

These classifications are based loosely upon Pape's descriptions (*SUM/PAR* Pape composition p. 18).

Estrada further claims that the way we *perceive* the elements is that sound frequency perceptually qualifies pitch, and that rhythm perceptually qualifies time in a completely analogous way. The sound and rhythm frequencies are treated like waveforms in terms of their physical structure. The unifying links are that both sound frequency and rhythm have three corresponding characteristics that can be assigned common labels: (1) temporal, (2) amplitudinal, and (3) harmonic content (Estrada website p. 3). This creates six characteristics that may be scored/controlled independently in a counterpoint of "individual sound and rhythmic components" (conceptualization *PAR* Estrada website p. 3).

In fact, that is exactly what Estrada did. He systematized a scheme of six separate graphs, one for each component, allowing each to evolve independently. The goal was to synthesize these sets to generate what Estrada calls a macro-timbre (or a more complete construct of the term timbre as being related to harmonic content), or the "net harmonic result", using traditional notation (Estrada website p. 3). So the six sonic components were controlled in isolation, allowing for maximum control and variety of musical materials. Hundreds of possible combinations can thus be woven in an incredibly intricate sonic fabric. *This intricate notation is very complex and enables Estrada to capture extremely small, refined differences, inflections, nuances, and sonic evolutions in time. In this way, Estrada could intuitively capture any dreamt musical matter, regardless how difficult it would be using traditional means! This includes the unique sound colors indigenous to ancient Indian cultures.*

Furthermore, unlike in integral serialism, the constructs of which operate upon and within fixed, discrete pitch values, this model enables the composer to explore in-between values continually: hence Estrada's term the "continuum".

Estrada's translation of the "chrono-graphical recording" (Estrada website p.2) into musical notation requires two distinct staff-lines for each instrument. These staff-lines serve components that unfold simultaneously (sound frequency and timbre). The pitch and timbral evolutions are handled this way, being as they lend themselves best to this rigorous definition. The other components (duration, micro-rhythm, intensity, and attack) are applied to the double staff set via standard notations, as a pragmatic adaptation to tradition. The controls exerted by the composer that are available through the splitting of staves are more intensive than ever possible using standard staff assignments. The performing complexity is prodigious.

Two additional thoughts bear comment. Estrada shuns the usual pitch intervals inherent in standard Pythagorean divisions, because they incorporate the harmonic series that favors the *dis*continuous. By selecting a small enough unit interval, 'steps' merge into the perception of continuity, the very goal of his compositional model (Estrada website p. 4). Also, the composer, when manipulating 'macro-timbre' cannot isolate rhythm from sound parameters. Each needs the other for elucidation (Estrada website p. 4).

Estrada composes in roughly the following stepwise fashion: (1) he dreams a rich musical matter, the 'imaginary', which is barren of specified qualities such as instrumentation; (2) he discerns the values that define the sonic qualities, through thought; (3) he graphs the approximate waveform curves (six); (4) finally, he translates the graphs into traditional notation employing, however, atraditional complexes of staff lines (*PAR* Pape composition pp. 14-16 and pp. 38-42).

This system is exceedingly complex, and so far Estrada has composed almost entirely for the chamber ensemble medium. Large-scale works involve tremendous complexity. Still, however, two large-scale works have been completed: the opera **Pedro Páramo** (1991), and the orchestral piece **Eua'on'ome** (1995).

Immediately following his groundbreaking formalization of continuum theory, Estrada composed a series of profoundly important works in the new system. Like the *Canto* set, the *yuunohui* set contains several 'member' compositions. *Yuunohui* is a Zapotec word referring to 'clay'. Estrada was to title all works with numeric suffixes drawn from the Nahuatl language to designate register (e.g., se – one [highest, for violin]; *ome* – two [next lower, for viola]; *yei* – three [second lowest, for cello]; and *nahui* – four [lowest, for contrabass].) (*PAR* Warnaby p. 13/Estrada e-mail 3-16-00). The *yuunohui* set consists of all possible combinations, so that there are fifteen individual pieces: one for each soloist, six duets, four trios, and one complete quartet, exhausting all possible combinations. All versions have been completed.

The first completed was **Yuunohui'yei** (cello - 1983) (*SUM* Warnaby pp. 13/14 and Pape composition p. 41). Completion of the solos spanned the decade of the '80s: **Yuunohui'nahui** (bass - 1985), **Yuunohui'se** (violin - 1989), and **Yuunohui'ome** (viola - 1990), following **Yuunohui'yei**. The template for completion of the remaining set members was accomplished from 1983-90. The quartet, **Yuunohui'se 'ome'yei'nahui** was recorded in 1995.

In these works, Estrada did not fantasize sounds arbitrarily. He conjured sounds unique to the ancient Indian cultures that expressed myths to be passed on through music. Many sounds are very rich in unusual timbre. These dreams convey yearnings found in many similar cultures and evoke rich, nostalgic, and complex sensitivities. Estrada found ways to shape the wave-form graphs to capture timbral characteristics that are uniquely suited to each particular instrument, be it violin, cello, etc. Thus, each 'member' work of the *yuunohui* set has its own unique waveforms (*PAR* Warnaby p. 13). Each of the four scores contains two individual segments (*introduction* and *finale*) which are conceived in such a way as to amplify the unique qualities inherent in each instrument.

For the quartet *(Yuunohui'se'ome'yei'nahui)*, Estrada combined the basic attributes of each solo piece, with its characteristic graphs, but transported some of the graphs, by inversion, to shape *different* characteristics for *other* instruments. For example, pitch-timbre for violin might have become graphically reassigned to delineate micro-rhythmical fluctuation for the cello. So a common waveform shape describes several of the instruments' different components in a veritable visual counterpoint of contour (*PAR* Warnaby pp. 13-15).

These forms then unfold in a splendidly intricate, free counterpoint of evolving lines (synchronic and imitative, not classical or mechanical). The array is a glorious sonic coalescence of microtonal plasma, in sounds rarely ever encountered.

Many important new works have accompanied or followed the appearance of the yuunohui set. Most important are: *Eolo'oolin* (percussion - 1981-3), *Ishini'ioni* (string quartet - 1984-90), *Mictlan* (voice and bass - 1992), *Miqi'nahual* (contrabass - 1993).

*Ishini'ioni* is Estrada's most profoundly beautiful work for string quartet. It conjures an alien sound world in delectable flux. A spatial element is involved that transcends macro-timbral variations. The cellist should be centered and fixed on stage, while the other players are circling around him/her, all the while playing (*PAR* Warnaby p. 14). The spatial sensation is very fluid with a relentless progress to a goal. Auditory phantasms emerge in a rich variety of tone color. "*Ishini'ioni* consists of a technical, theoretical and aesthetic synthesis of my recent research on the 'continuum', an ideal means to let oneself go to the intuitions of forgotten or unknown musical universes..." (Estrada/Salabert). Estrada was awarded the Prix de Composition Prince de Pierre de Monaco by its jury for this work.

## • **His Style**

Estrada's style is concerned mostly with the evolution of timbre in time. There is no good way to relate his style to anything that Western music culture ever has experienced. Estrada resorts to many special effects to evoke tone flavors from ancient times, including scraping, 'whining', special harmonies, etc. on strings (*Yuunohui...*). Even in the (much) earlier *Canto* set, innovative sounds are employed on a macro level (as opposed to local individual timbres). An example is the counterpoint of independent lines that intersect and create pulsating effects with double trills.

In this music, the Varèsian ideal of obliteration of all sense of melody, phrase, and development is culminated with a vengeance! Time seems to go in wavering spurts, and then hovers. Rhythm is meticulously managed in a stream of intricate notations. Rhythm as we know it is disassembled into its bare parts, only to be tortuously reassembled, twisted, turned, and otherwise mangled, so that only beauty remains. This truly is music for olden times--and for *tomorrow*.

♦♦♦

- ### His Major Works

*Canto Mnémico*
*Canto Oculto*
*Canto Alterno*
*Eolo'oolin*
*Ishini'ioni*
*Yuunohui'se*
*Yuunohui'ome*
*Yuunohui'yei*
*Yuunohui'nahui*
*Yuunohui'se'ome'yei'nahui*
*Pedro Páramo*
*Mictlan*
*Miqi'nahual*
*Eua 'on*
*Eua'on'ome*

Books and Articles:
Compositional Theory: *Discontinuum-Continuum* (Ph.D. dissertation)

*Música y teoría de grupos finitos* (Estrada/Gil – UNAM, 1984)

*El sonido en Rulfo* (1989, UNAM).
(Basis for opera – *Pedro Páramo*)

Author and editor of other books, including *La Música de México* (1984-8, UNAM)

*Teoría de la composición: discontinuo-continuo* (UNAM 2000 – in press)

From: "Julio Estrada" <ejulio@julioestrada.net>
To: "James McHard" <release10@sbcglobal.net>
Subject: Re: Fw: HI THERE!
Date: Wednesday, November 21, 2007 1:37 PM


Dear Jaime el Grande,

I'm writing you quickly this time because soon I leave to Mexico City.

I perfectly understand your idea about the method you propose for the music analysis: that has been my perception since the beginning, no doubt. I know it [the method] is not predictive but it shows how the music moves and lets us know its qualities in terms of being or not being organized in relation to a central kind of equilibrium. I perceive this as a necessity of a total risk in my creative process. I need that risk for freedom and to operate without constraints. Being closer to an abismatic new space is precisely that freedom. I guess you're studying and putting in the shot through the analytical method. That is what you name platykurtic and I understand better now. It took me a time, but I'm getting it for sure.

I can see that differences between X [Xenakis] and I will come out more clearly than through analysis concentrated on other factors. You're right! Please go on with all this in the new chapter: I found it magnificent and really new. Also, I'm convinced about the opening it could mean for the listener and the experts on continuum.

Yes, no one needs to die in the hurricane but I almost do it to perceive it intensively while creating my music.

Let's evolve toward that state of Nirvana.

The score will go out today.


Yours,

Julio

# Conclusion
## The Future of Modern Music –
## A Heretic's Perspective
❧

Thus far, we have surveyed the historical background to the recent work in today's music exploring the structure of sound. I believe the evolution of modern Western art music, as presented in our historical survey, points strongly toward the foundation of a new aesthetic. This new aesthetic is being pursued mostly at studios in which composers are conducting research into the nature and structure of sound. Of course, studios come and studios go. Much good work is also being conducted in seminars, and in courses worldwide. Plus, a great amount of innovative work has been conducted by composers in private settings.

For instance, a Canadian composer, Bert Cooper (1925- 2006), who has been working in isolation for decades, enjoyed a world premiere presentation of two of his electronics works at the TWICE (VII) festival, in April of 1993, in Ann Arbor, Michigan. Cooper has conductedlifelong work in electronics, and he has developed techniques and sounds that anticipated some of the work of Karlheinz Stockhausen. His work has culminated in *WOES* (1995) and WOES 4 (1995), the two works premiered.

The **WOES** template involves a sophistication of processes that Cooper set in motion early in his career. He experimented mechanically with new sounds for years until the appearance of the first electronics devices in the 1940s. By 1948, Cooper began to create sound environments using crude tape recording manipulations. In 1948, Cooper generated tape delay output controlled with a wire recorder. Two pickup heads were connected electrically at varying distances. As sound issued from one head, the other was moved during resonance until an echo-like effect was obtained. Further, continued movements changed the sound pattern. By playing sounds from one head back through the other, a constant, multiple echoing effect was obtained. This work anticipated some of the environmental work of David Tudor in the 1960s.

Another effect was obtained using a metal ribbon anchored at one end and twisted using a motor at the other end, providing varying torsional tension. Rain and other natural elements added much timbral variety to a wondrous, unfolding sonic environment. This is one of Cooper's signal characteristics: using the environment to amplify and modify sound output.

The **WOES** set introduces computers to systematize this intuitive process. Cooper creates a 'theme'-sound and alters the parameters (pitch, timbre, duration, etc.) independently. The sounds are mixed and subjected to recurrent re-entry through the sound system. The output is turmoil in a phantasmagoric billowing of sound effects.

Also, Luigi Nono's work was formalized, mainly in isolation, although he did effectively use Heinrich Strobel's Experimental Music Studio in Freiburg, Germany. The importance of this studio and others-- like IRCAM, directed by Pierre Boulez-- should not be minimized. They provide important materials for research into new sound-making apparatus. Electronics equipment abounds in these studios. Devices like the sonoscope, harmonizers, halophone, digital delay, band-pass filters, and vocoders are indispensable for the contributions they make for shaping sounds into effects that are otherwise not possible.

The problem is, though, that in the four decades preceding the 1990s, emphasis has been focused completely on experiment in, and development of, new methods and materials to evoke and generate sounds. This focus is mostly technique and equipment-oriented. There has emerged an abundance of devices, techniques, and ordering systems. Most of this has concentrated on the external creation of sounds and their arrangement. Far too little effort has been expended in determining why these researches are being, or should be, done. The less glamorous, but more fundamental philosophical questions are mostly being avoided.

Consequently, all this gimmickry has generated little enthusiasm in the public mind. Some of it even may have *undermined* the search for a real 'new music'. The public's rejection of modernism, I believe, is rooted in some of today's composers suffering from a basic misunderstanding of how we perceive sound, and in what is needed to attract people to new alternatives. The preceding efforts in devising new materials, having failed to confront fundamental issues regarding perception of sound patterns, have repelled the public in ways costly to progress towards a new musical aesthetic. Wanton, random new sounds for their own sakes don't enthuse or attract our listeners, and, after all, isn't the audience the composers' target?

Besides the technical gimmicks, extremely sophisticated ordering principles aren't enough for listeners, either. Too much of what has come out of this research generates arcane, abstruse gyrations within a dry, angular context. Serialism is self-limiting. It lacks, terribly, the means to create sufficient contrast in sound quality, and in transition-bearing capabilities, because of its focus on discrete values rather than on the continuum. Functional tonality had maximized the transitional process. When atonality was restricted within serial gestures, the functionality, and the sense of contrast, as well as transition-making means, were abandoned. The public just got tired of attending concerts to be bored with isolated screeches and clunks. The patterns in serialism look great in a mathematical environment because isometries do look good. But what works visually doesn't always translate into interesting aural experiences. So, the public uttered a resounding *"No!"*

The responsibility of the composer is to find a way to hook into the public consciousness, to engage the collective mind and spirit towards an enthusiastic search for new sonic adventure in the pursuit of joy. However, the response of far too many composers has been to seek refuge from the public's wrath in styles that pander to the public's desire for entertainment, and comfort. Hence, a surfeition of minimalism (e.g., 'disguised Mahler', rendered formally vapid, or bad psychedelic meanderings), neo-Romanticism, and other borrowings from past styles pervades the compositional landscape. We need to heed Julio Estrada's admonition that the composer ought not become irresponsible by withdrawing from his/her call to advance the cause of music. Using borrowed materials that have long since been created and discarded by others makes one neither creative, nor original, nor responsible, nor courageous.

Isn't the real responsibility of the composer to be a teacher, mentor, leader, motivator, and stimulator to entice the public in the exploration of previously uncharted regions of our experiential world? Music is the purest, most abstract discipline, with the possible exception of mathematics. Music, though, is more accessible than mathematics and avails itself more readily to a receptive, expectant crevice in the public's minds. Through music, it is possible, *desirable*, to engage our minds in discipline through the confrontation of challenge, to *stretch* our imaginations and to hone our logical and interdisciplinary skills so that we may grow, not stagnate. What better way to accomplish this than through an experience that also *excites?* Music is uniquely qualified to fulfill all these roles. And we will obtain some pleasure in the process! The composer, then, must find a way to keep our minds free of cobwebs, and to help us avoid stagnation that comes with purely hedonistic pleasureseeking. The composer must remain the primary alchemist in the stimulation of our ability to *think*. Without this we perish individually, and culturally! Musical challenge is the doorway to our evolution as sentient beings.

On the other hand, simply plunging into the world of technology is not enough without sufficient background in the understanding of the way we perceive. That is, mechanical and electronics devices alone don't create music, just as systems don't generate sound formal principles. Malipiero's engagement of intuition in molding patterns that 'obey a secret logic', is a wise model, especially if taken together with more explicit, external gestures. The creation of interesting sonic colors and shapes is most effective when there is a well understood reason to do so, and when the most effective means to manage new methods are understood. This sort of understanding is enriched best by composers who study the psychology of perception, the physics and biology of perception, and the corresponding natural systems that are available, in order to invoke the most promising sound results.

If Debussy, Schönberg, Malipiero, Bartók, Varèse, Nono, Cage, Xenakis, Lutoslawski, Scelsi, and Estrada have one thing in common, it is this: they *knew* that something new and *worthwhile* loomed on the horizon, and that they were on the precipice of its discovery. They, as well, knew that they had unique understanding of the nature of sound, of how we perceive it--and of how to marshal their special magic to brew their miracles in the genesis of a new sound aesthetic. The ultimate epiphany has come in the formation of studios directed by the guiding hand of Iannis Xenakis. Corelevant work, performed since this genesis, has been guided and accomplished by Gerard Pape (1955-), and by the profoundly disciplined and innovative theorist/composer, Julio Estrada. They have expanded upon the foundations constructed by Xenakis to pave pathways for the emerging revolutions in thought, perception, and musical aesthetics. The studios, CEMAMu (see Xenakis summary presented earlier), and Les Ateliers UPIC spawn new ideas, concepts, and methodology pregnant with inspiration gleaned from investigating nature's special secrets. Thus, these studios are crucibles for discovery.

The emphasis of the work at the studios is on psychology, the challenge of stimulating insightful perception, and upon relevant means by which to invoke rich sound tapestries. That is not to say method is irrelevant, and that music comes from a vacuum, though. Algorithms (quasi-formulas or stepwise recipes) to serve as midwives in the formation of these ghosts, the sonic-phantasms, are continuously devised to extract from nature those shapes with which we most successfully relate. This is *sound-based* musical composition driven by nature-based methods and devices. CEMAMu continues to marshal the services of leading thinkers from a vast array of disciplines, including those of psychologists, mathematicians, musicians, and others. These studies involve philosophy as it relates to the creation of an automatic music from the use of complex non-trigonometric waveforms. Results are noise-rich and lend themselves to a richer sound fabric that is more interesting aurally than that invoked by most other types of electronics or computer-generated music.

Les Ateliers UPIC studio concerns itself in more direct ways with the study of perception, and with more accessible, if not altogether simpler, algorithmic sound generation. Courses proceed continuously throughout the year. Classes and seminars are conducted. The emphasis is on what's nature-based, in order to maximize applicability to the human mind and its secrets of perception. For instance, by analogy, the human ear and brain, being of natural origin, will be sensitive to these natural sound environments. Therefore, pointless mathematical abstractions, rampant in the work done during previous decades, give way to sounds generated by natural transformation. Algorithms become tools to reach the goal. They don't drive the need. It's the other way around.

The afore-mentioned course work is provided under the careful tutelage of experts (e.g., Gerard Pape, Curtis Roads, and Brigitte Robindoré, all prominent composers). Guest lecturers also provide informative insights into new concepts being researched independently. For example, Julio Estrada lectured and worked on-site for a while. Now he teaches intermittently at the studio. Also, composer Michel Philippot, musicologist Harry Halbreich, and the great Renaissance figure, Iannis Xenakis (*himself*), have lectured. Course work includes studies of psychoacoustics (how the ear prefers certain formal structures over others, and how it responds to varying aural stimuli), of sound-based methods (as opposed to abstract mathematizing), and of algorithmic composition (that is, work in formal procedures that can help generate unique patterns; this is not so new--*functional harmony* embraces simple algorithms). The work of this studio is driven primarily by considerations first proposed by Xenakis and continued through the more recent work of Julio Estrada and Gerard Pape (*SUM* Pape Les Ateliers website).

More detail on this structured setting should increase understanding of this profoundly important work. Les Ateliers UPIC was founded in 1986. Nine-month educational programs now are offered to supplement the long-established music production at the studio. *Techniques of Computer Music* is a course consisting of thirty-two lectures on materials in a textbook, *Computer Music Journal*, published by Curtis Roads, a composer of highly advanced and technical computer music. This course examines the theory of computer music techniques with listening sessions and hands-on training geared toward advanced work in computer music. Gerard Pape has published a pamphlet summarizing the course contents as follows: "teaching the history of electronic music and fundamentals of digital-audio techniques; teaching the introduction to digital sound synthesis; presenting the MIDI Protocol; teaching techniques associated with sound synthesis (sampling, etc.); investigations into sound analysis (pitch and rhythm recognition, etc.); and teaching disciplines that provide many other practical tools, including the software that will run an amazing assortment of input and output devices" (*SUM* Pape Les Ateliers ... org).

Each of the two studios at Les Ateliers UPIC *(studio Xenakis and studio Nono)* contains sophisticated composing modules, including the Apple Macintosh (8600 and G3) computers. Other tools include UPIC graphic composing module, Mars system, super colliders, cloud generators, and related software.

Other classes have been taught by Brigitte Robindoré, and by other young composers. The course in *Electronic Music Studio Technique and Acoustics* includes study of acoustics principles applicable to oscillators, and classical musical instruments: acoustic analysis of timbre, dynamics, physiological aspects of auditory perception, and psychoacoustics are taught, as well. Another aspect of that class focuses on Electroacoustics and studio techniques (theory and practice). Fundamental notions of electricity and electronics are explored. Analog and digital technologies are compared. Finally, algorithmic composition is explored.

The *Theory and Practice of Composition* course is comprised of seminars and lectures by prominent composers and musicologists. In 1995, Julio Estrada conducted seminars in 'continuum' theory, based on the theory he developed in the 1980s and refined in the early 1990s. He still teaches there intermittently. His Continuum I-V concepts receive presentation in lectures. A three-part seminar by Gerard Pape is included. It consists of analyses of perception and composition, Microstructures in timbre and harmony, and microstructure in formal order and disorder evolutions. (Pape is a Lacanian psychologist, as well as a composer and musicologist.) The musicologist, Harry Halbreich, lectured on Varèse and Scelsi. Special guest lecturers have included Iannis Xenakis, Tristan Murail, Bernard Parmegiani, Jean-Claude Risset, Francois-Bernard Mâche and Jean-Claude Eloy, all important European composers *(SUM* Pape Les Ateliers ... UPIC).

Now, what of the future? This type of work focuses on the mind, and of what it is capable. Its goal is to expand the realm of thought to discover a continuous field of new sources and resources. Discoveries beget more discoveries. For instance, Nono studied the ways that different facial patterns alter vocal sounds. This in turn led him to develop uses for special techniques, like time-delay equipment, to capture these sounds in a disciplined fashion. Stockhausen's studies on pitch and timbre resulted in sophisticated electronics manipulations of rhythmic speeds. Xenakis' studies at CEMAMu resulted in advances in the uses of complex waveforms that, in turn, yielded the composition of a family of automatic music pieces, the *GENDY* series.

Pape's work at Les Ateliers UPIC combines concepts developed from these, along with those of Estrada and Scelsi, and extends them to encompass theories borrowed from the science of *Chaos*. He recognizes four basic dimensions in sound: frequency (pitch), amplitude (intensity or volume), timbre (tone color), and space (location of the sound source, and motion within the musical-generating environment) (Pape composition p. 17).

The composer operates on all dimensions at three levels of organization. Those three levels are (Pape composition p. 16):

Micro-form (the "counterpoint of the micro-parameters of sound")

Meso-form (harmonic transitions between the four basic sound dimensions)

Macro-form (heterophonic structures - independent linear patterns - order-disorder-chaos transitions).

So, we have an in-between level of organization -- 'meso' --in addition to the familiar micro, and macro levels. He further claims that the creation of interesting pieces needs to involve the manipulation and transformation of at least three of the four dimensions *in all three levels of organization* (my italics - Pape composition p. 17). The operation on the sound values at the different organizational levels requires differentiation between time scales of the changing values. For example, attack envelopes of different types occur at the micro-level, whereas sounds in continuous transition (e.g., a smooth curve) occur over a greater time span (meso-level). Heterophony, or the mingling of distinct lines, unfolds over large-scale (macro-level) time values, rendering an overall contour to the work.

At this juncture Pape introduces the notion of variable order levels. For example, order is perceived most vividly when one hears a continuous curve. However, when one encounters a disjoint set of unpredictably changing interval patterns, he/she perceives disorder. Pape then marshals the concept of chaos to describe the confused perception that results when there is a conflict between what is simultaneously perceived as order at one level, and what is perceived as disorder at another level. This model, including chaos, is an extension of ataxy, proposed previously by Xenakis. Pape also claims that pointillistic serialism generates just such a chaotic perception, because of the inherent internal conflict raised by its simultaneous evocation of order and disorder. Thus, a work so composed (serially) becomes a chaotic event (Pape composition p. 20).

Pape proposes that chaos can be evoked in far more productive ways to achieve more interesting music, by operating with the simultaneous counterpoint of evolving order perceptions at different organizational levels. For example, a pattern of ordered tone oscillations (micro) that is couched within a disorderly heterophony (macro), with chaotic timbral changes (meso). One way to achieve this would require the composer to acquire an exhaustive knowledge of the workings of all instruments. One result is that excessive pressure from a bow onto a violin string excites *non-periodic* vibrations, the very characteristic associated with chaos. Other possibilities include traditions in Eastern music that employ asynchronous (Pape composition pp. 23/4) merging and diverging lines in the same, but not quite simultaneous, melodic patterns. He uses asynchronicity concepts with 'detuning', (Pape composition p. 21) (or 'scordatura' in the case of stringed instruments).

Chaos can be applied to other dimensions, too. By special methods one can split sounds into period-doubling stasis repeatedly, until a non-resolving pattern is excited.

These can combine with orderly and disorderly patterns at all levels, thereby evoking a polyphonic plasma of varying order in constant evolution (Pape composition p. 25). He does caution against injecting chaos directly, using mathematical formulas, without exerting accompanying care in creating a through-composed counterpoint of changing sound dimensions (Pape composition p. 28). Only this care can guarantee the richest, most interesting outcomes. Pape's **Weaveworld** (1995 - in progress) employs sudden and unpredictable patterns in streams of sound in a plasma that draws from chaos models (Pape composition p. 29). These concepts are a few of the many studies underway at studios investigating the nature of sound.

For example, Xenakis continues his work at CE-MAMu, exploring the potentials outlined in his *New Proposals In Microsound* (Formalized Music - Xenakis). He envisions a musical fabric rich in noise patterns, and avoiding the spaghetti-like strands and thin-textured sounds of traditional electronic music. The barren sound of such music results, he claims, from a misapplication of Fourier-Analytical concepts to classical electronic music generation (Xenakis p. 242).

The traditional waveforms in classical electronic sounds come from simple trigonometric functions, like sinewaves, that contain none of the overtones from the harmonic series, only the fundamental. The sounds remind him of the heterodyning in radio signaling, common during the Second World War. His distributions, which employ random walks (Brownian Movement) through a noise-rich spectrum generated by applying complex wave functions (Bessel-curves, etc.) to the unit sound-kernels, imbue dense textures at both the micro (kernels) and macro (structural) levels. The music can be incarnated instantaneously by computer impulse, marshalling the musical 'shapes' characterized in the formulas. This is an extension of his general principles for the creation of an automatic music from minimum rules of composition. Conversely, the composer himself may intercede and write the music directly, from those rules (Xenakis pp. 246-9).

Also, Julio Estrada continues to explore the gamut of timbres, and he has armed himself with additional tools to do so by extending his theory of the 'continuum' systematically. In addition, he continues to study ancient music and its characteristic sounds, and he integrates these sound formations into Western composition theory and practice through his teaching activities.

It seems that work concentrating on the single tone and its evolution through tone-color variations, based on the work started by Giacinto Scelsi, would be rich in theoretical possibilities. A group of European composers, for example, has worked and lectured on this problem. Several of these composers, some unknown in the USA, are making important contributions to the theory of sound formation. For instance, sound-based exploration into the realm of the color-characteristics of harmonic series have been conducted musically by the contemporary French composers, Tristan Murail and the late Gérard Grisey, both one-time pupils of Messiaen, born in the 1940s. These explorations are analogous to parallel work initiated by Scelsi in the realm of single tone oscillations. Curtis Roads, who has taught at Les Ateliers UPIC, and published the *Computer Music Journal,* has adapted Xenakis' theory on granular sounds directly to computer music in his own compositions. The 1940s-born Rumanian and naturalized French citizen Horatiu Radulescu continues this work with teaching and composing. Finally, some promising trends are emerging through the noise and chance explorations of Helmut Lachenmann, Stefano Scodanibbio, and Salvatore Sciarrino.

## <u>Sound-based Composition</u>

It is apparent that this tightly focused historical survey is not all-inclusive of modernist trends of the 20th century in music. There are two reasons: the obvious one is that there simply is insufficient room to closely examine all major avant-garde composers and their works; the second and more telling reason is that not all 'new' music falls within the boundaries defined by the scope of this book. Much is made of many composers' contributions to the profusion of 'new sounds'. But most musical authors refuse to examine certain crucial differences in approach that reveal real distinctions between competing styles.

Many composers are lauded simply because they dazzle through glittering auditory display. Others, though less glamorous (and even some equally glamorous), approach musical discovery rigorously through exploration of what constitutes sound and how we perceive it. For example, much of Penderecki's cluster work was startling in its time, but it has become timeworn. Lately, he has abandoned the style altogether. Berio's work of the '60s seemed fresh in its bewildering speed and display of effects that seemed to have placed it at the leading edge of the avant-garde. He has become passe, as well. The trouble isn't so much that their work isn't valuable, but that it relied too heavily on effect, without intimate exploration of primal considerations of what constitutes sound.

The qualities that inhabit the seminal work of Xenakis, Scelsi, Estrada, Nono, and even Cage are fundamentally different from those that characterize the surface sheen of the works of Berio, Penderecki, Ligeti, and Górecki. The glittering effects contained within the works by the latter group are the by-products of these composers' manipulations of tones, albeit the creation of a *counterpoint of indi-*

*vidual,* or *isolated sounds.* On the other hand, it is almost always true that 'new' sounds in the work of the former group result from a painfully won control over the evolution and the transformation of *each tone.* This is a counterpoint of tonal *dimensions,* not simply of different *tones,* as defined by pitch attributes. These dimensions became well understood only through investigation of philosophical, perceptual, and technical concepts: how sounds are derived and varied or contrived, and how humans perceive them. This qualification required its practitioners to become expert at mastering tonal *three*-dimensionality --that is, timbral variations *within* a pitch level, in addition to the other more common two dimensions: frequency (pitch) and durational fluctuations. More than just the sound effects garnered by less fastidious and thorough composers, these sound-entities are the very stuff of sound in all its glory. The masters-- Xenakis, Nono, Estrada, and Scelsi (and John Cage, through his beguiling, unforeseen epiphanies) --became archangels of this peculiar sorcery to which we refer, and that is what informs *sound-based* composition.

It is this defining characteristic that has forced the choice of which residents were invited to inhabit this special world of the new modernism (modernist music). Our journey of necessity encompasses this specially defined terrain.

## The Future of Modern Music

These new ideas will spawn other new models. The common thread in all of this is to *maximize the interest of the listener!* "... But the question is one of how to apply the model musically in a way so that its consequences are most profoundly felt perceptually by the listener" (Pape: *Composition* p. 28). No matter how well grounded a composer is in theoretical concepts, he/she still has to be good, and interesting.

I hope that this short excursion into new worlds of sound will be as exciting to the listeners and readership as its presentation has been to me. My goal has been to stimulate the listener to search the existing world of art music, and to discover the many wonders it offers. I have tried to show that the exploration of new sound territory does not imply encountering only bad or uninteresting music. The problems inherent in much of the 'new' music of the '50s were recognized quickly by a public put off by pseudo-scientific, arcane music that was not intended to reach the mind of the listener, or that failed in its mission to do so. A return to the past is an unnecessary admission of defeat for both the composer and the listener. It is like saying, "We can't create original music" (composer); or "We can't stand anything after Debussy, and unlike previous times, we won't try" (audience). Neither eventuality is satisfactory.

Musical composition, if approached from the proper perspectives--keeping the value of sound preeminent over the value of method, and keeping the audience preeminent over ego--can continue to fulfill its ancient role of pleasurably educating, even in its use of ever more modern concepts.

♦♦♦

# Additional Composers and ideas for the Future

**Karl Amadeus Hartmann** –Born in 1905, was a near contemporary of Hindemith and a countering balance to Hindemith's weighty neo-Baroque romanticism. He stayed out of the limelight to escape attention; he was philosophically, in the sense of Bartók, a humanist; and his music, though at times dressed in serial garb, has a searching aspiring quality. Hartmann's music has a chiseled classical sound with a slightly granite edge, as well as a dissonant, muscular and athletic power. His best known works are: eight numbered symphonies (1936-62), the recently uncovered *Sinfonia Tragica* (unnumbered – 1940), the symphonic song cycle *Gesangsszene* (1962-3 unfinished), *Miserae* (1935), *Concerto Funebre* for Violin and orchestra (1939; rev. 1959), and the opera *Simplicius Simplicissimus* (final form 1955). He died in 1963.

**Luigi Dallapiccola** – Dallapiccola (1904-75, Italy) was an important composer from the first generation after the 'generation of the '80s' (Malipiero, Casella et al.) He inherited the affinity for a great, lyrical melodic line that spanned the centuries. He became one of the earliest Italians to adopt the dodecaphonic style, although his interest reflected Berg's orientation. He was inventive in his use of the row, constructing mutually exclusive triads in harmony, apart from Schönberg's overlapping schemes. This helped him maintain a delicate melodic flow even in a difficult serial atmosphere. Among his best works are included: *Il Prigioniero* (opera 1944-9); *3 Questions with 2 Answers* (Orchestra 1962); *Piccola, Musica Notturna* (1954, rescored for chamber orch. 1959); *Canti di Prigionia* (1938); *Preghiere* (1962); and *Canti di Liberazione* (1951-5)

**Goffredo Petrassi** – Petrassi (1904- 2003, Italy) was a compatriot and contemporary of Dallapiccola. However, the two were dissimilar in their interest and orientation. Dallapiccola had been drawn to opera and song; Petrassi was a composer of song, but also a large orchestral catalog. His early interests were primarily in the extensions of neo-classical spirit under the spell of Casella. It was later that he became interested in dodecaphony, well after Dallapiccola. The span of his evolving interest is no better seen than in the eight brilliant Concertos for orchestra (1933-72.) The first reveals a solid tonal neo-classicism spiked with dissonance; by the sixth the sound is dense and atonal.

**Giorgio Federico Ghedini** – (1892-1965, Italy) This introvert composer has suffered unjust neglect in the concert hall, especially in the U.S. He is in the seam between the generations of Malipiero and Dallapiccola. He never adopted twelve tone dodecaphony, but exuded a lyrical neo-Baroque style that draws some of its flavor from the Italy of olden times. His works are sensitive and quite beautiful. Early in his development he revealed a refined interest in concerto work and subsequently became known as the modern concerto composer. Most important among his works are the austere *Concert dell'Albatro* (1945), *Partita* (1926), *Architetture* (1941), the limpidly beautiful *Musica Notturna* (1947), *Invenzioni* for Cello and Strings (1940) and numerous other concerti for various solo strings or piano with orchestra.

**Sergei Prokofiev** –Prokofiev (b. Russia 1891, d. 1953) was one of history's major master composers. Prokofiev's early astringent, dissonant works of athletic rhythmic power are his most historically important. They reflect the then current Russian fixation on the industrial age. Prokofiev, along with other, less prominent composers contributed to a Russian Futurism, with its penchant for hammering, rippling of metal sheets and other effects associated with machines. For a time he was a rival to Stravinsky for the Russian leadership in music. The most famous of these aggressive earlier pieces are *Scythian Suite* (1914), *Chout* (ballet - 1920), *Le Pas d'acier* (ballet - 1924), the second and third (to a lesser degree) symphonies (1924 and 1928 respectively), and the second Piano Concerto (1917). Popular works in his later, more accommodating style include the *Classical Symphony* (no. 1 – 1916-17); *Love for Three Oranges* – Suite (1925), symphonies nos. 4-7 (1930-1952), *Romeo and Juliet* ballet suites (1936-7) and music for the film *Alexander Nevsky* (1938 – lost, then recovered). *Peter and the Wolf* is very popular, as are the first and fifth symphonies.

**Albert Roussel** – Roussel (1869-1937), was a near exact French contemporary of Ravel. He adopted Ravel's impressionistic style for a short time (Symphony *Le Poème de la Forêt* – 1908, and the ballet *Le Festin de l'araignée* 1913). By the 1920s, however, Roussel became one of the earliest advocates of neo-classical symphonism. His brand was particularly rugged and tonally uncompromising. His best works in this style are *Symphony number Three* (1930), and the ballets *Bacchus et Ariane* (1931) and *Aeneus* (1935). He also composed *Psaume LXXX* (1929).

**Alfredo Casella** – Casella (1883-1947) was one of the composers who, along with Malipiero, Pizzetti, and Respighi contributed to the re-emergence of instrumental music in an Italy that had been laden with operatic creation through the works of Rossini, Verdi and Puccini. Along with Malipiero, he soon split from the Respighi/Pizzetti axis of conservatives and worked tirelessly toward a new modernism through classical structure and expressive dissonance. He and Malipiero forged an important new group for the furtherance of modernism, Maggio Musicale Fiorentino, which sponsored production of a wide range of modern works, including R. Strauss' *Elektra*, and A. Berg's *Der Wein* (scheduled, then cancelled). Unlike Malipiero's, Casella's work emphasized stately, classical forms in a forging of a new neo-classicism. His most prominent works include *A Notte Alta* (1917), *Elegia Eroica* (1917) Italia (1910), *Serenade* (1927), *Concerto Romano* (1927) and three symphonies (1905; 1908; 1941).

**Bohuslav Martinů** – Martinů (1890-1959) was Czechoslovakia's main international figure in music after Janáček. But whereas Janáček attained fame through composing a series of remarkable operas based on folk-speech, Martinů was through and through a committed neo-classicist. Like that of his teacher Roussel, Martinů's classicism was heavily tainted with spiky dissonance. His music is noteworthy for its high precision and economy; yet it is very expressive. He expanded the expressive quality of the orchestra with inclusion of a piano, though in a percussive, non-soloistic manner, much like Bartók and Malipiero did. His works include 6 symphonies (1942-1953), several operas, ballets and concertos (several remarkable). Also important are his *Memorial to Lidice* (1943); *Les Fresques de Piero della Francesca* (1955), and *Double Concerto for Two String Orchestras, Piano and Tympani* (1938).

**Arthur Honegger** – Honegger (1892-1955) was born in France of Swiss parents. His proclivities remained French throughout his life. Consequently he became an admirer of Satie in the 1920s and even associated with others of 'Les Six' for awhile, though his style had a certain Germanic epic character. He was briefly ensconced in the urbane 'Six' tradition of witty brash music that characterized the 1920s. However, also, for a short time, he flirted with machine age music, in the spirit of Mosolov and others. He also composed densely dissonant neo-classical symphonies that 'Les Six' considered out of character. In this sense his was a spirit more kindred with Prokofiev's. His most advanced contributions include Symphonies 3

(1946) and 5 (1950); the tone poems *Rugby* (1928), *Pacific 231* (1924), and *Mouvement Symphonique no. 3* (1932-3), and the mimed symphony *Horace Victorieux* (1920-1.)

**Julián Orbón** – Orbón (1925-1991) is unfairly overlooked as a significant contributor to advanced modern music. He is Cuban-American of Spanish heritage. He made important contributions to rhythmic complexity as well as harmony. Both in matters of orchestration and harmony his music conveys a refined sense of tonal play in expert contrapuntal fashion. He is a distinct nationalist in the manner of Falla. His two most important orchestral works are: *Tres versions sinfonicas* (1953) and *Tres Cantigas del Rey* (Alfonso X, el sabio - 1960), three original works for Harpsichord and chamber orchestra selected from a set of songs from *Cantigas del Santa María* by Alfonso X.

**Jón Leifs** – Icelandic composer Jón Leifs lived from 1899 to 1968. He developed a profoundly original folk expression. His characteristic off balance rhythms and crushing explosive bursts are revelatory of a highly effective expression. The music for chorus with orchestra (e.g. *Guðrúnarkviða* – The Lay of Guðrun 1940) makes effective use of unbalanced rhythms and texts common in Old Norse legends. His phrases reflect the rugged, idiosyncratic contours of his native language. Tremendous climaxes and sudden ruptures recall the rugged Nordic landscape. His best works include *Hafís* (Drift Ice 1965); *Geysir* (1961); *Hekla* (1961 volcanic mountain); *Dettifoss* (Icelandic waterfall 1964); *Landsýn* (Landfall 1955); *Baldr* (1943-7 –drama with wordless choir and orchestra). Also important is his *Saga Symphony* (1941-2 – 'Söguhetjur' – First Symphony). In these he frequently called for unusual percussion; rocks; ship's chains; anvils; petri (stones); sirens; large wooden stumps; pistols; and cannons, some items electronically enhanced. *Fine I* (1963) and *Fine II* (1963) are beautiful works composed toward the end of his life.

**Manuel de Falla** – Falla is less conspicuously a solid member of this fraternity, although, by at least one piece he made a significant contribution to modern music. Lived 1946-1976 mostly in the Spanish province Cadiz, his work captures the nationalist folk sound ambience and local color of native Spain. He absorbed a certain Debussyan impressionistic quality, while pursuing formalistically a more cosmopolitan neo-classicism in vogue in the 1920s. In this he managed to avoid too close a local descriptive flavor. His best works include *Nights in the Gardens of Spain* (1916) that thrust his name into international attention. There followed three important works, two of them ballets: *El Amor Brujo* (1915) and *Three Colored Hat* (1919) ; the crucial work of modernism is the *Concerto for Harpsichord* (1926). It was a pungent, sparse, nearly barren, unrelenting masterpiece. Other pieces are minor in modern annals.

**Ernst Toch** - Ernst Toch (b. 1887 Austria) was Jewish; as such he was one of a number of important German/Austrian Jewish composers who were officially outcast and labeled degenerate (*'entartete'*) by the German Nazi regime. During the 1920s he had composed a number of very advanced works in serial style that earned him disfavor. From this negative climate Toch had to move to the US. After his exile, he turned to writing primarily for the movies. This gained him breathing room, but little acclaim from the more serious 'advanced' critical circle and he was long forgotten. CPO recently has released his complete set of symphonies (seven in all) to wide acclaim. His most notable works are: *Symphony no. 1* (1950); *Symphony no. 2* (1950-1); *Symphony no. 3* (1955 - 1956 Pulitzer Prize.) The style in these works is one of pungent dissonance over long, winding plastic rhythms in constant evolution. Abrupt bursts of sound are common. Tone poems *Big Ben* (1934) *Pinocchio* (1935), and *Peter Pan* (1956) also have achieved popularity, as has *Jephta, Rhapsodic Poem* – a.k.a. 'Symphony no. 5'. He died in 1964.

(Olav) **Fartein Valen** – Valen (1887-1952) has been a curious, isolated representative among the Norwegian composers. He was a pathfinder. Early he adopted Schönberg's twelve tone method, albeit in a very original, personal way. Within the strictures in that style he was able to create music of real sensitivity that emerges only after repeated intense listening. Once the granite veneer of atonality is cracked, though, the special beauty is revealed, and found to be distinguishable from that of Schönberg. He is most well known for his four formidable symphonies, but a number of smaller scale pieces are especially attractive, too. Among his works are: Symphonies 1-4 (1937-1949); *Epithalamion* (1933); *The Churchyard by the Sea* (1933-4); *An die Hoffnung* (1933); and the beautiful *Ave Maria* (1917-21.),

**Harald Sæverud** – Sæverud (1897-92) is Norway's foremost symphonist of the twentieth century. His symphonies are chiseled from the spirit of the mountains and fjords of Norway, as well as its legendary folk lore. The symphonies are polyphonic, yet quasi-tonal with some edginess that casts a peculiarly austere flavor. He eschewed atonality and dodecaphony. Among his best known works are the nine symphonies (1916-66), the sixth is subtitled *Sinfonia Dolorosa* bearing a quite melancholy air, and the ninth is somber and deeply moving, with very intricate lines. This was as near atonality as Sæverud ever approached. Other works include a cleverly expressive set of two *Peer Gynt Suites* (1947.)

(Gustaf) **Allan Pettersson** – This introvert Swedish (1911-80) composer worked for a long time in obscurity. His work was viewed critically as a repeating cycle of long, single-dimensioned and self-obsessed emotional works, nearly indistinguishable from one another. Recent opinion, however, has cast a new understanding that his symphonies are deep, brooding works that dwell on the emotional troublesome youth suffered by the composer. The symphonies are all in one long movement. The works are highly original, though they do share a quality of dark power with Mahler, and even somewhat with certain Shostakovich. Symphonies 1 (withdrawn) through 16 (1950-83) represent his main œuvre, although some concertos are noteworthy also.

**Aarre Merikanto** – Merikanto (1893-1958) was a Finnish composer who followed Sibelius chronologically, if not stylistically. He had long been attracted to the experimental aspects of musical expression, and this got him in trouble with a Finnish public that yearned for sentimental outpouring of the spirit of folk heritage characteristic of Sibelius' music. Later, in response, Merikanto recanted and even destroyed one work (later reconstructed by his student P. Heininen.) His subsequent work was much more traditional. His early, venturesome works include *Juha* (opera 1920-2); *Pan* (1924) *Symphonic Study* (1928; mutilated, then reconstructed 1980); *Notturno* (1929) and a *Nonet* (1926)

**Vagn Holmboe** – Holmboe (Danish 1909-1996) is an enigma in Danish music. His work, though basically tonal, has not generated significant interest until recently. His style owes much to Nielsen, a compatriot, and even Sibelius. His themes are long and broadly evolving. They are built from what he calls "germ cells" and 'metamorphosize' (his term.) The complexity is relieved by his intensity of expression. His main works are the thirteen numbered symphonies (1935-93), an orchestral *Sinfonia in Memoriam* (1954), four string sinfonias entitled *Kairos* (1957-62), and four Symphonic Metamorphoses – *"Epitaph"* (1956), *"Monolith"* (1960), *"Epilog"* (1961-2), and *"Tempo Variabile"* (1971-72.)

**Hanns Eisler** - Eisler (born Germany 1916; d there 1962) was a tragic figure in America. Like many intellectual composers of the time, such as Cowell, Copland and Nancarrow, Eisler ran afoul of the un-American House Un-American Activities Committee in the US congress. He had fled Germany in 1933 to live in America and to escape Nazism . He had to return to Germany due to his communist party affiliation in 1949. His early studies under Schönberg led him to an early atonal avant-garde style. By the 1920s he adopted a more 'proleterian' style, somewhat after Well. He soon had become, like Hartmann and Toch an *'entartete'* (degenerate) composer. His best works are the more dense serial pieces which retain an unassuming lyricism.: *Deutsche Sinfonie* (1937), one of his greatest works; *5 Orchestertücke* (1938); *Kammersinfonie* (1940); and the cantata *Die Mutter* (1931), another moving work.

**Roberto Gerhard** – Gerhard (1896-1970) was of Swiss parentage, but soon became associated with Spanish styles, most notably Catalonian. He was Felipe Pedrell's last composition student, and he also studied under Enrique Granados and Schönberg. Even before he joined Schönberg's class he was aware of, and had fallen under the influence of the several main new music currents raging in Europe in the twenties. He emigrated from Spain to Great Britain in 1960, becoming a subject. His later works are a curious mixture of dissonant tonality and Spanish folk atmosphere. He was a guest professor at University of Michigan in 1960, filling in for Ross Lee Finney during the latter's sabbatical. He got to know and taught the composers later associated with the ONCE Festival. His serialism is extended to apply to rhythms as well as tones. His main works are five symphonies (No. 5 unfinished) – No. 1 (1952-3), No. 2, *Metamorphoses* (1959, rev. 1967-8), No. 3 *Collages* (1961), and No. 4 *New York* (1967), *Don Quixote* (1940-1), and *Concerto for Harpsichord Strings and Percussion* (1955-6.)

**Egon Wellesz** – Wellesz, Austrian-English (1885-1974), had become a fairly popular composer in his early years, with his first two symphonies written after he emigrated from Austria to England in 1938. However, as his style moved further and deeper into Schönbergian atonality, he fell into obscurity until his 'rehabilitation' in his later years. He had studied privately with Schönberg alongside Berg and Webern. Soon, though, the eminent Mahler conductor Bruno Walter convinced Wellesz to set out alone and avoid the stultifying influence of such a powerful personality as Schönberg. Wellesz, nonetheless maintained a high interest in the musical history of Vienna, a process he set out to explore in his symphonies. The nine Symphonies (1945-72) show a compelling stylistic evolution that reflect Vienna from the just past romantic era of Mahler through to the revolutions of Schönberg (especially in nos. eight and nine.) This is almost a review of history, reenacted through the window of one lifetime. Other works include *Vorfrühling* (1912), *Symphonic Epilog* (1969), and the opera *Die Bakchantinnen* (1930.) The impression one gets on listening is that he was a master.

**Carlos Chávez** – Chávez (1899-1978) is the more famous of the two Mexican modernists, although his idiom is markedly less advanced than his fellow countryman Revueltas'. Chávez' main contributions to the modern canon of orchestral music consist of a few important works that reveal use of native Aztec materials, be they rhythmic (*Sinfonía India* – symphony no. 2, 1935), or instrumental (*Xochipilli Macuilxochitl* - **1940**.) *Xochipilli* **scores f**or native percussion instruments and has a very atmospheric sound reminiscent of ancient Aztec music. *Sinfonia India* contains high tension driving rhythms that carry the work to a powerful climax. *Tambuco* (1964) for 6 percussionists also is important in this fashion. Another work of atmospheric evocativeness is the *Sinfonía Antígona* (Symphony no. 1 – 1933.)

**Igor Markevitch** – This composer/conductor was, facetiously, long regarded as Russia's second Igor. Born in Russia in 1912, he commenced his career solely as a composer. From 1925 to 1946, he turned out one major work after another. However, the early acclaim turned to rejection for his unrelenting dissonances; accordingly, in 1946 he ceased composing entirely in order to become fully engaged as a renowned conductor. There has been a recent resurgence of interest in Markevitch's own music on Marco Polo CDs, notably *Sinfonietta in F* (1929); *Ouverture Symphonique* (1931); *Rebus* (1931); *Le Nouvel Age* (1938); and the notorious, deeply evocative, and provocative *L'Envol d'Icare* (The Flight of Icarus 1933; 1942). This last work exists in three versions, one each for large orchestra, for small orchestra, and for piano. He died in 1963.

**Artur Schnabel** - Schnabel (b. Austria 1882) is a very strange case indeed in the history of modern music. He was a fine and deeply professional piano player. In performance he was not usually willing to step across the great chasm that seperates a romantic expression from that of the avant-garde. However, as a composer, Schnabel felt no such boundary limit impringing on his creative drive. As a consequence, his compositions tend to be vigorous, yet driven by a special Schönbergian expression. He used a limited form of serialism in his symphonies; limited in that the system is contrived to reveal certain melodic relationships achieveable in no other way. The three symphonies (1938-48) are this testament. He died in 1951.

**Nikos Skalkottas** - Skalkottas is just recently receiving much deserved attention as "the other" great Greek composer (with Xenakis). Born in Greece 1904, he died tragically young of a strangulated hernia in 1949. For many years he suffered obscurity and neglect; but for his original settings of traditional Greek dances, he seemed destined for oblivion. Many thought of him as merely a dense version of Schönberg, his teacher, with whom he shared a penchant for twelve-tone methodology. Thanks to the enterprising release of much other of Skalkottas's works on BIS, the prejudice has begun to diminish as the audiences become more familiar with his original variant of serial music as a powerful and personal expression. His best works include: *The Return of Ulysses*, overture (1942-3); *36 Greek Dances* (1931-6;1948-9); *Death and the Maiden* ballet (1938); and three powerful piano concerti (1931, 1937-8, 1938-9).

**Silvestre Revuelta**s – Revueltas was born in Mexico on the very last day of the year 1899. During these times, Mexico was just beginning to emerge as a major musical culture, thanks to the early work of Manuel Ponce. Furthermore, Carlos Chavez was a rising star by the 1920s, contributing to a thoroughly native-based national sound. Revueltas, though, went much further along these lines than his compatriots. Combined with Conlon Nancarrow and Julián Carrillo, Revueltas forged a radical new path in the Mexican musical landscape. The music of Revueltas is alternatively raucous and wild, and deeply nostalgic in contemplation of the native Indian culture of times distant past. His music frequently comprises a mysterious mixture of the two stylistic tendencies. Along these combined lines the most engaging and forward looking works are: *Cuauhnahuac* (1931-32); *Ventanas* (1931); *Ocho per Radio* (1933); *Planos* "Geometric Dance" (1934); *Redes*, concert suite from the film (1935); *Homenage a Federico Garcia Lorca* (1937); *Le noche de los Mayas (1939)*, suite from the film; and the sensationally popular *Sensemaya* (1937-8). *Janitzio* (1933) and *Caminos* (1934) enjoy a certain currency, too. The music is rich with colorful dissonances and intricate rhythms. He died in 1940 of alcoholism.

**Douglas Lilburn** - Lilburn, born New Zealand in 1915 would not be included here but for a handful of great electronics works and one powerful symphony. He studies under Percy Grainger and Ralph Vaughan-Williams and from these he formed a study style in good Bristish tradition. His early work is exceptionally high quality but traditional stylistically. His works from that period include *Aotearoa Overture* (1940), *A Song of Islands* (1946), and two symphonies - 1949 and 1951 (rev. 1974). Then, 1970 he founded an electronic music studio at Victoria wherein he worked for the rest of his life turning out wonderfully original electronic music with limited resources. His most original works after 1961 beside *Symphony no. 3* (1961) include *Three Inscapes* (1972), *Sounds and Distrances* (1975), *Poem in Time of War* (1967), *Sings Harry* and *Spectrum Study*. The latter two are early, with no fixed date. He died in 2001.

**Ahmed Adnan Saygun** - Born in Turkey (1907), Saygun was one of a number of brilliant, original Turkish composers to burst upon the scene in the late 20th century. He was a noted teacher also. He accompanied Bartók on an ethnomusicological tour of Anatolia in 1936. He composed five rugged, highly original symphonies (1953-84) that used shifting rhythms and sudden bursts of richly scored sound in an epic form. He also wrote a stunning *Piano Concerto* (1956) and the beautiful oratorio *Yunus Emre* (1946). He died in 1991.

**Kamran Ince** - Ince, born in 1960 in America to Turkish parents, is the other promient Turk to burst on the world composing scene. He is even more original in his use of shifting rhythms than Saygun. His sound world is compelling for its reminiscence of Turkish heritage; yet it also promised a fusion of the near east and west - ancient and the new. The language, though tonal, is striking testament to the idea that original music need not be radical. Best known are three of his symphonies -no. 2 *"Constantinople"* 1994; no. 3 *"Siege of Vienna"* 1994-5; and no. 4 *"Sardis"* 1999-2000.

**Alois Hába** - Hába (1893-73) was a Czech pupil of Schönberg who explored new territory in microtonal sound systems. His system of quarter tones mostly predates the deeply thorough overtone-based 43 -tone construct of Harry Partch. His fifth- and sixth-tone works followed in the 1960s. Hába was fortunate to have an instrument maker (A. Förster) construct special instruments for his use in the field. His best known works are microtonal, although he has composed a solid body of tonal and twleve-tone music also. *Matka* (Mother-1927), opera in quarter tones is his most sensational work. It is truly dramatic and issues a queasy sense of off kilter sensation in keeping with an original text. Other key works include: a quarter tone *String Quartet no. 2* (1920); *The Path of Life* (1933) orchestral 'athematic' mix of twelve-tone and diatonics; the sixth tone *String Quartet no. 11* (1958); the quarter tone *String Quartet no. 12* (1960); and fifth tone *String Quartet no. 16* (1967). He also wrote quartet tone works for trombone, piano and clarinet.

**Josef Matthias Hauer** - Hauer, born in 1883, was an emerging figure in the nineteen-teens-until Schönberg's atonal works stole the spotlight. Hauer's music, never as spectacularly avant-garde-sounding as Schönberg's, was, nonetheless, very systematically headed toward revolutionary structural thinking right out of the get-go. Hauer had a vision for music that would link certain relationships between rhythm and pitch, and even bring tone-color into a systematic handling. His music proceeded towards that goal in careful evolutionary steps, each new work bringing in a new concept and redrawing interrelations never before considered. His works then evolved through a series of 'milestones' (his term.) Stage one occurred about 1913 with the introduction with the curiously attractive

*Apokalyptishe Phantasie.* This work revealed Hauer's treatment of tone color as resulting from intervals in pitch. The *Romantische Fantasie,* 1925 marked his introduction of *tropes ('Wendungsgruppen')* that organized all forty four possible combinations of two hexachords joining to form twelve tones. These were given a hierarchy to reveal the tone color potential in each trope. Shortly, Hauer distinguished between which interval sizes were appropriate for use in melody building and those that were best usable in harmony building. More intricate ordering gestures within the row or trope were developed into a continuum, allowing the four note chords to generate progeny with similar qualities. His later works were all titled *"Zwölftonspiel"* (twelve tone piece), the only distinguishing labeling among the set was the parenthetical note of the date for each successive piece. He died in obscurity; just now his work is beginning to attract interest (SUM/PAR Weiß/Hauer.

## Bibliography

Weiß, Robert Michael 1 and Hauer, Josef Matthias 2. *Milestones* 1 and *Manifesto* 2. 1 Translated by Praeder, Susan-Marie. CPO 777 154-2 Germany. 2007.

**Henry Cowell** – Cowell, born 1897 in California, was a revolutionary from his teens. An early work *Adventures in Harmony* (1910) included striking the keys with fists and forearms. Later, he started placing objects under the lid of the piano, and finally by playing the strings with his hands. *The Banshee* (1925) was thus composed for this 'string' piano. He even devised special notations for his sounds, and incorporated them as systematic expansions of the harmonic system. Also, along with Leon Theremin, he invented a harmonic/rhythmic device in the 1930s that used 16 rhythmic patterns on 16 pitch levels at various frequencies dubbed the 'rhythmicon'. He composed *Rhythmicana* (1932), an orchestral piece using the new system and instrument. Aside from these works he is most famous for his *Ongaku* (1957) for orchestra; *Aeolian Harp* (1923), *26 Simultaneous Mosaics* (1964), *Ostinato Pianissimo* (1930-34), *Quartet Romantic* (1915-17) and *Quartet Euphometric* (1916-19). The latter two were based on principles of the Rhythmicon. Estrada acknowledges Cowell's influence on him. He died in 1965.

**Conlon Nancarrow** – Nancarrow was American-born, 1912. He was refused his reentry Visa to the U.S. due to political affiliation in fighting on behalf of the Republican Brigade in the Spanish Civil War; he moved to Mexico. Like Cowell, he was an experimenter. He composed a series of *Studies* for player piano. Many of these were published for the first time in 1977; they are not dated, but appear to date from about 1948- 1990. They number ~55. He notated the pieces very painstakingly by punching holes into player piano rolls. This method enabled him to compose music of such speed and complexity that no human can perform it. Only player piano and rolls can activate these ingenious sonic miracles. Two short works for small orchestra are of interest, too. They are *Piece no. one for Small Orchestra* (1943) and *Piece number Two for Small Orchestra* (1986). His importance lies in his extraordinary rhythmic complexity and speed which seem to act on tone clusters in a way that the timbres fuse. In this he joins Cowell as playing a crucial influence on Estrada in the latter's development of the *continuum*. He died in 1997.

**Harry Partch** – Partch (1901-1974) worked on a music that would reflect the beauty of body movement, as well as capture complex scales and microtones. Among all the microtonal composers (including Alois Hába, Ivan Wyschnegradsy, Hans Barth, and Julián Carrillo) he was the most thoroughgoing in his use of the harmonic overtone series. He created an octave of 43 tones, unevenly spaced so as to reflect the cramping of intervals in the registers of higher harmonics. Generally, the others resorted to even tempered spacing of 24-36 tones to the octave. The music of Partch frequently accompanies dramatic dance. It is 'pleasingly' dissonant, if a little out-of-tune sounding. He constructed many new instruments specifically designed to play his music. Instruments include: chromelodeon, harmonic canons; cloud-chamber bowls and blow-boys. His best known works are: *Daphne of the Dunes* (1967 from the Film Score *Windsong* - 1958); *Castor and Pollux a.k.a. Plectra and Percussion Dances* (1949-52) and *Delusion of the Fury: Ritual of Dream* and *Delusion* (1965-6).

**George Antheil** –The other American bad boy, Antheil lived from 1900 to 1959. Antheil is most notorious for his contribution to music that glorified and celebrated the machine age. Several piano pieces of the 1920s were infamous for clashing clusters, especially *Mechanisms* (1922-3), *Airplane Sonata* (1922), *Sonatina (Death of the Machines -* 1922) and *Sonate Sauvage* (1922-3). Most famous, though, is his fantastic *Ballet mécanique* (1926; rev. 1953). The revision to the *Ballet...* was made for practical considerations, as the original work, calling for 8 pianos, extensive percussion and airplane propellers forged rhythms and sound simultaneities that were impossible to coordinate. Recently EMF (Electronic Music Foundation) has issued a CD of the original version that used sophisticated electronics. He, along with Luigi Russolo and Alexander Mosolov (*Iron Foundry* - 1927) brought the machine music movement to its apex. Other fine works include the six numbered symphonies (1926-49) and the orchestral overture *McKonkey's Ferry* (1948).

**Luigi Russolo** – Although he was born into Varése's generation, I include this radical pioneer here with younger composers because of his special influence on them. Russolo (b. 1885) was an Italian composer who was swept philosophically by Mussolini's Fascism and its promise of great social improvement through intellectual freedom of exploration. In 1909 he joined the then budding Italian Futurist movement founded by F. Balilla Pratella (music) and Filippo Marinetti (art, speaking on manifestos). Russolo put forth his own manifesto extolling the "art of noises" in his book **L'arte dei rumori**. He built several noisemaking machines, known as 'intonarumori', capable of emitting shrieks, clashes, explosions, groans, etc. Whereas Varèse concentrated on noise from electronics devices, Russolo sought noise from hand-built mechanical devices. His *Il Risveglia di una città* (Awakening of a City - ca. 1913) set the standard for the times. At least one recent masterpiece has been scored for these jewels: Yoshihide's *Anode #4*.

**Alexander Mosolov** – Mosolov (1900-1973) was the most infamous of the so-called Russian Futurists whose works were in vogue briefly in the 1920s. Although his work expands upon similar avenues hinted at in Prokofiev's early work in the Russian canon, he best fits here, with Russolo, the Italian Futurist, for his incorporation of realistic heavy machine sounds. Were it not for his ballet *Zavod* (1927 – "Iron Foundry"), Mosolov would be largely unknown to audiences today. His later drunkenness led to his expulsion from the Union of Soviet Composers. He was limited in his creative effort to a handful of folk songs and piano works, minor in both extent and impact.

**Gavriil Popov** – Popov (1904-1972) contributed to the mood of Russian Futurism as well, though in a somewhat less patent way. His early works were dissonant in almost frightening intensity. Notable among these are the now famous *1st Symphony* (1927-34) and the equally strident Septet (1927). The *1st Symphony* was so ear-piercing that it was known in Russian officialdom as dangerous. Popov soon fell headlong into serious trouble with authorities. He feared for his life. In response he did a turn-about in composing his *2nd*

*Symphony* (1944), noted for its complete lack of controversial sound make-up. This stylistic approach stayed with him throughout the balance of his career, through symphonies 3 to 6 (1947-1970) and other works. What is noteworthy in Popov's works, though, is his vivid originality. That so imbued his symphonies that, despite the reduced dissonance, these works exhibited very unusual forms and sound combinations. Popov really should qualify as a Russian master.

**György Ligeti** – Ligeti was born in Hungary, 1923 – died 2005) Ligeti's musical approach was a compromise between the serialism of Boulez and Stockhausen, both of whom he greatly admired, and the later dense styles forecast by Cerha. He heard Stockhausen's *Gesang der Jünglinge* (1956) on the radio and became interested in serialism, the concepts of which he later mastered by mathematically analyzing Boulez's aphoristically serial *Structures 1a* (1952). He then befriended Friedrich Cerha, whose *Spiegel I-VII* (1960-8), characterized by dense textures, may have interested him. Subsequently he learned electronics from the pioneer Gottfried Michael Koenig. Ligeti's mature style, found in the seminal works such as *Atmospheres* (1960) onwards, is 'Mikropolyphonic', a quasi-serial, dense exposition of internally complex, but gradually emerging counterpoint, wherein chords progress through minimal internal motion (e.g. changing one tone at a time.) Other major works include *Poème Symphonique pour 100 Metronomes* (1962), *Lontano* (1967), *Melodien* (1971), *Double Concerto* for flute, oboe and orchestra (1972), and two string quartets (1954, 1968). Julio Estrada studied his work and developed a highly intricate new form of counterpoint, *discontinuum*, from Ligeti's example. (See Estrada).

**György Kurtág** – Kurtág (b. 1926 Hungary) long lurked in the shadows behind his fellow countryman and near exact contemporary Ligeti. After shedding the mantle of Bartókian expression by 1960 he found his élan. Webern-like cellular movement contained within short durations, have marked his style since 1960. Of all the post-1945 serialists, he most closely approximates post-Webern serialism. His rows are compact, rarely as large as 12 pitches. Often his works are vocal with small instrumental ensemble. Whereas he didn't follow a similar path to that of Ligeti and the latter's mikropolyphonie, he exacted a purity and crystalline sound rarely found in recent music. His best known works include: *Messages of the Late R. V. Troussova* (1981 - vocal and ensemble), *Grabstein für Stephan* (1989 - orchestral), and *Stele* (1994 - orchestral.)

**Luciano Berio** – Berio was initially considered one of the early trailblazing avant-gardists, whose fluid, facile style of serialism opened the way for the development of 'third stream' expository treatment. Born in 1925, he studied under Giorgio Federico Ghedini. He assimilated classics, especially Italian lyrical masters, quickly. In the early 1950s, he, along with his friend Henri Pousseur, joined Maderna, Stockhausen, Nono, and Boulez in the Darmstadt summer courses as a teacher in the new integral serialism that was becoming in vogue. Several early masterworks emerged in the lyrical serial style, including *Nones* (1954), the *Chemins* series devoted to instrumental music (1965-80), *Differences* for tape and chamber orchestra (1959), *Visage* (1961 – tape), and *Eindrücke* (1974). *Laborintus II* (1965) foreshadowed a budding trend in Berio's work toward the emergence of collage styles, which, combined with jazz, would intensify the feeling of a moderating expressivity in the new music. The *Sinfonia* (1969) completed this trend, and is considered the first musical work of post-modern expression. Vocal works are prominent in Berio's output, especially *A-ronne* (1975) and *Coro* (1976).

**Bruno Maderna** – Maderna was born in Italy, 1920. He was an early advocate of the new serialism that Stockhausen and Boulez announced as the only alternative for the music of the future. Maderna joined them to teach for several years at the summer courses at Darmstadt. Maderna combined what he had learned of the olden Italian traditions from Malipiero with an expressive lyrical style under strict serial control. Major works featured *Grande Aulodia* for flute, oboe and orchestra (1969), and the three orchestral frescoes, *Quadrivium* (1969), *Aura* (1971), and *Biogramma* (1972). Ultimately, he joined Berio in search of a more moderate expression. His opera *Satyrikon* (1972) fully tilted his expressive world toward the realm of post-modernism.

**Henri Pousseur** – Pousseur, born in Belgium 1929, became a noted teacher, then a composer of influence with Stockhausen and Boulez in the summer courses at Darmstadt. He studied with Boulez, and befriended Berio. His approach incorporates some elements of collage, tape, serialism and lyricism. He strives to express the goal of man to achieve his maximum potential in expression in all arts. *Votre Faust* (1964-5) incorporates audience dictation of certain actions. Other important works include *Rimes pour Différentes Sources Sonores* (1958-9) for three orchestras and tape, *Trois Visage de Liège* (1961) for tape, and the *Madrigals* (I-II-III – 1958, 1961, 1962) for various instrumental combinations.

**Karel Goeyvaerts** – Goeyvaerts, born in Belgium in 1923, played a major role in early serial development, but didn't figure directly in the Darmstadt teaching activities. A series of letters between Goeyvaerts and Stockhausen reveals Goeyvaerts' early role in this development. Goeyvaerts started the serial methodology in its most formalistic sense in seven crucial experiments, each revealing a highly technical innovation. These works were simply titled 'Compositie nr...' (1 to 7 - 1951-7) in order to emphasize the extreme abstraction of their content; they included use of sine tones, dead tones, and acoustic instruments; his work foreshadowed later electronic works of Stockhausen as well. By the 1950s, though, Goeyvaerts abandoned total serialism dead in his tracks in the middle of the composition of *Compositie nr. 7* – 1955). What followed were works more suited to his highly religious sensitivity. Later works include *Litanie 1-5* (1979-82), *Improperia* (1959), *Avontuur* (1985), *Zomerspelen* (1961) for three orchestral groups, and the opera *Aquarius* (1992). These works exude a warm style only partially imbued with serial structures.

**Krzysztof Penderecki** – Born in 1931, Polish composer Penderecki has generated more controversy than most composers of his time. Vilified by musicians and audiences from both sides of the spectrum, Penderecki has managed to endear himself mostly to the audience in the middle: those who like a little spice, but not too much brutality and harshness. Critics within the avant-garde disdain his work for its blunt, straightforward sound atmosphere; too easy to approach; unsophisticated. The popular concertgoer, however, doesn't like the harsh string writing, no matter how direct it may seem. After the famous *Threnody: for the Victims of Hiroshima* (1960), he composed a few more 'advanced' works, notably *Fluorescences* (1962), *Anaklasis* (1960) and the *St. Luke Passion* (1966). He then turned to writing unabashedly romantic symphonies and was accused as a traitor to modernism. He changed directions again with his more modernist, third opera *The Black Mask* (1986).

**Henryk Górecki** – The beginning of the Warsaw Festival in the 1950s saw the emergence of a large group of Polish composers who were anxious to test their new works in public performance. The leaders were, as expected, Penderecki and Lutosławski. As radical as Penderecki seemed, Górecki was even more radical. Huge, dense microtonal chords were thrust into aural perception, and movement often included whole bands moving over repeated figures. The density was so heavy that Górecki was dismissed as an exhibitionist radical. In the 1970s, though, he spaced out his dense sounds, allowing breathing room and thenceforth followed a series of rather pleasing music, led by the now famous *Third Symphony (Symphony of Sorrowful Songs* - 1976). Other important works are: *Symfonia No. 1 "1959"*; *Zderzenia-Scontri* (Collisions – 1960); and *Symphony No. 2 "Kopernikowska"* (1972).

**George Crumb** – During the 1960s and 1970s, George Crumb was something of an idol among sophisticated American concertgoers too conservative for the radical 60s scene, and yet also too modish for the neo-classical genre. Crumb filled a niche, composing music stylishly cluster-borne, yet subtle in volume and only modestly dissonant. His most famous works are *Echoes of Time and the River* (1968) for which he received a Pulitzer Prize; *Ancient Voices of Children* (1970); *Night Music I* (1963 – rev. 1969); *Music for a Summer Evening (Makrokosmos III* - 1974); and *Black Angels* for electric string quartet (*13 Images from the Dark Land* - 1970).

**Toru Takemitsu** – Takemitsu led an honored life with teaching and lecturing posts worldwide. He is best known for his work as a leading Japanese composer of the avant-garde. In 1951 he and a few others founded Jikken Kōbō, an experimental workshop for the purpose of combining traditional Japanese sound sources with western modernist idioms. This he did most characteristically in a number of breathtaking works in the 1960s and 1970s. Included are *November Steps* (1967), *Arc* (1962), *Coral Island* (1962), *Dorian Horizon* (1966), *A Flock Descends into the Pentagonal Garden* (1977), and *From Me Flows What You Call Time* (1990). Although Takemitsu uses almost every technique in the modernist arsenal, his music comes across as gentle, subtle, exotic, and delicate. He uses silence as a means of achieving tension, rather than loud climaxes. His list of influences is wide and deep, notably John Cage and Iannis Xenakis. He also scored copiously for film (e.g. *Black Rain* – 1989).

**Toshiro Mayuzumi** – Mayuzumi (1929-1997, Japan) is an example of a one-time famous composer whose star fell badly shortly after early successful works. For a time he was heralded, with Takemitsu, as one of the leading Japanese avant-gardists. In fact he briefly worked with Takemitsu in the experimental studios in Japan, creating an important electronic piece *X, Y, Z* (1958.) Another important early work is the *Pieces for Prepared Piano and Strings* (1957.) His reputation suffered somewhat due to the negative perception among his fellow Japanese composers that he was politically too far right wing to warrant support in avant-garde circles. Lately, he has undergone 'rehabilitation' and his music is regenerating some limited currency. His best known works include *Mandala-Symphonie* (1960), *Nirvana-Symphonie* (1958), *Phonologie-Symphonie* (1957), and *Samsara* (1962.) Each of these exhibits his interest in campanology, the exceptional use of bells and gongs.

**Toschi Ichyanagi** – Ichyanagi (born 1933, Japan) was a peripheral experimental composer in the 1960s. He was a leader among composers in Japan who benefited from the example of John Cage, as he was Cage's pupil for a time. In the nineteen-fifties Japan was undergoing a cultural revolution that was marked by the appearance of such composers as Takemitsu, Mayuzumi, Ichyanagi, Takahashi and Matsudaira. Ichyanagi specialized in open forms. He was prodigious in his use of finely crafted notations, having invented certain of the notations for Cage's *Atlas Eclipticalis* (1961-2.) In the nineteen sixties Ichyanagi made a sensation with some works in open form, sometimes characterized as 'wild', by music critics, some of whom were by then accustomed to Cage's work! His best known early works include

*Piano Media* (1972) and *Life Music* (1966). His later works reveal a significant relaxing in his style, even allowing a certain romantic expression. Some later works include *Symphony No. 5* and *Piano Concert No. 3 "Cross Water Roads".*

**Yuji Takahashi** – Takahashi (1938, Tokyo) is the one composer from Japan to have been strongly influenced by Iannis Xenakis, with whom he studied in 1966. He is an outstanding pianist. He has played a number of Xenakis' works, notably *Herma* (1961), proving the piece not unplayable as opposed to reputed characterizations by critics. Takahashi's early music reflects Xenakis' concern for distributions of intervals as was introduced in the 'stochastic' music theory of Xenakis. Takahashi's style was terse and the music rigidly organized. The early works include *Maeander* (1973) and *Yé-guèn* (1970). His later works show a pronounced reduction in tension and are more typified by contemplation. There is even a tinge of Japanese folk flavor in them. Among the later works are *Sugagaki Kuzushi* (1993) and *Mimi No Ho* (1994.)

**Yoritsune Matsudaira** – Matsudaira, Japan (1907-2001) is one of a very few Japanese composers to have developed an interest in European serialism (notably that of Karlheinz Stockhausen). His style adroitly mixes it with Japanese traditional music expression. His music up to 1955 had been influenced strongly by Debussy and Satie, his favorite composers. But by the mid nineteen fifties he wanted to untie his stylistic expression combining romanticism and Gagaku in the European mold. He found a way to structure Japanese music with serialism that is surprisingly convincing. Among his best known works in this later style are *U-Mai* (1957), *Sa-Mai* (1958) *Danza Rituale e Finale (Enbou)* (1959), and *Danza Rituale e Finale (Chogeishi)* (1959.)

**Henri Dutilleux** – Dutilleux, (b. 1916) was another composer of very advanced music in a very subtle vein. This time, though, the subtlety was imbued from a French cultural orientation, rather than Far Eastern. The neglect accorded to Dutilleux is just recently being addressed and he is receiving long overdue performances worldwide. Overshadowed by both Messiaen and Boulez, Dutilleux merely continued to compose music that had the complexity of Berg, the expressiveness of Takemitsu, and the thoroughgoing formal cohesion of a Boulez. His work does not sound like Boulez or Messiaen, though. Beneath those sparkling jewels of sound lurks a neo-impressionistic soundscape that combines the best of Florent Schmitt, Maurice Ravel and Albert Roussel. He breaks little new ground, but sets a standard anyone would envy. His most notable works include: *Symphonie no. 1* (1951); *Symphonie no. 2 'Le Double'* (1959); *Cinq Métaboles* (1965), *Timbres.Espace.Mouvement* (1978), and *L' Arbre des songes* (Tree of Dreams - 1985).

**Jean Barraqué** – This Frenchmen, born in 1928, was by education and temperament a romantic mystic, after Messiaen; however, by age, he was a competitor to Boulez. The romanticism of his idol Beethoven was not fashionable, and he lacked the commanding spirit of Messiaen to attract devotion from any but a very small cadre of followers. André Hodeir, a French music critic in the 1960s once crowned Barraqué (in <u>After Debussy</u>) as the true successor to Messiaen in the annals of French modern music. Since then Barraqué has all but disappeared from the concert scene. Recently, though, a revival of his works has been undertaken. A recording of his complete works is now available on CD set. The dark, romantic undercurrent and the mystic sincerity shimmer, whereas the works of the more abstract serialists can be off-putting at times. His best known symphonic works include: *Les Temps Restitué* (from *The Death of Virgil* – 1957/68); *Chant après chant* (1966); and *Concerto for Six Instrumental Groups and Two Instruments* (1962-8).

**Pierre Barbaud** – Pierre Barbaud was another of a long line of strangely reclusive composers in modern music. He was born in Algiers in 1911, a fact only recently confirmed. He shunned interviews and photographs. He is slowly gaining attention now as the founder and project leader of INRIA (Institut de Recherche en Informatique et Automatique). He thus shared with Boulez and Xenakis a deep interest in research into sound and acoustics. This interest has blossomed into a number of spectacular works. It must be said about those works, though, that most are automatic: that is, they were composed via computer directly from serial algorithms. Unlike Xenakis, who honed the output to obtain ordering that was æsthetically acceptable, Barbaud generally made no such concessions. His best known works are orchestral: *Mu Joken* (1968); *French Gagaku* (Strings – date unknown); and *Hortulus coelicus* (1975) – his lone exception to blind acceptance to untempered computer output. He died in 1990.

**Sylvano Bussotti** – Italian composer (b. 1931) of extreme expression in works focusing on theater, opera, and ballet. He advocated incorporating extremes in his music. Whereas many composers (e.g. Nono) would call for extreme effects at different times for impact, Bussotti often went further, juxtaposing opposite extremes in the same time frame for the purpose of wrenching the opposites into collision. In this last regard he shared with Kagel and Schnebel (even Evangelisti) certain dialectic tendencies in which one can elicit a resolution through confrontation. Certain of these qualities have led him to ponder the deeper questions of the proper role of music and theater in society. He calls much of his work BUSSOTTI-OPERABALLET. He had been a theater director from 1956 to 1981. His most prominent works include *RARA Requiem* (1969), *Bergkristall* (ballet - 1973), *Lorenzaccio,* an opera from which he extracted a symphony (1972), and *Le Passion Selon Sade* (1965).

**Dieter Schnebel** – Schnebel (b. 1930) was a highly controversial musicologist who ushered in the notion of musical expression through bodily processes (breathing, heartbeat, etc.). Key to his work is the Hegelian concept of dialectic: juxtaposing a 'thesis' and an 'antithesis' hoping for annihilation that promises a new beginning. He is the master of null æsthetic, or anti-æsthetic. Key works include his choral masterpiece *für stimmen* (...*missa est*) (1956-69), the combination *Coralvorspiel I & II* (1966/1968-9), and *Lamento di Guerra I und II* (1991).

**Mauricio Kagel** – Kagel (b. Argentina 1931) is one of a group of composers whose use of extremes of sound and extreme opposites in simultaneity characterize works of progressive radical expression. His music before 1972 is characterized by harsh and dense serial structures of deep complexity. In this way he is regarded variously as a discipline of Cage, or, alternatively, of Stockhausen. Like his comrade in radical theater music Schnebel, Kagel prefers multiple action and multiple possible interpretations. Most characteristic of these extreme early works are *Halleluiah* (1967), *Transición II* (1959 – for piano, percussion and tape), *Music for Renaissance Instruments* (1966), and *Heterophonie* for large optional ensemble (1962).

**Franco Evangelisti** – Evangelisti, born 1926 in Italy, was one of Italy's most radical composers. In his short career (he died in 1980) he explored the extremes of all avant-garde expressionism. He composed only a dozen or so works. The critic Heinz-Klaus Metzger notes that Evangelisti was insulted at the turn of music by the mid 1970s, especially the new simplicity movement; he stopped composing altogether, as a result, shortly thereafter. What he did compose, though, provides a clinic in advanced techniques. He incorporated serialism, chance, and matrix control using extreme registers for players. His most representative works include:

*Random or not Random* for orchestra (1957-62); *Incontri di fasce sonore* (1956-7) for tape; *Proiezioni sonore, strutture* per piano solo (1955-56); and *Die Schachtel* (opera – 1962-3).

**Aldo Clementi** – Clementi, born 1925 in Sicily, is a shadowy figure in Italian music of the avant garde. Yet he composed some of the most deeply structured music among the Italians. His music is compacted and intense, weaving intricate polyphony in dense webs of sound. In this he anticipates Górecki in complex cluster sounds. His best works are the *AEB* for 17 instruments (1983); *Concerto* for violin, carillon and 40 instruments (1977) and *Intermezzi* for 14 winds and prepared piano (1977).

**Franco Donatoni** – Donatoni is an Italian composer born in 1927. In his formative years he was considered an especially radical composer combining serialism and chance in unusual ways. At that time he followed a procedure of progressive *de*-composition in which a finished serial work was used as a model for a succeeding family of works using but systematically reducing the structural content. Later works are less formalistic and more expressive, exploiting extremes in dense counterpoint. His main works of the early years include *Quartetto IV, 'Zrcadlo'* (1963) that follows the de-compositional concept through multiple performing versions. Characteristic of the later work are orchestral frescoes including *Portrait* (1975-6), another modern masterwork for Harpsichord and orchestra.

**Hans Werner Henze** – A German radical with Stockhausen in the early 1950s, Henze (b. 1926) soon split with systematic, rigid serialism and became an isolated composer of expressionist pieces, particularly operas employing a free serialism more reminiscent of Berg and Schönberg than of Webern. He was, like Nono and Xenakis, a committed leftist politically, and the subjects of his operas reflect that leaning. His best known opera, for a time, was *König*

*Hirsch* (1952-5; revised 1962 as *Il Recervo)*. Since then *Ondine* (1956-7), a ballet, has enjoyed success. Among his ten extant symphonies, number one (1948) is the most interesting early one; number six (1969) is powerfully expressive.

**Bernd Alois Zimmermann** – Zimmermann, a German, born in 1918, was one of the truly tragic figures in modern music. He was a leading serialist, yet was mostly concerned with tonality-serialism, as opposed to through-composed serialism. He was a flash point early, opposing the rigid formalism of most Darmstadt ideology. This left him isolated and bitter. This and other tragic circumstances (including failing eyesight) led him to commit suicide in 1970, a time during the height of his career. His music was explosive and dense; also, both harshly dissonant, yet expressionist in the manner of Berg and Schönberg. His most moving work, *Requiem für Einen Jüngen Dichter* (1967-9) for speaker, soloist, large orchestra, jazz combo, organ and tape uses texts by several poets, all of whom committed suicide themselves. This was an expression of his personal obsession with thoughts of suicide. Other works include the equally powerful opera *Die Soldaten* (1958-60), based on material similar to Berg's *Wozzeck; Photoptosis,* prelude for orchestra (1968) ; and the eloquent *Concerto for Cello and Orchestra* in the "*Form of a pas de trois*" (1965-6).

**Friedrich Cerha** –Cerha has become famous in composing for his expert completion of the third act of Alban Berg's *Lulu* (1937-79). Born 1926 in Austria, he had a thorough musical education. As a conductor he is important in the presentation of works in the modern repertoire including his own. As a composer, he has been the beneficiary of important first recordings of his *Spiegel I-VII* (1960-68), as well as other orchestral works, notably *Für K* (1993) and *Monumentum for Karl Prantl* (1988). The *Spiegel...* set is particularly important for its pursuit of dense textures, a style that had been shunned by the serialists, in their pointillistic works. Other than the music of Xenakis this work is one of the earliest of cluster music works and it set a new trend, adopted by Ligeti and others.

**Gottfried Michael Koenig** – Koenig, born 1926 in Germany, was an early electronics pioneer. His early studies with Stockhausen pointed the way for future electronics studios. He went to Utrecht, Holland to found the Institute of Sonology. He was director there from the late 1950s until the 1990s. Thereafter, Konrad Boehmer assumed leadership. The focus of the studio has been to find relationships between mental processes in general, especially those associated with sensory perception, and those normally associated with the musical arts. Study has been directed toward discovering sonic fields that link to general perception. Hence Koenig's titles, which include a series of 'color'-*Funktion* works (e.g. his series *Funktion Grün* (1967), *Funktion Rote* (1968) etc., for green and red. Others include orange, blue, grey, etc.). Additional works include the *Terminus* (I-X - 1963-7) series, and his most famous work – *Klangfiguren 2* (1955/57). Other notable composers who have visited this studio include Rainer Riehn and Wouter Snoei.

**Avet Terterian** - Terterian was born in Baku, the Caspian capital of Azerbaijan (1929), although he is normally considered Armenian. Like the following composer Ustvolskaya, he is one of a  very few profoundly original 'Soviet' geniuses who scream for greater attention. He defies classification, as 'avant-garde'. Yet, his music is based on cellular motives that wind their way through the discourse in intuitive ways that meld his essence into the infinite, timeless comos. His music is not exactly harsh, yet it is unconventional, using unusual rhythms in a mysterious weave guided only by the assurance of primal instinct. Orchestral effects in the symphonies can be sharp and piercing; sometimes insistent and primitive. At times electronic shards sear through all the sitting; and waiting for...a *something*...which somehow, 'knows' how and when to happen. His third (1975), fourth (1976), seventh (1987) and eighth (1989) symphonies are recorded and are gaining worldwide attention. He died in 1994.

**Galina Ustvolskaya** – Ustvolskaya (b. Russia 1919) remains one of the most enigmatic and elusive figures in all modern music. She studied under Shostakovich, with whom she briefly shared philosophical and musical focus. Very soon, though, she struck out into territory that was certainly her very own. Her works gradually became more and more austere and she herself became more mystically religious. Few women can be said to have been so sincerely, deeply pious; only Hildegard von Bingen and Lily Boulanger come to mind. In her secret sacred service to Christ through music she found expression through economy. Her textures grew increasingly sparse, nearly to the point of barrenness. Her most powerful works were the set of five *Symphonies* (1955-1990) and the three *Compositions* (1970-1975). *First Symphony* calls for large orchestra and 2 boys' voices. By the *Fourth Symphony - Prayer, (1985-7)* though, she had pared her forces to trumpet, tom-tom, piano and alto! The expression is slow, chant like and barren of special sounds or tone colors, almost as in a reverential contemplation worthy of the monks in medieval music.

**Wolfgang Rihm** – Rihm, German (b. 1952) is a late descendant of Henze stylistically, although he had attended Stockhausen's seminars; he also received counseling from Wolfgang Fortner. Rihm's tonal language varies somewhat within each piece, and more detectably from work to work. The music is highly skillfully structured and comes across as expressive, within a mildly Berg-Schönberg cast. His most famous works include *Ins Offene...* (in more than one version – 1990-2) and *Sphere* (1992-4).

**Gérard Grisey** – Grisey (b. 1946) followed in the footsteps of his teacher Boulez in developing an advanced serial music resplendent in tone color. Grisey was a prominent figure until his tragic death in 1998. He composed music of clear crystalline quality, in extreme colors and contrasts. He attached a name to his compositional process – 'Spectral music' – all the while disclaiming any such system; he states it is merely a frame of mind in composing rich, complex music. His best known works are *Vortex Temporum* (1995), *Talea* (1986), *L'Icone Paradoxale* (1993-4): *Quatre chants pour franchir le seuil* (1997-8) and *Les Espaces Acoutiques* (1976-85) which contains the explosive *Modulations*.

**Tristan Murail** – Murail was another of the 'spectral' composers after Boulez and Messiaen. He was born in Havre, (1947) He was an important founder of Groupe de l'Itineraire. Composers in this group are interested in links between electronics and acoustic instrumental sound. His music is described as Splashes of light-like sound colors that coalesce into waves of sound. His works *Gondwana* (1980) and *Désintégrations* (1982-3) are characteristically luminescent and glittering.

**Hugues Dufourt** – Dufourt (b. 1943) traveled a similar pathway to that taken by Grisey and Murail in his early work. He joined the 'spectral' group a little later (1975). Since, though, he has ventured on his own; his new style is less flowing, incorporating sound bursts and eschewing 'research'. He is a loner following an intuitive pathway. Important works include: *Saturne* (1979); *Surgir* (1984); *La maison du sourd* (1999); and *Lucifer d'apres Pollock* (2001).

**Kaija Saariaho** – Saariaho, Finnish, born 1952, is recognized as one of the leading post-Messiaen, post-Scelsi 'spectral' composers. She has focused for the better part of her composing career a musical expression that reflects upon images from nature or literature without being drawn into programmatic statements. This interest draws its source from her having studied music and fine arts. Saariaho works from a germinal idea as the basis upon which to start, then works gradually into more depth and detail, allowing the ultimate forms to emerge from their own impetus. Saariaho has been characterized as dicing up various textures and splitting them throughout, much as in a dream. Among her best known early works are included *Verblendungen* (1982-4), *Jardin Secret I* (1984-5) ...*sah den Vödeln* (1981), *NoaNoa* (1991). Her later works are represented by *Cinq Reflets* (2001), *Nymphea Reflection* (2001) and *Oltra Mar* (1998-9). She frequently combines unusual instruments, such as prepared piano *(...sah den Vödeln)*, as well as electronics *(Jardin Secret I)*.

**Olga Neuwirth** – Neuwirth is a true one-of-a-kind find. Born 1968 in Austria, she has managed to avoid being chained to any specific group in her very individual style. Although she did study with Murail 1993-4, and did work briefly with 'Stage d'Informatique Musicale' she is fiercely independent. Her music seems to follow mysterious pathways to unforeseen conclusions. It is variously startling, splashy and translucent. It is always vivid. Her best known works are: *Vampyrotheone* (1995) and *Hooloomooloo* (1996/7).

**Helmut Lachenmann** – Lachenmann (b. 1935) was one of a number of students of, and early supporters of, Karlheinz Stockhausen. His pointillistic orientation soon gave way to an extreme ascetic harshness. His new style was a result of his increased interest in the expressiveness of stringed instrument played in unusual ways and achieving unusual textural qualities. He also favored heavy batteries of percussion in his music. His early great string quartet *Gran Torso* (1971-2) is an aggressive masterwork exploring grinding, scraping and other sounds not usually found on string instruments. These are achieved primarily by special bow and finger positions at the bridge and other places. It is a nightmarish ride through extreme sounds that neverthe-less leaves the listener somehow moved. His *Kontrakadenz* (1971) and *Tableau* (1987) are representative of extreme or-chestral plasma with highly expressive percussion sounds.

**Salvatore Sciarrino** – Sciarrino (b. 1947) is an alche-mist of sound. His work, much of it for stage, shows a flair for refined, controlled sound that is unusual even for an Ital-ian lyricist. Sciarrino has a knack for eliciting sounds of the most minute shading and gradation in works that are pri-marily operatic and dramatic. He studied with Evangelisti and developed an avant-gardist taste for the detailed minu-tia that characterize his work at an early age. He frequently uses special electronics effects to enhance acoustic sounds. *Introduzione all'oscuro* (1981), *Lo Spezio Inverso* (1985), and *Perseo e Andromeda* (1990) are his most famous works. Some of his operatic effects are powerful, even in small settings, such as in *Perseo...*, wherein a few instruments are electroni-cally enhanced to elicit sounds of strange, beguiling power.

**Stefano Scodanibbio** – Scodanibbio (b. Italy 1956) has studied with Salvatore Sciarrino. Also, he collaborated with Luigi Nono and Giacinto Scelsi. He has earned a repu-tation of being the world's finest string bass player, having performed exceedingly difficult works of many composers of the avant-garde including Bussotti, Franco Donatoni, Estrada, Sciarrino and Xenakis. John Cage praised him highly. He has composed a number of very beautiful works for string bass solo, string quartet, and other string combi-nations. He uses the most advanced performing techniques in the works of, especially, Xenakis and Estrada, including multiple stops, playing at the extremes of the strings, play-ing underneath the strings, and harmonics. He uses these effects copiously in his own works, setting forth a dazzling array of lyric, expressive sounds. His early work concentrat-ed on extreme sounds and effects within highly controlled frames. More recently, he has allowed the string bass to 'breathe', in lyrical, expansive, still progressive gestures. His works include *My New Address* (1986-8), *Geografia amorosa* (1994), and *The Voyage That Never Ends* (1979-1997).

**Heinz Hoffman-Richter** – Very little is known about this electronics music pioneer publicly. He is composer, conductor and musicologist. His use of aliases has tended to mask his identity throughout his career. An ear lobe tumor seems to have interfered with his interest in continuing his career. Listening to his work, though, creates in the listener the impression of a major pioneer, who has conquered subtlety as well as technique. *Symphony for Tape Delay, IBM Instruction Manual, & OHM Septet* has been recorded. He also composed a *Cantata for Reverb-a-phone* and kitchen instruments.

**Chou Wen-Chung** – Chou (1923) long has been recognized as Varèse's main student. He is China's most prominent composer, although he moved to America and studied under Slonimsky in 1946 and Varèse in 1949. His work has begun to receive attention since its introduction in recording through CRI Records. Chou is a very meticulous composer and has introduced a large variety of new sounds for traditional Western instruments to make them capable of certain Chinese sounds, and he has introduced new instruments. *Yü Ko* (1965) is the most famous work for using Western instruments to adopt a Chinese character. Other works exhibiting a more traditionally modernist cast of serial dissonance include *Landscapes* (1949) and *Pien* (1966.)

**Isang Yun** – Yun (1917-1995) is Korea's prominent avant-gardist. Like many composers of the orient, though he has turned in his more recent works to a romantic idiom that combines some modest dissonance with somewhat standard symphonic handling. *Gasa* (1963) for Violin and Piano is an early example of his avant-garde expressionism. His more recent work includes 5 warmly expressive symphonies (1983-87.) He is famous for his having been spirited away from his teaching activity in Germany by the South Korean police, causing an international scene. Stravinsky and others intervened in his behalf. He was later discharged.

**Morton Feldman** – For years Feldman (1926 - 1987) stood on the sidelines in the shadow of the more ostentatious John Cage. In the early 1950s he joined the so-called New York school of composers, represented by Cage, Earle Brown, Christian Wolff and himself (pianist David Tudor was to associate himself with them shortly thereafter). At first Feldman was a composer of very quiet pieces, which he scored for small instrumental forces on sheets of graph paper. The charts helped him to isolate sounds and simultaneously capture a sense of elastic freedom. He soon discovered, though, that his graphic work was unduly restrictive in a dynamic, movement sense. He then reverted to more traditional scoring still using soft dynamics. His best known works include: For *Samuel Beckett* (1987); *Rothko Chapel* (1971); *Coptic Light* (1986); *Routine Investigations* (1976); and the *Durations...* series (I-V - 1959-60). Some of his works are given whimsical titles (e.g. *Crippled Symmetry* (1983), *False Relationships and the Extended Ending* (1968), and others, perhaps in memory of Erik Satie). Some consider him the germinal catalyst of minimalism.

**Earle Brown** – Brown (b. 1926 Massachusetts) was a long-time sidekick of John Cage. They, along with Morton Feldman and Christian Wolff (and later David Tudor) formed what was once known as the "New York School". They had met in the early 1950s, forming mutual friendships: they occasionally collaborated. Brown was to remain one of the more conservative members of the group. He used chance in a limited way. One of his characteristic methods was to compose in blocks, a mobile form, allowing players to play sections in varying orders from performance to performance. His style was more European in flavor, favoring Webern and some serialism. His most important works are: *Octet I* (1953 – spatially separated magnetic tapes); *November 1953 – Synergy*; *Chef d'orchestra/Calder Piece* (1967); and *Hodograph* (1959).

**Christian Wolff** – Wolff is a French born American, born 1934. As youngest member of the Cage circle he tended toward the most musically radical solutions. Like Cage, he employed generally free, open chance. However, he often tied the performing players' evolving sounds to reactions to what other players were doing. *Burdocks* (1970/1) and the *Tilbury* (1969-96) pieces are his most famous.

**David Tudor** – Tudor (b. 1926) was the most radical of the Cagean group. He joined with Cage in the early 1950s. He uses live electronics combining an intricate looping device and system to force feedback and interaction between tape segments. His music is sometimes referred to as 'environmental. Appropriately, his most famous work is titled *Rainforest I* (1968). Like all this type of music (see Mumma, Lucier, Tone, and Yoshihide) his work is hard as nails on the unaccustomed ear. He died in 1996.

**La Monte Young** – Young is hailed often as the grandfather of minimalism. John Adams, Philip Glass, Terry Riley and Steve Reich followed Young's lead by reducing melody and harmony to near repetition. This really wasn't what Young had in mind, though. Born Idaho, 1935 his early studies drew his interest to unusual scales and intonation. Several of his works involve long drones under tones in just intonation that last many minutes at a time. In his dream works, Young concentrates on extremely gradual evolution of sounds over lengthy time periods. This is notable in the titles of some of his works. Best known are: *23 VIII 64 2:50:45-3:11 AM the volga delta* (1964) for bowed gong and

The *Second Dream of the High Tension Line Stepdown Transformer from the Four Dreams of China* (1962-84) for brass.

**Pauline Oliveros** - Oliveros, US, born 1932, once had the distinction of being the most radical woman composer. Her composing activities involved constructions of tape devices and loop techniques. In 1966 she had become dierctor of the Tape Music Center of Mills College at Oakland, California. She contributed a piece to the ONCE Festival in Ann Arbor, Michigan (*Applebox Double* - 1965 - a piece performed by scraping and rubbing objects connected to a box with electronic attachments including a Buchla Box 100 series) Other works include *Beautiful Soop* (1966) and *Alient Bog* (1967).

**Donald Scavarda** – Scavarda (b. 1928) studied at the University of Michigan. Together with Gordon Mumma, Robert Ashley, George Cacioppo and Roger Reynolds in the early 1960s, he co-founded the now famous ONCE series of concerts in Ann Arbor, Michigan. This setting was a radical venue for the most extreme music until that time. Scavarda's contributions are many, and just now getting attention. He is most famous for *Matrix for Clarinetist* (1962) and *Landscape Journey* (1963) for clarinet and piano, accompanying a film by Scavarda. *Matrix* also was published in <u>Generation Magazine</u> in 1962 at the University of Michigan. In these works he explored the region of multiphonics (1960!) six years prior to Bruno Bartolozzi's (1911-80) publication (1968/82) on the topic. *Sounds for Eleven* (1961), pitting 'living' sounds (winds – held tones) against 'dying' sounds (percussion – brittle) explores new territory in time elasticity. *Groups for Piano* (1959), is a study in extreme distillation of time.

**George Cacioppo** – Like Scavarda, almost forgotten among the ONCE group of composers, Cacioppo set out to rescue modern music from the tides of oblivion. Born 1927 in Michigan, he studied at University of Michigan.

His classmates in Finney's classes included Scavarda and Mumma. He became one of ONCE's founding members. He was original in his use of time schemes that incorporated special play of wind instruments. He created an unusual scheme for his most famous work *Cassiopeia* (1962), one of three studies for piano titled *Pianopieces* (1962). The scheme is a diagram, mimicking a schematic of the brain. The nodes are notes with numbers the player must traverse according to Cacioppo's directions involving intricate metrical play. Equally engaging is his *Advance of the Fungi* (1964) based on Ernest Large's book on the potato blight of 1845-1940. *Time on Time in Miracles* (1964) contains very sensitive sounds by winds and soprano.

**Bruce Wise** – Wise (U.S. born 1929) can be described as more introspective than the main five ONCE composers. Although a founding member he never really meshed completely into the raw experimental pattern set by the others. His interests took him elsewhere in a doctoral program two year later. His best known works are *Two Pieces for Piano and Chamber Group* (1958) and *Music for Three* (1963).

**Robert Sheff (a.k.a. "Blue" Gene Tyranny)** – Sheff, born in Texas in 1945 formed the nucleus of a Texas group of composer/performers who joined ONCE in 1962. Others included Philip Krumm (*Music for Clocks* 1962), George Crevoshay *(7PTPC)*, and Larry Leitch (performer). Sheff composed *Ballad* (1960) and *Diotima* (1963) for the group. Since then he has become Ashley's personal piano accompanist under the name "Blue" Gene Tyranny. Under the latter name his best known work is The *CBCD Variations* (1980).

**Roger Reynolds** – Reynolds (b. Detroit 1934) was one of the original founding members of the ONCE group in Ann Arbor in the early 1960s. Of those composers, he is the best known to the audience at large because he has mainly shifted from the deeply American experimental tradition by around 1970 to a more urbane European avant-garde style. He won the Pulitzer Prize in music in 1988 for his *Whispers out of Time*, making him the first 'radical' composer to win that award. More famous to countercul-ture aficionados are his ONCE pieces: *Ping* (electronics - 1969); *Traces* (1968); and *A Portrait of Vanzetti* (1962-3).

**Robert Ashley** – Ashley (b, Ann Arbor 1930) was, with Mumma, the most radical of the ONCE compos-ers. With Mumma, Lucier and David Behrman he per-formed original works in the Sonic Arts Union during the late 1960s. His most famous works are divided into two periods: the ones composed during the ONCE years and the later theater works. Among the 1960s early works, most prominent are: *In Memoriam Crazy Horse – Sym-phony* (1963); the *Wolfman* (1964); and *Bottleman* (1960). Later works of note are the *She was a Visitor* (1967), and *Purposeful Lady, Slow Afternoon* (1968). The early works are characterized by extreme high ranges and volumes in electronics, mixed in very original ways. The later works are quieter, slower and contemplative, but often focusing on texts of trivial or even questionably tasteful subjects.

**Gordon Mumma** – Mumma (b. 1935 US) was the most radical of the ONCE group. He composed several works for the group, including *Sinfonia for Twelve Instruments and Magnetic Tape* (1958-60), and *Megaton for Wm. Burroughs* (1963). In these works, Mumma experimented with new tape and machine circuitry, forcing the machines to disgorge unimaginable sounds. Other notable works have followed, including several for the Sonic Arts Union, formed in the late 60s with Alvin Lucier, David Behrman and Ashley. The most famous use cybersonic devices (derived from *'cybernet-ics'*, relating to networks, circuits and human interaction.) *Cybersonic Cantilevers* (1973), *Mesa for Cybersonic Bando-neon* (1966), and *Hornpipe* (1967) lead the list. In *Hornpipe*,

Mumma plays an altered horn in concert duet with interactive computer circuitry that reacts to the altering sound space.

**Alvin Lucier** – Leading member (b. 1931 US) of Sonic Arts Union, friend of Mumma, Ashley and Behrman. His work explores very unusual landscapes, physical territory, etc. Brain Waves are converted into sound, echo devices seek confining frames within a dark space, and special electronic characteristics are explored in Lucier's sound schemes. His most well known works include: *Music for Solo Performer* for Amplified Brain Waves and Percussion (1965); *Vespers* (Echo clicker - 1969); *Clocker* for Amplified Clock, Galvanic Skin Response Sensor, Digital Delay System (1978-88); and *Music on a Long Thin Wire* (1977).

**David Behrman** – Americanized Austrian born in 1937, Behrman is a shadowy figure in ONCE and Sonic Arts Union music history. He was trained as an electronics technician and musician. As a producer for Columbia Records he met Mumma, Ashley and Lucier. He soon discovered that his activities were similar to those of the others. Himself a homespun experimenter with electronics gadgetry, he joined forces in the Sonic Arts Union. His most famous works are *Runthrough* an improvisatory piece on cheap (Behrman) electronics equipment (1960s) and *My Dear Siegfried* (2003 – five music pieces for players improvising and interacting to texts of letters between Behrman's father Sam and Sam's German friend Siegfried Sassoon in wartime 1939). Behrman's *On the Other Ocean* (1977) is also recorded. His style is less abrasive than that of the other Sonic Arts Union members.

**Yasunao Tone** – Japanese composer (b. 1935 – ) and friend of Cage. Tone incorporates logic-interruptive experimentation to turn controlled sound impulses into feedback. His work rests on a concept he calls 'wounded CD', in which normally processed sound patterns are interrupted on their way into the processing of CD imprint and converted via 'yes-no' inversion, creating seeming noise and sound-'junk'. The crucial question here is one of the creation of a new æsthetic, one in which symmetries are maintained under inversion, so as to create seeming random noise by rigorous initial logic. Best known work: *Wounded Man'yo 2/2000* (2000). This is bizarre, jarring music; but it teaches one to reach far down inside to challenge just what one's æsthetics *really* mean!

**Toshiya Tsunoda** - Some random vingettes on this enigmatic environment composer: *A signboard, wind blown* (1997) "A contact microphone was set in the gap between wooden frame and iron sheet" (Tsunoda); *Cicada and window* (1999) "This was recorded in my room on an early midsummer's afternoon" (Tsunoda); *40 oscillators - Hayasa installation* ("...The exhibition site space was a factory...") (Tsunoda); *Pier* (1998); *Heater and Amplifier* (1995). "A living space has two types of vibration: the vibration through air; and the vibration through solids." © *sirr.ecords 2003. sirr 2012* .

**Otomo Yoshihide** – He is known as leader of the current Japanese underground counterculture. He was born in (1959). Here, even more than in the case of Tone, we have noise-machine action, deploying such devices as turntable circuitry overload and feedback. His best known work is *Turntable Solo* (2002). Here again, new æsthetic territory is lain open. Is there an æsthetic inherent within a machine whose design was intended for altogether different purposes? Is the æsthetic in the machine or in the machine in combination with the 'performer'? The latter; and this is welcome new work. Another crucial work is the intonarumori piece *Anode 4* (date ca. ~2000?). Again, if one thinks of composers such as Mumma, Lucier, etc. as sonically extreme, try this. It is not for delicate ears, or the constitutionally weak!

◆◆◆

# APPENDIX A
## Re-Considerations of Some Musical Thinking

Here are some thoughts on Key musical ideas that go together in what we consider the building of a "sound-based" composition.

## Klangfarbenmelodie

We surveyed some new ideas in the text concerning tone-color melody. We showed the historical development in bits and pieces sprinkled through the original work of the composers. Let's take a look at how the compact discipline stands.

First, some background: by mid-20th century there appeared to be proliferation with no hope of unity. Free atonality, serialism, free chance, indeterminacy, stochastics, clustering, eclecticism, collage, protocubism, neo-classicism, dada, neo-baroque, neo-romanticism, impressionism and expressionism all were touted in various quarters as the wave of the future. Ultimately, post-modernism emerged as an 'antidote' to the complexities and difficulties inherent within certain of these trends, especially in total serialism and indeterminacy.

One of the prominent features of post-modernism lies in the use of collage in composition. This technique relies upon a gathering together of seeming-diverse sounds, patterns, styles, etc. in a soup of mixed effects. However, this 'solution' is really a refusal to choose. If one believes that one may escape the grueling demands of original work by hiding from disciplined choice behind that which has gone before, the art of serious composition need proceed no further. One may as well say, "I give the responsibility for original work to someone else. I can entertain listeners without it."

I believe that the signs of decay in a culture are reaped by such attitudes. The apex of the ancient Greek and Roman civilizations, for example, existed in the days of high literature and of original mathematical discovery. Those days gave way to ones of 'commentary' upon older original work. This led to decay. A civilization that cannot create afresh, but can only re-create, will decay.

Composition and new music, as research and teaching tools, best serve to achieve the goal of returning music to its triple role. Entertainment is good in its appropriate context; but only research and teaching can elevate art making to a lofty status. These are the activities that protect the mind from intellectual atrophy.

The work of one prominent composer of the last century serves as a pertinent example for all present-day composers. This composer, the greatest radical in music history, was basically self-taught. Arnold Schönberg needed no stereotypical crutch, though, to help him launch his revolution from which music has never recovered. His mantra was to explore; to be true to oneself. This severity of purpose resulted in his special gifts to us, not the least of which is "tone-color melody". It is a method that required of him travel along the hard road, a road that offered no simple answers. His Germanic term, *klangfarbenmelodie*, has stuck by virtue of its own ring. This approach requires an exceptionally keen rigor. It also requires deep understandings of the nature of sound, hard won through study and focus upon one's most advanced composing skills. Today, we can continue to create great and original work through similarly disciplined methods, thereby avoiding the pitfalls associated with easy eclecticism.

How can the concept of *klangfarbenmelodie* be marshaled to rescue musical discipline from torpid conformity? Music's rescue can be achieved through a real understanding of the historical development of *klangfarbenmelodie* and its role in the music of diverse 20th century composers. First, what is *klangfarbenmelodie*? Is it simply tone-color melody? What is that? The answer to these questions requires a little background, so the following survey provides a tracery for what occurred throughout the 20th century.

Schönberg freed music from the bonds of traditional tonality. This freedom enabled him to concentrate on sound qualities, as opposed to arrays. The regimen of expressionism demanded absolute focus upon appropriate sounds to capture an ambience that would conjure certain feelings. Some of these emotions were unpleasant and extraordinary. They required special sounds conveying unusual traits. In his work with this, Schönberg noticed that changing timbre was capable of carrying the freight of musical patterns. The transformation of color (the variance of preferred harmonics within the overtone series) acted in a manner akin to transformation of pitch. So, whereas pitch change conferred a melody upon a stream of sound, timbral change ought to be able to perform an analogous function. Let's examine two opposing techniques that Schönberg brought to bear: one was Sprechstimme, or speech-song, a kind of inexact pitch setting; the other was intense tone-color control within an exact pitch context. These diverse techniques actually worked harmoniously with one another to enrich the sound spectrum available to Schönberg. And they required high discipline in sound manipulation. Though this exacted considerable effort, Schönberg was up to the task!

A crucial work in this œuvre was the *Five Pieces for Orchestra* (1909.) The classic third movement, Farben (Colors), consists of a slowly emerging sound flux with changing instrumentation and special handling to elicit evolving timbres. In theory, Schönberg posited, a whole melody could be devised within a single tone --timbral variation alone -- thereby carrying the role normally associated with pitch variation. (In fact, the tones in Farben's setting do transform between pitches very gradually, leading to a slightly impure realization of the master's original concept.) He had actually confided his new approach to Mahler, who vehemently disagreed with him regarding its validity. Interestingly, shortly thereafter, Mahler was to develop a variant of his own on the idea of tone coloration that bears distant roots within the klangfarbenmelodic handling.

This variation upon Schönberg's 'theme' was a quasi-hocket handling of tones in a melody (the 12th century hocket form is a contrapuntal handling which prescribes sudden interruptions with alternation of voices.) In this method each separate tone was assigned its unique instrument so that tone color is changed within the phrase, almost note-by-note, but each color was assigned to a discrete pitch. This is not real tone-color melody, but a distant cousin; one, the distinction of which, I believe will clarify some crucial differences between certain seemingly similar trends in advanced music (e.g., between that of Penderecki or Ligeti, and that of Xenakis, which we examine later).

This particular handling of Mahler's can be seen in his masterpiece, *9ᵗʰ Symphony* (1909-10), in the opening measures. A tone is repeated, but stated in different instruments (horn, cello, and harp), then elaborated by pitch additions with harp and muted horn shaping the phrase in a set of answering mottos. This handling was expanded greatly in the work of Anton Webern, especially in his *Symphonie* (1929), and *Concerto* (1934.)

This concept of tone-color melody ushered in a new concentration upon special tone qualities that invites much further work. Not much is done in this arena in universities, inasmuch as collaging and set-ordering are emphasized, instead. Tone-color melody demands an understanding and a focus that are inherent in the disciplines associated with truly sound-based composition. The nature of sound and the way we perceive it are part and parcel of both sound-based composition in general, and *klangfarbenmelodie* in particular. Indeed, *klangfarbenmelodie* is a special technique within the general concept of sound-based composition.

Equally important to this ground-breaking development was a parallel current in the music of Debussy, Varèse, Messiaen, and Estrada - something I will call color-chord harmonics. We recall Debussy's use of chords in purely coloristic, non-functional ways. He went further. He used chordal patterns in repetition to carry a role analogous to timbre in the sound frequency sense. The chords mean something entirely new.

Varèse used chords as shifting planes of sound, so that the melodic discourse was framed by sound blocks that carried special meanings in different registers.

Messiaen went even further in his use of specific, special chords that carry meaning within a certain context such as the mode two sectioning of the tritone into two minor thirds, as opposed to mode three which contains a major third and a major second. The modes were reserved for special handling. His traversing through the chords took another turn analogous to timbre.

Within more recent developments, Xenakis' work has introduced a couple of very interesting variations on Schönberg's concept of tone-color melody, as unexpected as this interrelationship may seem to be. A special case is found in Xenakis' delicate earlywork, *Atrées* – (*Hommage à Pascal* - 1962.) The opening of section one unfolds a static single tone subjected to some sophisticated color variations. Flat (non-vibrato) tones in clarinet and violin transform to tremolo (violin) on the same pitch, and back. These and similar fabrics evolve and emerge on that same pitch for a period of a couple minutes. More in a theoretical context, Xenakis discusses in great detail his handling of timbral (or cloud amalgamations) evolutions in his groundbreaking book, *Formalized Music: Thought and Mathematics In Music* (Iannis Xenakis, Pendragon Press , Stuyvesant New York, 1962), pp.50-63, chapter II "Markovian Stochastic Music – Theory". He outlines here his use of logic screens by which timbre may be evolved through time. His *Orient-Occident III* (1960) reveals some breathtaking, evolving timbral sound via his having used logic screens. A more controversial look at tone color in Xenakis' work concentrates upon examining his handling of clouds of sound in *Pithoprakta* (1955-56), or the granularities in *Bohor I* (1962.)

I implore the listener/reader, upon encountering these two latter works, to treat the massive array of individual particles of sound not as a collection of individual, discrete tones, but as a single, sound-mass in flux: one that bubbles, gurgles and erupts. Here lies the basis for a crucial distinction, previously suggested, to be made between Xenakis' work and that of other seemingly related composers of the so-called cluster camp (especially Penderecki and Ligeti.) This distinction emerges from the fact that Penderecki and Ligeti, in their work of this kind, do not really handle masses containing innumerable, inseparable, packets in flux, as does Xenakis. Their early pieces (notably *Threnody: To the Victims of Hiroshima* – Penderecki - 1959-61; and *Atmospheres* – Ligeti – 1961) handle massed bands of sound that usually move as a unit, rather than in flux. They do handle points, but when they do, these points remain discrete and separable. Timbral variation in the work of these composers is more like that in Webern's work: discrete tones, discrete timbres. Xenakis' work has the characteristic of a large mass under real timbral evolution, part of which is internal granularity. This quality of single-tonal transformation is elaborated even more in the work of Giacinto Scelsi, albeit on a very miniature scale.

Scelsi's work brings *klangfarbenmelodie* to a focal point. Never in musical history has a single tone received more intense scrutiny than it does in Scelsi's work. (One critic even considered Scelsi's work to consist entirely of transition!). The best example here is the epic *Quattro Pezzi* (1959.) In this work, microtonal variations within variable amplitudes combine with variable vibrato and dynamical variations, as sound breaks into split octaves. These split sounds thusly amplify the harmonics. This is strange music in which serpents from another world seem hurled through unimagined dimensional barriers. Sounds 'orbit', then hover. This is delightful plasma of sound in turmoil! I wonder if Schönberg could ever have imagined this, or the sound world of Xenakis!

As a last journey, we trace *klangfarbenmelodic* discipline straight through into Estrada's *continuum*! Estrada's *Ishini'ioni* (1984-90) follows incredibly complex pattern-transforming that treats timbre, sound frequency and intensity in a unitary complex, part of the evolving macro-timbre.

(Note that Estrada uses TWO sets of staves, to enable him to place extraordinary controls over the changes in sound.) The ghosts unfurled in shards of sound will infuse the listening mind with an indelible impression of wonder in the making. Through this concentrated effort, the listener will become sensitive to the care and diligence spent in the composer's effort to communicate something original, and of *value*! The best music making demands no less. This is gorgeous stuff. But it transcends entertainment value; it teaches possibilities that I know some composers don't realize exist. It also provides a template for further research. Estrada's *Continuum Theory*, the unfolding of which is so rich in this example, will be examined in a book (in French - *Le Continuum*.)

No discipline worth its salt rests solely upon the rock of comfort. These morsels provide a promise of musical enrichment, and of new disciplines promised for the music of the future. *Klangfarbenmelodie* has many forms. Its understanding will pave the way for the special understandings demanded for the field of sound-based composition.

♦♦♦

## APPENDIX B
## Perceptual Transformations in
## Modern Music

Progressive modern music exhibited a tremendous change in all objective elements between the years of 1890 and 1945. With Debussy harmony lost its mooring. Harmony no longer worked in step with melody to create and underscore a tonality. Chords were handled in a fashion analogous to timbre. Tonality could be suspended with the introduction of whole tone, octatonic, acoustic and chromatic scales. Stravinsky and Bartók introduced frequent and dense dissonance to create a polytonal atmosphere of sound. Then Schönberg took what appeared to be the final step: dissolution of the diatonic tonal system altogether in his introduction of 'pan'-tonality (his term). This term is used to imply the inclusion of all twelve equal tempered keys simultaneously and equally! Most often the term atonality is used to signify a total lack of any tonality, a rendering which Schönberg detested. Berg's particular contribution was attachment of specific significance to numbers and the place in structure (numerological construction.).

In the 1940s Webern and Varèse took music to its most radical extent then-to-date, in the entire abandonment of traditional phrase structure. For Webern, it was the distillation of expression to the essence contained within the isolated single tone, as though to shrink a complete melody to its stark skeletal value. For Varèse it was the clashing densities and planes of sound that avoided any semblance of phrase whatsoever. So at this time music had been shorn of its traditional meanings in melody, rhythm, harmony, and phrase. Surely, one would wonder, this must be the last step possible in the dismemberment of musical composition.

How must it have been, then, that an advanced avant-garde could emerge after 1945? What we would see was new emphases on densities and timbre. More revolution at first seemed to create wide-spread confusion and a dissipation of concentrated effort; we would see bewildering panoply of special cases with no rigorous establishment of any overarching master plan. This in fact was the case, but only for a short period, after which an emergence of new fundamental principles would take center stage. What had seemed aimless began to take on a radical new shape that would ultimately shake the very foundations of æsthetics!

First, we engage a brief journey into early uncharted territories. Around about 1960 the short-term fixation on method and serialization finally disintegrated. Soon composers began finding ways to enhance the sound stuff directly. In this sense I suppose Varèse would be a first model, as in his work all effort was directed to experimenting with sound sources to find and elicit new sounds. Any mechanical aid was directed toward the structuring of intervals to heighten the sense of sonic uniqueness in carrying the musical argument forward. Put bluntly, Varèse almost never employed a row or serial technique. His orderings were guided by the value in the sounds, and transformation, and not in ordering pitch frequencies. Pitch frequencies in and of themselves contain little information compared to the richness evident in evolving overtones driven by alterations through the harmonic series.

The result of serial manipulation is flat emotional construct with varying frequency levels. It's boring. However, around 1960, just as Varèse was completing his sound miracle, Scelsi and Xenakis entered the scene to provide a complete expansion and overhaul of æsthetic context as had been understood. Cage had entered the scene in the forties, but it had taken until the sixties for his mark to be fully measured. These three composers engaged in revolutions that were at opposing ends of the scale. Before consideration of their work I inject here a brief commentary on cluster music that was beginning to appear. The Polish and Hungarian composers, prominently Lutosławski, Górecki, and Penderecki (Polish), and Kurtág and Ligeti (Hungarian) sought to free music from its limitations of sounding either pointillistic or spaghetti-like in strands that resulted from serial concentration. They brought dense chord clusters into play to introduce a depth sense. Their handling was usually intuitive and not systematic (although that is not always so in Ligeti's case.) Even if dissonance had been dense there was a flow of motive that still behaved in concordance with older practice. Beauty could be reframed in terms of mass motion.

Scelsi embraced his revolutionary concept of internal counterpoint in his seminal **Quattro Pezzi** (1959). Here, for the first time, counterpoint could be applied to what was happening inside the unit tone in terms of transforming timbre. The revolution had passed harmony and melody and entered into micropolyphony. This concept is marshaled to organize evolutions of sound on the small scale. Estrada would formalize the concepts here in his revolutionary theories on the *continuum* and *discontinuum* that have been discussed already. Beauty is energized by the minute organism.

On the opposite side, Cage introduced chance as a means of breaking down a feeling of rigidity. Fortuity eliminates any argument of progress in the usual Western sense. The obvious question here is what is the meaning of æsthetics in this sound environment?

On the way along these explorations æsthetics was a concept under increasing assault. Truly, what had seemed to be an underpinning of an agreed upon and fixed understanding of what was beautiful was coming apart.

## The Vaporization of Constancy

Xenakis provided us with the first real clue that we were in for a rough ride unless we would completely examine what we meant by æsthetics, indeed beauty. Dictionaries invariably invoke the words "of or pertaining to beauty" in defining æsthetics. But then that begs the reader to look up beauty; yet, here we find little help, as beauty is characterized as that which gives pleasure. These ideals are hopeless and need rethinking. What I find "pretty (?)" is not guaranteed to provide pleasure to others. A conglomerate of sound may, in the classical sense, be disarmingly sumptuous and limpid. And, granted, the way we have been conditioned in our upbringing, we would usually call that "beautiful."

Is a bird-song beautiful? Taken in context as merely a collection of euphonious sounds, one argues, yes, of course; however, notice that the bird-song in its unvarnished sound-array is not diatonic. Immediately we have created a setting of contexts to elicit what we consider beautiful, *given the setting.*

Even cluster music, (say of Penderecki or Crumb) may seem euphonious, if also dissonant. Is it pleasurable, or "pretty"? Some say yes, some no. One will find it necessary to establish a predominating edifice within each work one may compose to "set the bar" for what is, within the piece, beautiful, or æsthetically pleasing; then plan around the basis or foundation to allow for an evolution of æsthetic meaning. In these contexts, one may even argue that the concept moves along a spectrum so that what may seem ugly in one context is beautiful in the one at hand!

A mathematics professor, George David Birkhoff, 1884-1944, sought to establish æsthetic foundations deductively (Livio p. 12-14). The results of this were published in his book Æsthetic Measure. Yet, as well based as this approach may seem, the final arbitration is still intuitive and ephemeral. Mathematical argument cannot establish taste á priori as a natural force. Æsthetics still comes down to learned experience. If we assume that what we normally experience as pleasure is a given, anyone, math professor or not, may establish deductively its validity. That is circular. It can be challenged on every ground. Rather than being a fixed entity on a static or unchanging scale, æsthetics is a dynamic concept, variable in its existence and completely contextual. Æsthetics, then, is truly "in the eye of the beholder!"

Getting back to Xenakis, he introduced the ugly into musical discourse on equal footing with all values along the scale[1]. As a piece establishes its particular ambience it sets the scale of its æsthetic content. As more and more of "that ugly stretch" unfolds, the more ones ear becomes acclimated to it and one would actually distrust the sudden appearance of normally diatonic sounds; they would be *unbeautiful* in the context!

---

1 Luigi Nono introduced ugliness into his music, also, in a different way and for a different purpose. Estrada has employed this collision of opposites most regularly.

Estrada explores this reality quite rigorously in his *continuum* scheme.

## **Value Neutral Æsthetics**

Let's reevaluate what should be understood in the unfolding of an æsthetic in the framework of progressive modern music.

>>An *æsthetic* is a value ascribed to an event. <<

This value need not be preferential, and especially need not be prejudicial within considerations of cultural or personal taste norms. Value is useful as a means of establishing hierarchical manipulation of music operators in the act of changing event quality or transformations. The æsthetic taken in this fashion is a quality indicator in the way 'red' or 'orange' may signify an abstract, or objective color quality; not good, bad, preferred, or otherwise, as a subjective formulation. Likewise sounds handled in the fashion of evolution under transformation set up certain abstract templates necessary to the discourse.

We must, of course, first agree upon what a value is. A value is an agreed upon characterization of a module. We ascertain how we wish to characterize this module. It may not be pretty, ugly, desirable, or euphonious. Perhaps it is overtone heavy, or truncated. Maybe it's in a shape, such as a fixture or template. This template, or setting, may then act as the fountainhead of the work as a whole. One major flaw in trying to apply emotionally heavy meanings is that, surprising though this may seem, the expansiveness of possible expression becomes limited, and new territory is preferentially closed off to exploration in the piece.

The music of the progressive avant-garde is interested in the widest possible range of expression. So a composer's employing unrestricting classifications are preferable.

Let's view this in a more general sense. Æsthetic constructs are torsional forces in an operational field. Such constructs are used to set sound in motion, creating a sound-wheel; the sound-wheel being a musical argument. How do we perceive it? How does the composer desire us to respond to it? A composer may approach an audience as final arbiter of musical value, and thereby treat listener prejudice as final paradigm for expression. Normally this does not demand much from the listener; standard practice is all that is necessary in the offering of enjoyable experience for the listener. Music thus framed becomes an entertainment tool. Æsthetics are limited and prejudicial here.

On the other hand, I postulate the introduction of a value-neutral æsthetic field with a much wider scope that takes in the prejudicial ring as a special case. In the new wide-arrayed æsthetical field we have possible soundscapes as much new as familiar. The familiar moorings attending the old limited ring are missing, at many times, in the newer, wider field. Avoiding the tendency to get lost, signposts must be provided; but there is much greater expressive flexibility as a reward. Expression may venture into further regions of discourse than those to which we are habitually accustomed. In an abstract æsthetic context, the listener cannot grasp a sense of position without some base as a frame of reference. All unusual construct must somehow be linked through memory to its opposite! Think of a magnetic bar, with two poles, one at each opposite end. Each end shimmers in a quasi-magnetic glow appropriate to its opposing position. The composer will employ an æsthetic frame suitable to his/her argument, and the particular ambience contained therein. (Think of Arnold Schönberg's expression of fear;

he eschews the feel-good preferential æsthetic in favor of a less well-known one.) The new construct is not meaningful without some memory of its opposite. Fear and repose are extremes. The gamut may be explored through time from one end to the other. This provides richness and contrast (and balance.)

At the beginning, a composer may overtly employ only one end, but the effects of the other end are still present, even though submerged. As the play progresses, the other end may surface, causing a rupture or tear in the musical fabric, in a confrontation of opposites. Here catastrophe may appear. The range may be systematically explored until all values conjoin; *this becomes the point whereby the "pretty" and the ugly commingle and even exchange positions – and real beauty emerges!*

## Æsthetic complexes, multiples, variables and the null æsthetic

The vast selection-field of æsthetics has been subjected to vigorous exploration recently by avant-garde and experimental composers of all persuasions. These developments are worth exploring here to reveal the richness of the new æsthetic horizon.

A fast look at certain key composers will suffice for this brief survey. One may propose, for instance, a multiple æsthetic. This proposition was widely explored in the 1960s in the works of Sylvano Bussotti (b. Italy 1931) and Mauricio Kagel (b. Argentina, 1931.) In mixed handling, these composers scored for very unusual instrumental combinations, often pitting extremes of range, intensity, timbre etc. against their opposites. Bussotti was quite direct in his expressive approach, as he frequently explored extreme expressionistic sounds in vocal and instrumental scoring traversing the entire sound range. *Lorenzaccio-Symphonie,* an extract from the grand opera of the same title, (1972) provides a good example of this.

Kagel often went even further; he pitted different instruments against one another in opposition, by assigning to each an opposing extreme of sound-type in turmoil! Several works may be exemplary. One is tempted especially to cite *Hallelujah* (1967) and *Heterophonie* for orchestra (1962) as two frightful, yet effective settings.

The other extreme case rich in this kind of potential is the strange case of Dieter Schnebel (b. Germany 1930). His *Coralvorspiel I/II* (1966/68-9) is an eerie setting of sobbing vocal sounds interjected into, over, under, and through a totally flat-line expression, led by an uninvolved/anti-involved organ/'nebeninstrumente' (auxiliary instruments) mélange into disquietude and unease. The qualification of this oblique world would be close to a null æsthetic. This possibility is given rise by virtue of a complete lack of emotional engagement between sound sources and audience emotional state. It is a music space about sound and empty expression in a surreal world of opposites.

The analysis of the latter position would necessarily conclude that such strange lack of connection results most likely from Schnebel's position as closer to Cagean experimental music than to 'ordinary' avant-garde expression. Thusly put, the obvious next question becomes: might there be two distinct positions possible in null-æsthetical discourse? That would request both a null æsthetic born of unconcern as a choice, and a null æsthetic born of necessity! Is it either, or both? Can there be a situation in which an experimental music environment demands null-æstheticism?

I believe that such an option is valid as a quality in European avant-garde music; of the music of Schnebel and perhaps a few others. I believe this is so because the European mind-set is more expressive by culture than that of recent American experimentalism.

In America, experimentalism takes deliberately extreme forms. I touch on three examples; John Cage (b. 1912), Alvin Lucier (b. 1931) and Gordon Mumma (b. 1935). Cage's case is well known by now. His work is characterized by chance, and, of necessity eschews any æsthetic whatsoever. The work of Mumma and of Lucier is more complex. There are ways to argue that we may encounter here a sort of 'found' æsthetic. In Mumma's case, we could have an æsthetic of the machine; of the electronics equipment itself, sliced out from the composer himself, entirely. Or, the other, more obvious way to view it is to concede that there is no æsthetic at all. Need this to be the case in the works of Mumma and Lucier, and any who may follow in their footsteps? I don't know. More work is required here in analyzing live electro- or 'box' music. One might interpret this either way.

An interesting case arises from the recent Japanese countercultural, alternative music scene. Although, technically Yasunao Tone (b. Japan 1935) is really more fluxus movement than a member of the latter-named movement, he poses the strangest case for interpreting æsthetical content in music yet. His most famous recent activity involves what he considers "wounded CD", in which the work at hand may be carefully composed and yet the digital CD instructions are interrupted at the point of realization by turning "1's" to "0's" and v.v. We have a thoroughly composed initial concept, with, presumably, a composer driven æsthetic. However, the cleavage at realization creates an apparent chaos. The resulting sounds are seemingly chaotic gibberish and splotchy electronic squawks and gurgles. This seems null æsthetically. However, that is only at first glance. When one thinks about it, the instructions in the original array would carry an æsthetic. The interruption only turned the output sound into gibberish; however, not so that the relationships between the "1's" and "0's" are destroyed! So we are left with an æsthetic that is disguised entirely from view. This is an example in which a single 'æsthetic' (a template) is altered in its output but is preserved relationally, so that a single æsthetic can be viewed as containing opposing output sound environments!

Lastly, we encounter the extreme case of Otomo Yoshihide (b. Japan 1959.) Yoshihide contrives physical environments in which to set unusual electronics apparatus. One of his pieces is titled **Turntable Solo**, in which the peculiar and particular ambience within the construction of a turntable is explored. The special electronic hookup and miking creates a screeching shard of sound-debris that defies categorization. The æsthetic lies in the machine. The machine's inherent construction features dictate the possible outcomes.

Are these null? Not entirely. Do these sound universes convey content, and therefore an æsthetic? I am inclined to say "yes"; and therein lay a story. We have examined a wide range of æsthetic variations. One of the most fascinating possibilities is the mixture of values; an æsthetic complex and æsthetic multiples.

Future composers who function across an æsthetic spectrum may find it possible to traverse wide spans using either intuitive protocols or a mathematical transformation operator (geometrical, as in Xenakis' **Akrata** (1966.))

## Motion

Now we confront a crucial issue. We have dwelt upon the concept of æsthetics as consisting of a field of possibilities. By this we not only mean a structure of values in a continuous array, increasing or decreasing infinitesimally as the case may be, but also as a means of travel in varying degrees of rigor. In mathematical algebraic theory a field is a domain with a set of values that remain as members of that field under any of the four standard operations of addition, subtraction, multiplication or division. Some domains are not continuous and lack this characteristic under division (e.g. the set of integers 1, 2, 3, which consists only of whole integers, and does not always return an integer under division.) Under operations, the set forms a group: a set of values under an operation that maintains symmetry.

At the risk of going astray in mathematical theory, we now turn to and examine what this bestows upon our magnificent candle of colors: the æsthetic field is a group. We saw previously that the composer of avant garde, progressive, or experimental music may enrich the æsthetic spectrum by introducing confrontations and complexities where none previously existed. This has the benefit of expanding and enriching the field in ways that ultimately can force a mixture or even transformation of opposing values. The listener is enjoined in a travel during which previously fixed values become compacted and friends (pretty) can turn into enemies (ugly) or v.v. Xenakis proposed this in entirely new ways of listening in music such as **Gendy 3** (1991) where Brownian motion of sounds is explored (the random motion of molecules under imposed sonic 'pressure' resulting in unpredictable bumps and jumps.)

Estrada's **Búsica** (2005) was composed via the imaginary, which then becomes a default operator of organic significance. Other means to 'move' along a changing spectrum exist. Chance in varying degrees can interrupt expectations. More direct means entail explicit use of the algebraic field operators themselves: addition, subtraction, etc.

An unexpected possibility is a walk in tandem with the composer and the values in the æsthetic field itself in interactive communication! This is a possibility that warrants considerably more exploration. Essentially, that is what happened in *Búsica*. Estrada and the æsthetics roiled and churned until the state of the musical value took on the characteristic of a kaleidoscopic evolution. At the end the listener no longer cared if the sounds could be viewed as pleasing, for the element of beauty had become abstract, as the harsh, grating sounds become unusually attractive in mysterious ways obviating the need for pleasure.

Another example of this kind of 'walk' is more immediately apparent in the music of Gordon Mumma, especially in his *Hornpipe* (1967) in which Mumma engages in direct, if subversive communication with his cybersonic console. These remarks are offered as facilitators for discussion in explorations for the future of modern music.

So, the values in the field not only exist, but they evolve! The composer, too, explores his/her unique imaginary complex and evolves in real time down to the infinitesimal. The ground moves!

**"Et ecce terrae motus"**
**(Missa – Antoine Brumel's "Earthquake Mass")**

# Chaos, Catastrophe, Density and other major matters

Estrada is the first composer to admit openly the existence of catastrophic impulse as a significant and rigorously designed component in his music. In order to understand catastrophe we need to focus on a normal flow of musical argument and what happens when it is interrupted.

Second, we need to determine a way to capture the 'shape' of a catastrophic event so we can identify it clearly as a significant rupture in the musical discourse. This latter investigation will lead us to graphing density against time and seeing what characteristic shapes represent a given high density work. This will enable us also to isolate fabric tears.

Let's take a brief look at what might be a visual model of catastrophe, so we can appreciate what is the musical analogy in Estrada's work. Let's see how catastrophe may shock the æsthetic variable complex into a new state. In this way catastrophe renders a 'moment' of dislocation generating irregular activity (usually of high degree of density change content.) Here is a freehand rendering of a cusp (Random House, p. 473), a figure that contains a singularity.

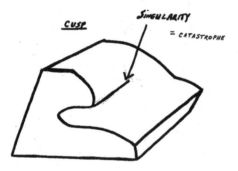

The symmetry in the flow of music is broken. This rupture becomes a formal fulcrum. Any tangent will wobble wildly; the music is set into a high degree of unpredictability and variability. Upon its subsequent return to normalcy, the fabric subsided in its intensity and there became a snapshot of an event signaling new directions. This is one way to generate form. Perhaps a visual analogy will help. Let's take another look at catastrophe and see how this musical event is analogous to physical models under which catastrophe normally functions.

The mathematician René Thom (1923- ) created the theory of catastrophe in 1966. He specializes in differential manifolds and topology, two classes of mathematics wherein one is most likely to encounter catastrophe. Small scale gradual changes are triggered by large scale and sudden 'jumps'. This is the essence of catastrophe. Such change is discontinuous. A smooth surface may end in a point, such as in a 'cusp', the figure above.

The value in recognizing this comes from the derived ability to differentiate works of different composers and even different works of each composer individually.

In preparing a book examining the biography of Julio Estrada, I noticed that I could obtain a glimpse of how sharp would be the violent shifts in his texture of a given piece. I also could find ways to distinguish his density qualities from those of his major teacher, Xenakis. Consequently, I set Estrada's *yuunohui'se* and Xenakis' **Pithoprakta** to a graph of manuscript notational change density against time. I confirmed a number of interesting things via this procedure: there, before my very eyes, I could *see* the first onset of catastrophic change as a severe spike in density of change events. This turmoil lasted several seconds. The musical fabric had suddenly shifted to a higher level of angst. This held for a time, lending a wholly new character to this section in question.

Other things became apparent. I could track the speed of change and compare it to Xenakis, to obtain a confident feel for how much more intense were Estrada's shifts in expression. I could obtain a 'moment' of speed, that is, a characteristic level for the piece as a whole. Other measurement paradigms may be useful, but great care must be exercised when resorting to them. One very interesting result would have been to establish a difference in degree of central tendency of density and speed of density change.

Caution must be exerted here. For one must first determine the 'faithfulness' of the graph of density level frequencies of occurrence to the target distribution type. Usually one would (from personal bias) expect a bell or normal curve. In fact this is the case with Xenakis; but, after all, this should be no surprise, inasmuch as Xenakis resorts to use of stochastic distributions of interval sizes, so these are usually bell. However it is possible to obtain a rare event distribution of density frequencies of occurrence as well. So a Chi-square test should be applied to particular data output of the score under question before drawing any conclusions.

One can measure explicitly degrees of central tendency by calculating the kurtosis (amount of spread in the graph) and the skewness (shift of the graph away from center. But these tools are exceedingly intricate and complex. Is this effort worth the information value obtained? I had expected Estrada's piece to reveal a graph that perhaps might be severely skewed, or contain more than one center (double-humped) because of his lack of reliance on stochastics as a driver. Much to my surprise I discovered Estrada, too, had a single, centered measure! The unexpected result might well be the innate habits of a given individual composer that may result in a sub-conscious bias toward single-centeredness. Certainly, it seems the intrusion of a well-directed impulse such as an 'imaginary', as is the case in Estrada's works, could skew otherwise abstract statistical output.

I believe this approach, therefore, to be less helpful than the approach previously discussed on the graphing of density and speed of density change. The analyst may none-theless use a variety of tools to quantify music of high density in which melody, harmony, and phrase play little part.

The major point is that the tools and methods discussed here will be a key to new analytical methods used in the qualification and quantification of progressive modern music.

Ultimately the ear is the best tool. Certainly the listener need not concern him - or herself with the analysis tools. The tools help understand the foundations of the new music, but listening can still be gratifying without them.

## Ghosts and Transformations

Density then is added to our arsenal of musical components for a composer to subject to transformation. Even the variable æsthetic field is grist for this mill. However, the future in music really goes to all elements, not just density and timbre. Yes, the older elements, too, including sound frequency, intensity, envelope of attack, duration and, yet another new one – micro-rhythm – are to be tamed in the wide boundaries of music-making. No longer, though, does music consist solely of semi-specific notation for pitch change (melody) or harmony, with a few subjective instructions sprinkled for intensity and duration.

The element just mentioned anew, micro-rhythm, is excited by sympathetic vibrations generated from the environment of other sound molecules. It is duration's analog to frequency's timbre. One may recall the chart in the chapter on Estrada detailing the *continuum* template. Each of the six newly associable elements is laid forth to show the panorama of candidate control elements. The elements: sound frequency; duration; intensity; envelope of attack; timbre; and micro-rhythm are subjected to close and intricate scrutiny and controlled transformation. This looks like six dimensions, since each is accorded roughly similarly intense manipulation. In fact, we may say that the new, full paradigm is a nine-dimensional field. Add density, time and æsthetic content to the other six. It is possible to graph the six fold evolution of the six above-listed elements in their evolution through time, as has done Estrada, by employing the use of a chrono-acoustic graph. See figure below:

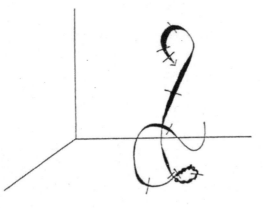

This is an essentially six dimensional drawing reduced to three dimensions. The three visible dimensions are shown in the axes (call them x, y, and z.) The other three dimensions are signified by the strip itself, which would normally consist of lines without width. The width shown here assigns action in a 'related' dimension simultaneously (e.g. sound frequency and duration are such a frequency-to-rhythm pair.) The extent of the figure shows the travel through time. All elements are subjected to careful attention, control and evolution visually. The end result is then translated into musical notation, albeit of a very intricate degree, in two-staff sets (see chapter on Estrada.)

The complexity of movement is often intense, as mathematical operators, an 'imaginary' or other less rigorous operators are brought to bear on the field. Each dimension is a field in that it consists of a group of related values that, when subjected to an operator returns another member of the value field. The values are assumed to be densely continuous: that is there are no 'spaces' between the values.

Another interesting conjecture is whether this field-set of Estrada's is complex enough that it qualifies as a Riemann space. Such a space is a manifold, wherein the complete cycle of values is not exhausted until at least two 360° calculation circuits are generated. An example of this would be, in two dimensions, the complex plane under multiplication. Riemann represented that as two planar circles slightly tilted in orientation to one another.

Here is the reason for this question. The multiplication operator is available for use. Additionally, Estrada employs very cleverly sounds and sonic shadows, especially in his opera *Murmullos del páramo* (2005) to assist in casting the 'ghosts' as wraithlike figures in sight and sound. Sound memories vie with full sounds, following, for the audience's attention. This discussion may flesh out the richness, depth and breadth of the concepts in use by composers of today's progressive avant-garde.

## Material in Turmoil

In no way should we consider these arguments simple or elementary. These are beyond the scope of this book making it necessary to reveal only as an appendix. Without this analysis, any in depth survey of progressive modern music is futile. But I introduce it here in the lightest possible way as merely to provide the readership with a way to appreciate the depth of the musical revolution. Without at least a taste of this the Future of Modern Music is indeed a distant concept. [2]

♦♦♦

## Bibliography

**Random House Webster's Dictionary of Scientists**. Ed. Jenkins-Jones, Sara, et al. © Helicon Publishing Ltd. London 1996. © Random House, Inc. New York. 1997.

Livio, Mario. **The Equation that Couldn't Be Solved**. *How Mathematical Genius Discovered the Language of SYMMETRY.* Simon and Schuster Paperback, New York. 2005.

---

[2] These concepts are being included, nearly verbatim, in the forthcoming biography of Julio Estrada. Appearance of this book is scheduled tentatively for mid-2008.

## APPENDIX C

An important historical revolution in music took place from 1960-69, just years after John Cage's revolution in music-making. The ONCE group of composers has received long overdue recognition with the release of a 5-CD set by New World records in early 2003. The revolutions sparked by this group were so trend-setting as to garner astonishment even today. Therefore a record of this series of events is demanded.

No coverage of these contributions has yet to find its way into a concise tome. Let's be the first.

## ONCE – A Cauldron of Progressive Music

Every one hundred years or so, a musical experience of spectacular originality leaves a lurking, potent mark upon the future. Initially, events such as these may be met with incomprehension and neglect; subsequently, though, these phenomena emerge from slumber to leave a profound world-wide impact on the musical culture. In certain instances, the participant composers even emerge as masters whose works anticipate many major future trends. One such event has been memorialized in a remarkable set of CDs released in September 2003 by New World Records. This CD set presents for the first time a recorded anthology of music composed for the famous ONCE festivals that took place from 1961-1968, mostly in Ann Arbor, Michigan. The time frame covered in the CD set extends only to 1966, as this period encompassed the most fruitful of the festival years.

The CD release is accompanied by an attractive, well researched 156 page program note booklet that describes in detail for the first time the evolution of the ONCE festivals. Also included are copious notes on and by the major composers (only Cacioppo is unrepresented among composers' personal notes for the booklet. He passed away prematurely in the 1980s.) The author of the major portion of the notes, Leta E. Miller, a professor of music at the University of California, Santa Cruz, describes the history of the funding for the festivals and the concert presentations. The following survey is based on her text in the program booklet.

When this music first appeared it was radical by inception and conception. At a time when music was being subjected to several wrenching innovations, and when audiences were still struggling mightily with the music of Arnold Schönberg and his school, the young revolutionaries of Ann Arbor were soon to shock even those accustomed to the near cacophony of John Cage. That this revolution was taking place right under the long noses of the University of Michigan's staid professorial music leadership speaks well for the tolerance of some of that leadership, especially Ross Lee Finney. Finney, composer-in-residence, and himself a devout Bergian, showed careful leadership and understanding of the artistic efforts of most of the ONCE participants, if also less patience with the 'antics' occurring within the actual confines of the festival. Each of the major composers: Donald Scavarda and George Cacioppo initially; Gordon Mumma and Robert Ashley shortly after; and finally, Roger Reynolds, were students at U of M, taking courses led by various music faculty members.

The festivals, though, were another matter entirely. The festival activities were rife with "wildly" new techniques that later were to become permanent modus operandi in future experimentalist canon. Such rash compositional and performance methods raised more than one eyebrow of university musical officialdom (and more than once! – no pun intended!) So, philosophical support of Finney for the individual *composers* was unmatched by that of other teachers within the university musical milieu for the *festivals*, themselves.

Nevertheless, this setting was a cauldron of activity for major performers, composers, and newspaper critics over those years. The festival received considerable attention worldwide. All five major composers issued works, both for the festival and subsequently, that were to reveal wholly new methods of music making. Activity so new is very difficult to sustain without solid good fortune. Normal concert settings usually are insufficient financial generators to support raw creative miracles such as these that ignored the usual matters of musical sensibilities. The composers had to find a special means of support. They did.

The fortuity that befell ONCE and enabled its continuity is latent in the story of the group's emergence. ONCE was different from most festivals that were presented around the globe in the 50s and 60s, especially in that it was, foremost, an interdisciplinary group. This fact was crucial to the specific musical development of the composers, and to their ability to obtain financial support at the University of Michigan.

The story begins in the early 1950s when Robert Ashley graduated with a bachelor's degree in music theory. He moved to New York City to work on his master's in piano and composition at the Manhattan School of Music. He rented an apartment and by chance roomed next to a young painter, George Manupelli, who was attending Columbia Teacher's College. They became close friends and started a collaboration that lasted throughout the early 60s.

Ashley returned to Ann Arbor to seek a doctorate. Ashley's attempts to place into the program were rejected, as his candidate pieces were deemed unplayable. Undaunted, Ashley investigated electronic music resources and this brought him to the Speech Research Institute. Ashley became a 'special' student in these labs during his efforts to gain acceptance into the music department. "Ashley took anthropological courses in speech habits, linguistics, and logic (Miller p.17)". This is crucial to the understanding of Ashley's later work that so focuses on speech and electronics.

By circumstance, Manupelli, whom Ashley had met previously in New York, changed his interest to focus on film. Ashley collaborated with Manupelli on the latter's thesis with an electronic music piece to accompany Manupelli's dissertation. Thus, the initial cross-disciplinary seeds were sown that would bear fruit in the ONCE festival. Subsequently Manupelli joined the U-M faculty.

Soon afterward, Ashley met assistant professor Milton Cohen in the art program faculty. Cohen was working on a light show called "Space Theatre". This was central to the development of the ONCE festival's famed inter disciplinary activities. At the time, Gordon Mumma was working with Cohen to accompany the latter's shows with electronic music. Mumma encountered his own difficulties with Finney and dropped out of the university music department. Mumma built electronics equipment and worked odd jobs on the side.

However, Finney welcomed Mumma and others on an *unofficial* basis into the seminars called "composiums (Miller p. 23)", where non-music students were welcomed alongside music students to attend. Large numbers of people including professionals were encouraged to attend. These seminars had a great impact on the ONCE composers.

Mumma continued to work on electronics equipment designs for use in accompanying plays presented by the literature department. Mumma found ways of altering the operations of the tape machines used in the plays. This began his real work in electronics.

Mumma also worked with the College of Architecture and Design, where he, as had Ashley previously, met Cohen. Mumma taught himself electronics from books and built some of his own equipment. Soon, the key collaborations formed that would provide the basis for the compositional styles of the two ONCE composers, and, crucially, for the financial support for the festivals (SUM/PAR Miller pp. 16-24). Scavarda had begun his career path previously and was a successful composer in his own right before ONCE. He developed a unique approach to ONCE and to electronic music in particular (PAR Scavarda pp. 127-8.) Cacioppo, for his part, also had been composing prior to ONCE; however, in his case, real success had to await his experiments within ONCE.

Cohen launched the Space Theatre shows in 1958 with the aid of an architect, Harold Borkin. Borkin designed special equipment to enable light flashes to fly around the auditorium. Manupelli provided slides and films. Mumma and Ashley provided electronic music. Sounds ushered forth from a bewildering variety of actions, and reconstructing antics (SUM/PAR Miller pp. 16-25). Some techniques, such as breaking down a piano and playing the strings, and stretching and releasing weighted wires, remind one of Cage's prescriptions for later pieces such as his *Cartridge Music* (1960). Mumma's experiments in electronics widened as he developed "gate-trigger-controlled envelope-followers (Miller p. 25)". This was the seed for much of Mumma's later work with cybernetics and cybersonic consoles. Ashley's *Fourth of July* and Mumma's *Sound Blocks* were two seminal light show pieces for Space Theatre programs. The audiences were subjected to multi-media to which they had been heretofore unaccustomed.

The previous summary shows the background for the composers' finding a way to obtain funding through the auspices of the College of Architecture and Design (!) rather than through expected channels within the music school proper. Miller's excellent synopses also reveal the events that shaped the emergence of electronics music as a source for cross-disciplinary presentations. Scavarda's cross-disciplinary work emerged from his serious work that dated back to his high school days and his intense interest in all the arts. Such was the foundation that lay the groundwork for ONCE.

George Cacioppo entered the scene upon having met Mumma in a record store in which they worked. Soon they were friends. Cacioppo introduced Mumma to his classmate, Scavarda. Scavarda had won the BMI student composer contest during Scavarda's stay in Germany on a Fulbright Fellowship for his *Fantasy for Violin and Orchestra*. Around 1955 Scavarda entered the doctoral program. Two of Scavarda's works from this period attracted attention, and were subsequently performed by ONCE: *In the Autumn Mountains* (1959); and *Groups for Piano* (1959). Of the two, *Groups...* generated considerable reaction when performed by pianist Paul Jacobs at Tanglewood. *Groups...* is a work of great precision, sophistication, and intricacy. It is comprised of five very brief patterns consisting of 7, 8, 10, 8, and 7 seconds. The numerical relationships are deeply embedded and account for a very tight structure. Scavarda's later work reveals a connection with ONCE's philosophical foundation as it centers on cross-disciplinary concepts including film structures that contain moving images that form the basis for musical performing scores (SUM Scavarda pp. 127-153). Scavarda's major film works breaking new ground that became part of the festivals include *Filmscore for Two Pianists*, and *Greys*, (1963), *Landscape Journey* (1964), and *Caterpillar* (1965). *Filmscore...* relied upon techniques Scavarda developed in 1960 on a movie camera he had purchased in 1960.

Roger Reynolds studied in Ann Arbor at this time, also. Reynolds' relatively late development as a pianist resulted in his initial choice of studies to be in engineering, rather than in music. This background would serve him in his work with ONCE, also. After working in engineering in California, Reynolds returned to Ann Arbor to begin work toward a degree in music. Reynolds took an unconventional path by connecting with H. Wiley Hitchcock, whose unique approach enabled Reynolds to follow an unusual one-on-one coursework pattern. Hitchcock was later president of the American Musicological Society and authored many articles and books. He also wrote reviews of some of the ONCE composers' works. Later Reynolds became editor of a university arts magazine, *Generation*. He published, through this magazine, musical scores, including Scavarda's *Groups...* and *Matrix...*, and Mumma's *Suite for Piano*. He took Finney's 'Composition for non-composers' course. Finney's influence, then, affected in some way all five ONCE composers.

Two decisive incidents in 1958 spurred the individual composers to find a fruitful way to combine their efforts and organize productions, even at a recalcitrant university that was unwilling to provide any 'official' financial arrangement. By 1958, the European musical community had seen its own avant-garde movement established, just as America had seen its new star, John Cage, rise to fame. Cage had traveled to Darmstadt to present works he had composed just previously, including works performed by the experimental pianist David Tudor. The impact on the audience, that included famous composers such as Karlheinz Stockhausen, was considerable. Stockhausen then visited the US to lecture at the University of Michigan. He urged the composers not to rely solely on official sources of funding, but to find original means of financial support for themselves, in order to 'take the bull by the horns' and control performance circumstances (SUM Miller p. 28).

Then Mumma sought the advice of a then literature student and explored creating a performance model successfully adopted by the theatre students. Performances would be held in spare rooms or basements if more usual space couldn't be found (PAR Miller p. 28). As these avenues remained only potentialities for the time being, things began to change with a well-timed visit to the University of Michigan by prominent composer Roberto Gerhard. Gerhard was a successful composer who had been a pupil of Arnold Schönberg in the mid 30s. What was important was his enthusiasm for new music. He was a vocal supporter of the efforts of the ONCE five. His enthusiasm was contagious as it energized the group in its aspirations. Many informal discussions were held between Gerhard and the students. In a lecture, Gerhard countered Theodore Adorno's assertion that contemporary music was in a decline artistically. Gerhard asserted that the "contemporary confusion" was indeed healthy (PAR/SUM Miller p. 33). Gerhard further argued that such confusion was a necessary result of the search in art for ultimate ways to stretch intellectual boundaries, a process indeed vital if art is to survive and not stagnate (PAR Miller p. 28-30). Thoughts such as these would not have been pronounced from the mouth of Finney, who had invited Gerhard to fill in for Finney's sabbatical; or from the lips of any other University of Michigan professor.

This spark of insight added further stimulus for the budding of new ideas fresh in outlook, as opposed to the 'professoreze' normally associated with those beacons of rigor mortis who prod their student soldiers onward to regurgitate mechanical copies of old Mozart, or serial abstractions too abstruse to comprehend.

John Cage had met Reynolds in 1960 in New York after a concert of a work by La Monte Young in which Cage was a performing participant. Reynolds invited Cage and Tudor to visit Ann Arbor and perform their works. The Dramatic Arts Center (DAC), organized earlier in the 50s was focused on providing an environment for quality art in the interest of community enhancement. This center would later figure in annual funding of ONCE presentations from 1960. A calculus professor at UM, Wilfred Kaplan acted as a philanthropist of sorts by personally helping DAC finance the concerts. He had been a musician on the side and his enthusiasm bore fruitful results.

The stimulus that tipped the scale was a subsequent trip to Stratford by four of the five (Scavarda was not present.) The event was a conference for international composers, at which several major composers, including Edgard Varèse, were present to produce their own works and to discuss the planning and execution of major events such as festivals, as well as other topics. Although the four ONCE members had a very hard time contacting the guest composers to cull some ideas for their use, they were stimulated more determinedly than ever, even if in frustration, to fulfill their dreams by themselves.

October 16, 1960 saw Reynolds and Mumma approach DAC for funding to include concert events; three events including guests such as Luciano Berio, Paul Jacobs and others, and three more featuring local composers (Ashley, Reynolds, Mumma, Scavarda, Cacioppo, and Bruce Wise, a doctoral student who worked briefly with the other five original constituents.) The funding story is traced by author Miller to show how its success grew each year.

The foregoing survey is based upon the fine booklet provided by Professor Leta Miller. This synopsis is paraphrased, summarized, and condensed from her account taken from pages 1-50 of the booklet. Also liberally extracted are sections from Donald Scavarda's summary-thesis toward the end of the same booklet, pp. 127-153 entitled *"New Sounds, New Forms, New Ideas..."* The above summary is sprinkled also with observations and conclusions that are solely my personal views, particularly with regard to Mumma's techniques anticipating those of Cage in *Cartridge Music*, and also to the valuation of professor-composed 'music', and others.

This account is offered primarily to emphasize the overwhelming impact that traveling to such unusual lengths to get funding for works of such uncompromising originality makes. I believe that it is important to understand this, because so much crucially creative work is stunted by the lack of support from unsympathetic teachers and recalcitrant organizational sponsors (councils for the arts, etc.). It is startling to see what can happen in a milieu in which money is not an undue restriction. These composers were set free; as a result, some of the most radical, inspiring, soul-shaking, inventive music making in history came from the pens of five nearly neglected, idiosyncratic masters in a quiet nondescript Midwestern university town.

The sweep of their innovative powers resulted from a single key source of genius: their willingness to travel untested territory by exploring the raw communicative power of sound in a truly primitive, yet mysteriously rigorous and progressive fashion!

♦♦♦

## Bibliography

Miller, Leta. **Music from the ONCE Festival**. New York. New World Records. 2003.

Scavarda, Donald. *"New Sounds, New Forms, New Ideas…"* In Miller's **"Music from the ONCE Festival"** (pp. 127-153). New York. New World Records. 2003.

# Works Cited

Albera, Philippe. *"Recital for Violin".* Translated by Hebbelinck, André. CD **Montaigne Auvidis. MO 789003**. 1960.

Babbitt, Milton. *"Béla Bartók String Quartets 5 and 6."* **Columbia** Record **ML 4280** (Liner Notes). ca 1955.

Baron, Carol K. *"Dating Charles Ives's music, facts and fiction".* Kohl, Jerome Ed. **Perspectives of New Music.** Vol. 28. No. 1 Winter 1990.U. S. A. Perspectives of New Music, Inc. Hamilton Printing Co. 1990.

Batstone, Philip, N. *"Multiple order functions in twelve tone music".* Boretz, Benjamin. Ed. **Perspectives of New Music.** Vol. 11, No. 1. Fall/Winter. 1972. Princeton, New Jersey. Perspectives of New Music, Inc. Edwards Brothers, Inc. 1973.

Berg, Alban. *"Why is Schoenberg's music so hard to understand?".* Schwartz, Elliott and Childs, Barney, Eds. (with Fox, Jim). **Contemporary Composers on Contemporary Music**. Expanded Edition. New York. Da Capo Press. 1998.

Bois, Mario. **Iannis Xenakis: The Man and His Music - a conversation with the composer and a description of his works**. Westport, Connecticut. Boosey & Hawkes. 1980.

Boynick, Matt. **Leoš Janáček**. 1996. http://www.rz-berlin.mpg.de/cmp/janacek.http.1996.

Burke, Jane. **20th Century Music-Leoš Janáček - student project**. Emory University. http://www.cc.emory.edu/MUSIC/ARNOLD/janacek.content.html.

Cage, John. *"Composition as Process".* Cage John. **Silence**. Middletown, Connecticut. Wesleyan University Press. 1961.

Cage, John. *"Experimental Music: Doctrine".* Cage John. **Silence**. Middletown, Connecticut. Wesleyan University Press. 1961.

Carner, Mosco. **Alban Berg**. New York. Holmes & Meier Publishers, Inc. 1983.

**Composers Voice.** *"Matthisj Vermeulen as critic"*. Record **CV 8384/2**. Donemus, Amsterdam. (Liner notes - insert).

Cremones, Adriano. *"Giacinto Scelsi"*. Translated by Taylor, Michael. Paris. Salabert **Actuels** CD. **SCD 8904-5.** Distributed by Harmonia Mundi HM. 1990.

Darrell, R. D. *"Darius Milhaud"* **Candide**. Record. **CE 31008**.

Davies, Laurence. **Ravel Orchestral Music**. Seattle. BBC Music Guides. University of Washington Press.1971

De Voto, Mark. *"Berg, Alban"*. Vinton, J. Ed. **Dictionary of Contemporary Music**. New York. E. P. Dutton & Co., Inc. 1974.

Downes, Edward. *"Atlas Eclipticalis with Winter Music - John Cage"* Kostelanetz, Richard. Ed. **John Cage.** New York. Praeger Publishers. 1970.

Drake, Jeremy. *"Quantum Scelsi"*. **Salabert Actuels**. CD. **SCD 8904-5.** Paris. Distributed by Harmonia HM. 1990.

Emory University 20th century music. **Claude Debussy.** http://emory/edu/MUSIC/ARNOLD/debussy_content.hmtl.

Estrada, Julio/Butin, Patrick. *"Canto Occulto"* and *"Ishini'ioni"*. **Julio Estrada.**Paris. Salabert Editions. 1994.

Estrada, Julio. *"Focusing on Freedom and Movement in Music: Methods of Transcription inside a Continuum of Rhythm and Sound"*. http://www.prodigyweb.net.mp/ejulio/Julio.html.

Ewen, David. **The World of Twentieth Century Music**. U. S. Prentice Hall, Inc. 1969.

Fennelly, Brian. *"12-tone techniques"*. Vinton, J. Ed. **Dictionary of Contemporary Music.** E. P. Dutton & Co., Inc. 1974.

Goodfriend. James. *"Glagolitic Mass - Leoš Janáček"*. **Columbia. Record. ML 6137.**

Griffiths, Paul. **Modern Music.** - *"A concise history from Debussy to Boulez."*. New York. Thames and Hudson, Inc. 1976.

Griffiths, Paul. **Olivier Messiaen**. - *"And the Music of Time."*. New York. Cornell University Press. 1985.

Halbreich, Harry. *"Giacinto Scelsi: Aion-Pfhat-Konx Om Pax"*. Translated by Buzzard, Elizabeth. Paris. **Accord** CD **200604**. 1986.

Halbreich, Harry. *"Quattro Pezzi-Anahit-Uaxuctum"*. Translated by Buzzard, Elizabeth. Paris. **Accord** CD **200612**. 1989

Halbreich, Harry. *"The Five String Quartets/String Trio/Khoom"*, Brussels July 1989. Translated by Buzzard, Elizabeth. **Salabert Actuels** CD **SCD 8904-5**. Paris. Distributed by Harmonia Mundi HM. 1990.

Hausler, Josef. *"Boulez, Pierre"*. Vinton, J. Ed. **Dictionary of Contemporary Music**. New York. E. P. Dutton & Co., Inc. 1974.

Holmes, Paul. **Debussy**. London. Omnibus Press. 1989.

Howat, Roy. **Debussy in Proportion** - *"A musical analysis."*. Cambridge, Massachusetts. University Press/Press Syndicate of the University of Cambridge. 1983.

Johnson, Robert Sherlaw. **Messiaen.** New Ed. Berkeley, California. University of California Press. 1989.

Kaltnecker, Walter. *"Luigi Nono"*. Translated by Dobbin, Frank. **Astrée** CD **E 8741**. France. 1990.

Ketting, Otto. *"Matthisj Vermeulen (1888-1967)"* The Hague/Donemus Amsterdam. **Composers Voice** CD **CV 36/37/38.**

✻ Koch, Gerald R. *"Luigi Nono"*. Translated by Bell, John. Germany. **Wergo** CD. **WER 6229-2.**1993.

Kostelanetz, Richard. Ed. **John Cage**. New York. Praeger Publishers. 1970.

Lebrecht, Norman. **The Companion to 20th Century Music.** New York. Da Capo Press. 1996.

Lendvai, Ernö. **Béla Bartók** - *"An analysis of his music"*. London. Kahn and Averill. 1971.

Lesznai, Lajos. **Bartók**. Great Britain. J. M. Dent & Sons, Limited. 1973.

Machlis, L. **Introduction to Contemporary Music**. U. S. A. W. W. Norton Company. 1961.

Matossian, Nouritza. **Xenakis.** New York. Kahn & Averill. Taplinger Publishing Company. 1986.

McAllister, Rita. *"Igor Feodoritch Stravinsky"*. Thompson, Oscar Chief Ed. Bohle, Bruce Ed. 10th Edition. **The International Cyclopedia of Music and Musicians**. Dodd, Mead & Co. 1975.

Newsweek. August 24, 1992.

Pape, Gerard. Ed. **Les Ateliers UPIC**. http://mitpress.mit.edu/e-journals/Computer Music-Journal/Documents/UPIC.hmtl.

Pape, Gerard. Ed. **Les Ateliers UPIC**. http://www.emf.org/organizations/upic/index.hmtl.

Pape, Gerard. *"Composition and the Structure of Sound"*. Publication Pending (Projected for book in France **Le Continuum**). 1995.

Pape, Gerard. *"Luigi Nono and His Fellow Travellers"*(sic.). pp. 57-65. Issue Ed. Davismoon, S. **Contemporary Music Review.** Vol. 18, Part 1 *"Luigi Nono - The Suspended Song"*. Pub. by License under Harwood Academic Publishers Imprint, part of Gordon and Breach Publishing Group. c. 1999 OPA (Overseas Publishers Association). N.A.

Pareyón, Gabriel./Espinosa, Pablo. *"Maya Ramos y la recriación de la vida teatro-musical en México.* Translated by Santa Anna, Laura.http://serpiente.dgsca.unam.mx/1996/mar96/960313/cultura.hmtl.

Pauli, Hansjörg. *"Austria and Germany - since 1945".* Vinton, J. Ed. **Dictionary of Contemporary Music.** New York. E. P. Dutton & Co. Inc. 1974.

Protheroe, Guy. *"Iannis Xenakis - Palimpsest".* Mainz Germany. **Wergo**. Record. **WER 6178-2**. Schallplatten GmbH. 1989.

R. N. **Leoš Janáček.** *"The Musical Times"* (editorial). No. 1000 - vol. 67. 1926. http://www.measure.demon.co.uk/dos/Janacek.hmtl.

Rae, Charles Bodman. **The Music of Witold Lutosławski.** London. Faber and Faber. 1994

Randel, Michael, Ed. T**he Harvard Dictionary of Music.** Cambridge, Massachusetts. Belknap Press of Harvard University Press. 1996.

Restagno, Enzo. *"Giacinto Scelsi and the Sound Sphinxes".* Translated by Taylor, Michael. Paris. **Salabert Actuels.** CD. **SCD 8904-5.** Distributed by Harmonia Mundi HM. 1990.

Rich, Alan. *"Karlheinz Stockhausen".* Thompson, Oscar, Chief Ed. Bohle, Bruce Ed. 10th Edition. **The International Cyclopedia of Music and Musicians**. New York. Dodd, Mead & Co. 1975.

Rickards, Guy. **Hindemith, Hartmann and Henze**. London. Phaïdon Press Limited. 1995.

Russcol, Herbert. **The Liberation of Sound**. *"An introduction to electronic music".* U. S. A. Prentice-Hall International, Inc. 1972.

Schwartz, Elliott and Childs, Barney. Eds. (with Fox, Jim). **Contemporary Composers on Contemporary Music.** Expanded Edition. New York. Da Capo Press. 1998.

Slonimsky, Nicolas. Ed. **Baker's Biographical Dictionary of Musicians**. 8th Ed. New York. Schirmer Bros. Division of Macmillan Inc. 1992.

Snyder, Ellsworth J. *"Chronological Table of Cage's Life"*. Kostelanetz, Richard. Ed. **John Cage**. New York. Praeger Publishers. 1970.

Stenzl, Jürg. *"Fragments - Stillness, for Diotima"*. Translated by Stenzl, C. and Pan, L. Hamburg, Germany. **DG**. CD. **DG 415 513-2 GH**. 1983.

Stravinsky/Craft. *"Stravinsky on Varèse"*. U.S.A. **Columbia.** Record. **MS 6362**.

**TAHRA.** CD. *"Gian-Francesco Malipiero - L'Orfeide"*. France. **TAH 190-1**. 1996.

Tremblay, Gilles. *"Messiaen, Olivier"*. Vinton, J. Ed. **Dictionary of Contemporary Music.** New York. E. P. Dutton & Co., Inc. 1974.

van den Toorn, Pieter C. **The Music of Igor Stravinsky.** Forte, A. Gen'l Ed. New Haven & London. Yale University Press. 1983.

Varga, Bálint András. **Conversations with Iannis Xenakis**. London. Faber & Faber, Ltd. 1996.

Vinton, J. Ed. **Dictionary of Contemporary Music**. New York. E. P. Dutton & Co., Inc. 1974.

Warnaby, John. *"Julio Estrada: Works for Strings"*. Paris. **Montaigne Auvidis.** CD. **MO 782056**.1993.

Waterhouse, John C. G. *"Gian-Francesco Malipiero"*. Germany. **Marco Polo 8.223602.**1993.

Waterhouse, John C. G. *"Gian-Francesco Malipiero"*. Germany. **Marco Polo 8.223603.** 1993.

Waterhouse, John C. G. *"Gian-Francesco Malipiero"*. Thompson, Oscar. Chief Ed. Bohle, Bruce. Ed.10th Edition. **The International Cyclopedia of Music and Musicians**. New York. Dodd, Mead & Co. 1975.

Wolff, Christian. *"Cage, John"*. Vinton, J. Ed. **Dictionary of Contemporary Music**. New York. E. P. Dutton & Co. Inc., 1974.

Xenakis, Iannis. **Formalized Music** - *"Thought and Mathematics in Music."* Revised Edition. Stuyvesant, New York. Pendragon Press.1992.

Xenakis, Iannis. **Arts/Sciences: Alloys**. *"The Thesis Defense of Iannis Xenakis"*. Translated by Kanach, Sharon. New York. Pendragon Press.1985.

# Complete Bibliography

Albera, Philippe. *"Recital for Violin"*. Translated by Hebbelinck, André. CD **Montaigne Auvidis. MO 789003.** 1960.

Babbitt, Milton. *"Béla Bartók String Quartets 5 and 6."* **Columbia** Record **ML 4280** (Liner Notes). ca 1955.

Baron, Carol K. *"Dating Charles Ives's music, facts and fiction"*. Kohl, Jerome Ed. **Perspectives of New Music**. Vol. 28. No. 1 Winter 1990.U.S.A. Perspectives of New Music, Inc. Hamilton Printing Co. 1990.

Batstone, Philip, N. *"Multiple order functions in twelve tone music"*. Boretz, Benjamin. Ed. **Perspectives of New Music.** Vol. 11, No. 1. Fall/Winter 1972. Princeton, New Jersey. Perspectives of New Music, Inc. Edwards Brothers, Inc. 1973.

Bois, Mario. **Iannis Xenakis: The Man and His Music - a conversation with the composer and a description of his works.** Westport, Connecticut. Boosey & Hawkes. 1980.

Boynick, Matt. **Leoš Janáček.** 1996. http://www.rz-berlin.mpg. de/cmp/janacek.http.1996.

Burke, Jane. **20th Century Music-Leoš Janáček - student project**. Emory University.http://www.cc.emory.edu/MUSIC/ ARNOLD/janacek.content.html.

Cage John. **Silence.** Middletown, Connecticut. Wesleyan University Press. 1961.

Carner, Mosco. **Alban Berg**. New York. Holmes & Meier Publishers, Inc. 1983.

**Composers Voice**. *"Matthisj Vermeulen as critic"*. Record **CV 8384/2.** Donemus, Amsterdam. (Liner notes - insert).

Cremones, Adriano. "Giacinto Scelsi". Translated by Taylor,

Michael. Paris. Salabert **Actuels** CD. **SCD 8904-5.** Distributed by Harmonia Mundi HM. 1990.

Darrell, R. D. *"Darius Milhaud"* **Candide**. Record. **CE 31008.**

Davies, Laurence. **Ravel Orchestral Music.** Seattle. BBC Music Guides. University of Washington Press. 1971.

Drake, Jeremy. *"Quantum Scelsi"*. **Salabert Actuels**. CD. **SCD 8904-5**. Paris. Distributed by Harmonia HM. 1990.

Emory University **20th century music: Claude Debussy.** http://emory/edu/MUSIC/ARNOLD/debussy_content.hmtl.

Estrada, Julio/Butin, Patrick. *"Canto Occulto"* and *"Ishini'ioni"*. **Julio Estrada.** Paris. Salabert Editions. 1994.

Estrada, Julio. *"Focusing on Freedom and Movement in Music: Methods of Transcription inside a Continuum of Rhythm and Sound"*. http://www.prodigyweb.net.mp/ejulio/Julio.html.

Ewen, David. **The World of Twentieth Century Music**. U.S. Prentice Hall, Inc. 1969.

Goodfriend. James. *"Glagolitic Mass - Leoš Janáček"*. **Columbia**. Record. **ML 6137.**

Griffiths, Paul. **Modern Music**. - *"A concise history from Debussy to Boulez."*. New York. Thames and Hudson, Inc. 1976.

Griffiths, Paul. **Olivier Messiaen.** - *"And the Music of Time."*. New York. Cornell University Press. 1985.

Halbreich, Harry. *"Giacinto Scelsi: Aion-Pfhat-Konx Om Pax"*. Translated by Buzzard, Elizabeth. Paris. **Accord** CD **200604.** 1986.

Halbreich, Harry. "Quattro Pezzi-Anahit-Uaxuctum". Translated by Buzzard, Elizabeth. Paris. Accord CD 200612. 1989

Halbreich, Harry. *"The Five String Quartets/String Trio/Khoom"*, Brussels July 1989. Translated by Buzzard, Elizabeth. **Salabert**

**Actuels** CD **SCD 8904-5.** Paris. Distributed by Harmonia Mundi HM. 1990.

Hansen, Peter S. **An Introduction to Twentieth Century Music**. Boston. Allyn and Bacon, Inc. 1971.

Hayes, Malcolm. **Anton von Webern**. London. Phaïdon Press, Ltd. 1995.

Holmes, Paul. **Debussy.** London. Omnibus Press. 1989.

Howat, Roy. **Debussy in Proportion** - *"A musical analysis"*. Cambridge, Massachusetts. University Press/Press Syndicate of the University of Cambridge. 1983.

Johnson, Robert Sherlaw. **Messiaen.** New Ed. Berkeley, California. University of California Press. 1989.

Kaltnecker, Walter. *"Luigi Nono"*. Translated by Dobbin, Frank. **Astrée** CD **E 8741.** France. 1990.

Ketting, Otto. *"Matthisj Vermeulen (1888-1967)"* The Hague/Donemus Amsterdam. **Composers Voice** CD **CV 36/37/38.**

Koch, Gerald R. *"Luigi Nono"*. Translated by Bell, John. Germany. **Wergo** CD. **WER 6229-2**.1993.

Kolneder, Walter. **Anton Webern.** Translated by Searle, Humphrey. Berkeley and Los Angeles. University of California Press. 1968.

Kostelanetz, Richard. Ed. **John Cage.** New York. Praeger Publishers. 1970.

Lebrecht, Norman. **The Companion to 20th Century Music.** New York. Da Capo Press. 1996.

Lendvai, Ernö. **Béla Bartók** - *"An analysis of his music"*. London. Kahn and Averill. 1971.

Lesznai, Lajos. **Bartók.** Great Britain. J. M. Dent & Sons, Limited. 1973.

MacDonald, Malcolm. **Schoenberg**. Great Britain. J. M. Dent & Sons, Ltd. 1976.

Machlis, L. **Introduction to Contemporary Music**. U.S.A. W. W. Norton Company. 1961.

Matossian, Nouritza. **Xenakis.** New York. Kahn & Averill. Taplinger Publishing Company. 1986.

Meyers, Rollo H. **Ravel**. Westport, Connecticut. Greenwood. 1973.

Newsweek. August 24, 1992.

Nieto, Velia. *"Recherche-Création dans l'oeuvre de Julio Estrada"*. Ph.D. Thesis. Universite de Paris VIII. 2000.

Ouellette, Fernand. **Edgard Varèse.** Great Britain. Calder and Boyars, Ltd. 1973.

Pape, Gerard. Ed. **Les Ateliers UPIC**. http://mitpress.mit.edu/e-journals/ComputerMusic--Journal/Documents/UPIC.hmtl.

Pape, Gerard. Ed. **Les Ateliers UPIC.** http://www.emf.org/organizations/upic/index.hmtl.

Pape, Gerard. *"Composition and the Structure of Sound"*. Publication Pending (Projected for book in France **Le Continuum**). 1995.

Pape, Gerard. *"Luigi Nono and His Fellow Travellers"*(sic.). pp. 57-65. Issue Ed. Davismoon, S. **Contemporary Music Review.** Vol. 18, Part 1 *"Luigi Nono - The Suspended Song"*. Pub. by License under Harwood Academic Publishers Imprint, part of Gordon and Breach Publishing Group. c. 1999 OPA (Overseas Publishers Association). N.A.

Pareyón, Gabriel./Espinosa, Pablo. *"Maya Ramos y la recriación de la vida teatro-musical en México* Translated by Santa Anna, Laura. http://serpiente.dgsca.unam.mx/1996/mar96/960313/cultura.hmtl.

Peyser, Joan. **Boulez - Composer, Conductor, Enigma.** New York. Schirmer Books, a Division of Macmillan Publishing Co. Inc. 1976.

Protheroe, Guy. *"Iannis Xenakis - Palimpsest"*. Mainz, Germany. **Wergo**. Record. **WER 6178-2**. Schallplatten GmbH. 1989.

R. N. **Leoš Janáček**. *"The Musical Times"* (editorial). No. 1000 - vol. 67. 1926. http://www.measure.demon.co.uk/dos/Janacek.hmtl.

Rae, Charles Bodman. **The Music of Witold Lutosławski.** London. Faber and Faber. 1994.

Randel, Michael, Ed. **The Harvard Dictionary of Music**. Cambridge, Massachusetts. Belknap Press of Harvard University Press. 1996.

Restagno, Enzo. *"Giacinto Scelsi and the Sound Sphinxes"*. Translated by Taylor, Michael. Paris. **Salabert Actuels**. CD. **SCD 8904-5**. Distributed by Harmonia Mundi HM. 1990.

Reynolds, Roger. **Mind Models**. *"New Forms of Musical Experiences"* New York. Praeger Publishers. 1975.

Rickards, Guy. **Hindemith, Hartmann and Henze**. London. Phaïdon Press Limited. 1995.

Russcol, Herbert. **The Liberation of Sound.** *"An introduction to electronic music"*. U.S.A. Prentice-Hall International, Inc. 1972.

Schwartz, Elliott and Childs, Barney. Ed. (with Fox, Jim). **Contemporary Composers on Contemporary Music.** Expanded Edition. New York. Da Capo Press. 1998.

Slonimsky, Nicolas. Ed. **Baker's Biographical Dictionary of Musicians.** 8th Ed. New York. Schirmer Bros. Division of Macmillan Inc. 1992.

Stenzl, Jürg. *"Fragments - Stillness, for Diotima"*. Translated by Stenzl, C. and Pan, L. Hamburg, Germany. **DG.** CD. **DG 415 513-2 GH.** 1983.

Stravinsky/Craft. *"Stravinsky on Varèse"*. U.S.A. **Columbia**. Record. **MS 6362**.

Thompson, Oscar. Chief Ed. Bohle. Ed. 10th Edition. **The International Cyclopedia of Music and Musicians.** New York. Dodd Mead. & Co. 1975.

**TAHRA**. CD. *"Gian-Francesco Malipiero - L'Orfeide"*. France. **TAH 190-1**. 1996.

van den Toorn, Pieter C. **The Music of Igor Stravinsky.** Forte, A. Gen'l Ed. New Haven & London. Yale University Press. 1983.

Varga, Bálint András. **Conversations with Iannis Xenakis.** London. Faber & Faber, Ltd. 1996.

Vinton, J. Ed. **Dictionary of Contemporary Music**. New York. E. P. Dutton & Co., Inc. 1974.

Warnaby, John. *"Julio Estrada: Works for Strings"*. Paris. **Montaigne Auvidis**. CD. **MO 782056**.1993.

Waterhouse, John C. G. *"Gian-Francesco Malipiero"*. Germany. **Marco Polo 8.223602.**1993.

Waterhouse, John C. G. *"Gian-Francesco Malipiero"*. Germany. **Marco Polo 8.223603**. 1993.

Wörner, Karl H. **Stockhausen, Life and Work.** Berkeley and Los Angeles. University of California Press. Revised/Translated. Faber and Faber. 1973.

Xenakis, Iannis. **Formalized Musi**c - *"Thought and Mathematics in Music."* Revised Edition. Stuyvesant, New York. Pendragon Press.1992.

Xenakis, Iannis. **Arts/Sciences: Alloys.** *"The Thesis Defense of Iannis Xenakis"*. Translated by Kanach, Sharon. New York. Pendragon Press.1985.

# Index

## Q

## R

## X

## Y

## Z

Lachenmann Gran Turse

# JAMES MCHARD

McHard is a freelance composer, lecturer, and author on music history. He was educated at the University of Michigan, where he completed his BS in mathematics. He lives with his wife in Livonia, Michigan, and is a French horn player for various local symphony orchestras and concert bands.

His original compositions include *Tremors* and *Virtuals*. The former is scored for ten specially positioned instruments, taped sound effects (including jet aircraft and bomb noises), and UPIC computer console output; the latter is scored for UPIC console output, alone. Both were performed and enthusiastically received at the Twice Festival of Experimental Music concerts in Ann Arbor, Michigan.

Mr. McHard has guest lectured several times on experimental music, and on mathematics in musical composition. He has lectured on modernism and it's future in music at UNAM (Universidad Nacional Autónoma de Mexico) for Dr. Julio Estrada's class in experimental music composition and at CCMIX (formerly Les Ateliers UPIC) in Paris.